THOUGHTS ON REDESIGNING TRIBAL EDUCATION: THE WHY AND WHAT?

THOUGHTS ON REDESIGNING TRIBAL EDUCATION: The Why and What?

Dr. Nanjunda D.C.

Publications

KALPAZ PUBLICATIONS
DELHI-110 052

Thoughts on Redesigning Tribal Education: The Why and What?

Rs. 750/-

ISBN : 978-81-7835-725-6

Published in 2008 in India by
Kalpaz Publications,
C-30, Satyawati Nagar,
Delhi-110 052
Phone: 9212729499
E-mail : kalpaz@hotmail.com

Laser Type setting by: Isas System, Delhi
Printed at: G. Print Process.Delhi

Contents

Foreword

The Indian sub-continent has the largest population of tribals. They born and grows the children of the nature; but they are deprived of many civic facilities even today. They are spread across the country mainly in forest and hilly areas. Most of them are living below poverty –line. The absence of institutional schooling; distinctive customs regarding birth, marriage and death; a moral code different from that of Hindus and Muslims; specialties of religious beliefs and rituals etc. are the distinguishing features of tribals. In India- most of the tribals are suffering from illiteracy, unemployment, poverty, indebtedness, liquor habits, health problems and insufficient infrastructural facilities. In the given institutional set up, they have no access to the various economic social development programmes implemented by the Government. Due to some governmental efforts, considerable changes have taken place in the tribals. Yet, for more improvement of tribal conditions; their forest - rights should be protected, some employment generation programmes should be made, special health programmes must be promoted, number of primary schools in tribal areas should be increased and the infrastructural facilities should be improved.

Education is also the most powerful instrument for achieving an egalitarian type of the society. The framers of constituent, therefore, took a special care of the condition in which the people from these communities are provided several safeguards for the promotion of their educational and economic interests. No country or nation can become prosperous without achieving high literacy rate. The main reason for low literacy among the ST was due to the fact that they were profited from learning since time immemorial however the literacy rates for the STs is increasing at a very high rate after independence due to protective discrimination in many states. The rate of literacy has gone up substantially of all social groups in 2001 as compared to 1991 in Karnataka. The rate of literacy was high among non-ST as compared to STs in Karnataka. There was a fluctuation in the rate of literacy by districts in Karnataka. The education status of urban population was high as compared to rural population. Further, the educational status of males was high as compared to females. The education status of Scheduled Tribes is low when compared to that of other social groups in Karnataka. The recent repot says, the number of teachers in ashram schools was 1,171, and the number of teachers employed in primary, upper primary and high schools was 1,821. The number of students in receipt of postmatric scholarships was 1,950, 468 tribal students were admitted to reputable private schools and public schools, and 90 students were enrolled in the special residential school for tribals in Karnataka state.

Elementary education was a priority area in the Tribal sub-plans from the 5th Five Year Plan. Education of ST children is considered important, not only because of the Constitutional obligation but also as a crucial input for total development of tribal communities. One of the goals of SSA is to "bridge all gender and social category gaps at primary stage by 2007 and at elementary stage by 2010". The issues and challenges in tribal education can be categorized as external, internal, socio-economic and psychological. The external constraints are related to issues at levels of policy, planning and implementation while internal constraints are with respect to school system, content, curriculum, pedagogy, medium of instruction etc. The third set of problems relates to social economic and cultural background of tribals and psychological aspects of first generation learners. The literacy level of Scheduled Castes and Scheduled Tribes is very low compared to the general literacy rate in the state. Since education provides opportunities for a permanent change in the socio-economic status of these people, this Government have given top priority to education. Hence out of a sum of Rs.448.91 crores provided in the Budget Estimate for 2007-2008 to this Department, more than70% is earmarked for schemes related to education. There is a need to evolve a sensitive model of tribal education rooted in the psychological strengths of tribal children.

I hope a sincere effort of my beloved student Dr. DC Nanjunda's effort would be useful to the policy makers regarding tribal education in India.

Dr. R K Mathur
New Delhi

Preface

Tribal development programmes in India have significant achievements to their credit. A widespread administrative infrastructure has provided the confidence to launch an expensive anti-poverty programme unmatched anywhere in the world. The expansion of physical infrastructure of schools, village roads, health centers, drinking water facilities, housing for the weaker sections, sale centers for production requisites are to be compared with what we had when we started on the planned development path, to be believed. The expressions of rising frustration only prove the truism that we demand more only when we have achieved part of our ambitions.

Realizing that Scheduled Tribes are one of the most deprived and marginalized groups with respect to education, most of the programmes and measures have been initiated ever since the Independence. Elementary education was a priority area in the Tribal sub-plans from the 5th Five Year Plan. Education of ST children is considered important, not only because of the Constitutional obligation but also as a crucial input for total development of tribal communities. One of the super goals of SSA (serva shikshan abiyan) is to "bridge all gender and social category gaps at primary stage by 2007 and at elementary stage by 2010".

The issues and challenges in tribal education can be categorized as external, internal, socio-economic and psychological. The external constraints are related to issues at levels of policies, planning and implementation while internal constraints are with respect to school system, content, curriculum, pedagogy, medium of instruction etc. The third set of problems relates to social economic and cultural background of tribals and psychological aspects of first generation learners. The literacy level of Scheduled Castes and Scheduled Tribes is very low compared to the general literacy rate. Recognizing that education provides opportunities for a permanent change in the socio-economic status of these people, this Government gives top priority to education. Hence out of a sum of Rs.548.91 crores provided in the Budget Estimate for 2007-2008 to this Department, more than70% is earmarked for schemes related to education. There is a need to evolve sensitive model of tribal education rooted in the psychological strengths of tribal children.

The strength of a society lies in the role of education in training, development and allocation of its manpower resources. Education has been conceived as training for better life and better social adjustment in a community or group. It is a phase of the social process which is fostered by society for life in-group. It can be said that education is the complete development of individuality so that one can make an original contribution to human life according to one's best capacity.

It is clear that in an under developed tribal community, where the poor people form the majority, owing to sheer poverty, they could not avail of the educational opportunities. Thus, the educational development of the marginalized people is inter linked with their socio economic condition. Hence, prior to solving the problems associated with the educational backwardness of the tribals, the problem of bread must be satisfied. Among the these people who hardly get meal twice a day, education is a tall talk, taking into account the predominant role played by socio economic factors in determining the utilization of facilities by the ST and SCs.

Education cannot change in any fundamental way unless we change our basic patterns of thinking and interacting so that learning can become a way of life. Teachers, parents, administrators, district resource and community people should come together throughout hundreds of school communities to learn how to revitalize their schools with a process known as

"Tribes." Evaluation of Tribes Learning Community Schools (TLC) has examined the impact of the Tribes process on student behavior, academic performance, school culture, and teacher collegiality. Studies have shown that, Tribes TLC has a positive impact on classroom environment. Teachers report spending less time managing student behavior, students are significantly less likely to be referred for disciplinary problems, the Tribes process helps teachers address performance and content standards, students in well-implemented classrooms score significantly higher on standardized tests than students from comparison groups. "Responsive Education" is an essential pedagogy for academic achievement and school reform. It is the synthesis of artful teaching practices. It is based on understanding the critical developmental needs of a student age and cultural group. The Goal is to engage all teachers, administrators, students and families in working together as a learning community that is dedicated to caring and support, active participation and positive expectations for all students.

In spite of sixty years of independence and more than fifty five years of planned development and social provision for accelerated socio economic development of weaker sections, the gap in literacy levels among the general population and the socially disadvantaged sections is persisting and in some cases this gap is further widening. There were 16 million ST children [13.87 million of 6-11 years and 6.12 million of 11-14 years) as of March 2008, out of the total child population in India of about 198 million in the age group of 6 to 14 years. [Selected Educational Statistics – 2006 Government of India] – Education of ST children to considered important, not only because of the constitutional obligation but also as a crucial input for total development of tribal communities. Most tribal children do not understand the textbooks, which are generally in the regional language. The appointment of non-tribal teachers in tribal children's schools is another problem. The teachers do not know the language the children speak and children do not understand the teacher's language.

First of all I would like to Solute *Shri Shirdi Sai Baba* for his blessings. I would like to thank University Grants Commission (UGC-) for providing fellowship to work on Tribal Education Project in Karnataka. I would like to thank all the Editors of various Journals, Books and Magazines. I am very thankful to my friend, guide and philosopher Dr. Steven wind (USA). Next, I am most grateful to Prof. Annapurna M, Dr. Hari Mohan Mathur, Prof. P R G Mathur, Dr. B R Ghosh, Prof. Fleming Just, Dr.Jakka Partha Sarathy, Dr. Shiva Prasad, Dr. Midatala Rani and Dr. Anjali Kurane for their logistic help. I owe a deep sense of gratitude to Nagesha D, Linga Raju, Venu Gopal P.N., Jyothi Lakshmi S, Suresh Kumar M and Raji for their vital role. Heartful thanks to my parents also. Moreover, I am grateful to the promoter of Kalpaz Publications for publishing my book. This book is dedicated to the Indian Tribals and Anthropologists. Further, I extend my acknowledgement to the research staff of my NGO sharing their knowledge.

Dr. Nanjunda DC

1
Indian Tribal Population: A Brief Review

Indian tribes constitute roughly 8 per cent of the nation's total population, nearly 68 million people according to the 1991 census. One concentration lives in a belt along the Himalayas stretching through Jammu and Kashmir, Himachal Pradesh, and Uttar Pradesh in the west, to Assam, Meghalaya, Tripura, Arunachal Pradesh, Mizoram, Manipur, and Nagaland in the northeast (see fig. 1). Another concentration lives in the hilly areas of central India (Madhya Pradesh, Orissa, and, to a lesser extent, Andhra Pradesh); in this belt, which is bounded by the Narmada River to the north and the Godavari River to the southeast, tribal peoples occupy the slopes of the region's mountains. Other tribals, the Santals, live in Bihar and West Bengal. There are smaller numbers of tribal people in Karnataka, Tamil Nadu, and Kerala, in western India in Gujarat and Rajasthan, and in the union territories of Lakshadweep and the Andaman and Nicobar Islands. The extent to which a state's population is tribal varies considerably. In the northeastern states of Arunachal Pradesh, Meghalaya, Mizoram, and Nagaland, upward of 90 percent of the population is tribal.

However, in the remaining northeast states of Assam, Manipur, Sikkim, and Tripura, tribal peoples form between 20 and 30 percent of the population. The largest tribes are found in central India, although the tribal population there accounts for

---

* Extracted from a Website

only around 10 percent of the region's total population. Major concentrations of tribal people live in Maharashtra, Orissa, and West Bengal. In the south, about 1 percent of the populations of Kerala and Tamil Nadu are tribal, whereas about 6 percent in Andhra Pradesh and Karnataka are members of tribes.

There are some 573 communities recognized by the government as Scheduled Tribes and therefore eligible to receive special benefits and to compete for reserved seats in legislatures and schools. They range in size from the Gonds (roughly 7.4 million) and the Santals (approximately 4.2 million). Central Indian states have the country's largest tribes, and, taken as a whole, roughly 75 percent of the total tribal population live there.

Apart from the use of strictly legal criteria, however, the problem of determining which groups and individuals are tribal is both subtle and complex. Because it concerns economic interests and the size and location of voting blocs, the question of who are members of Scheduled Tribes rather than Backward Classes (see Glossary) or Scheduled Castes (see Glossary) is often controversial. The apparently wide fluctuation in estimates of South Asia's tribal population through the twentieth century gives a sense of how unclear the distinction between tribal and non-tribal can be. India's 1931 census enumerated 22 million tribal people, in 1941 only 10 million were counted, but by 1961 some 30 million and in 1991 nearly 68 million tribal members were included. The differences among the figures reflect changing census criteria and the economic incentives individuals have to maintain or reject classification as a tribal member.

These gyrations of census data serve to underline the complex relationship between caste and tribe. Although, in theory, these terms represent different ways of life and ideal types, in reality they stand for a continuum of social groups. In areas of substantial contact between tribes and castes, social and cultural pressures have often tended to move tribes in the direction of becoming castes over a period of years. Tribal peoples with ambitions for social advancement in Indian society at large have tried to gain the classification of caste for their tribes; such efforts conform to the ancient Indian traditions of caste mobility. Where tribal leaders prospered, they could hire Brahman priests to construct credible pedigrees and thereby join reasonably high-status castes. On occasion, an entire tribe or part of a tribe joined a Hindu sect and thus entered the caste system en masse. If a specific tribe engaged in practices that Hindus deemed polluting, the tribe's status when it was assimilated into the caste hierarchy would be affected.

Since independence, however, the special benefits available to Scheduled Tribes have convinced many groups, even Hindus and Muslims, that they will enjoy greater advantages if so designated. The schedule gives tribal people incentives to maintain their identity. By the same token, the schedule also includes a number of groups whose "tribal" status, in cultural terms, is dubious at best; in various districts, the list includes Muslims and a congeries of Hindu castes whose main claim seems to be their ability to deliver votes to the party that arranges their listing among the Scheduled Tribes. A number of traits have customarily been seen as establishing tribal rather than caste identity. These include language, social organization, religious affiliation, economic patterns, geographic location, and self-identification. Recognized tribes typically live in hilly regions somewhat remote from caste settlements; they generally speak a language recognized as tribal.

Unlike castes, which are part of a complex and interrelated local economic exchange system, tribes tend to form self-sufficient economic units. Often they practice swidden farming—clearing a field by slash-and-burn methods, planting it for a number of seasons, and then abandoning it for a lengthy fallow period—rather than the intensive farming typical of most of rural India. For most tribal people, land-use rights traditionally derive simply from tribal membership. Tribal society tends to be egalitarian, its leadership being based on ties of kinship and personality rather than on hereditary status. Tribes typically consist of segmentary lineage's whose extended families provide the basis for social organization and control. Unlike caste religion, which recognizes the hegemony of Brahman priests, tribal religion recognizes no authority outside the tribe.

Any of these criteria can be called into question in specific instances. Language is not always an accurate indicator of tribal or caste status. Especially in regions of mixed population, many tribal groups have lost their mother tongues and simply speak local or regional languages. Linguistic assimilation is an ongoing process of considerable complexity. In the highlands of Orissa, for example, the Bondos—a Munda-language-speaking tribe—use their own tongue among themselves. Oriya, however, serves as a lingua franca in dealings with Hindu neighbors. Oriya as a prestige language (in the Bondo view), however, has also supplanted the native tongue as the language of ritual. In parts of Assam, historically divided into warring tribes and villages, increased contact among villagers began during the colonial period and has accelerated since independence. A pidgin Assamese developed while educated tribal members learned Hindi and, in the late twentieth century, English.

Self-identification and group loyalty are not unfailing markers of tribal identity either. In the case of stratified tribes, the loyalties of clan, kin, and family may well predominate over those of tribe. In addition, tribes cannot always be viewed as people living apart; the degree of isolation of various tribes has varied tremendously. The Gonds, Santals, and Bhils traditionally have dominated the regions in which they have lived. Moreover, tribal society is not always more egalitarian than the rest of the rural populace; some of the larger tribes, such as the Gonds, are highly stratified.

Economic and Political Conditions

Most Indian tribes are concentrated in heavily forested areas that combine inaccessibility with limited political or economic significance. Historically, the economy of most tribes was subsistence agriculture or hunting and gathering. Tribal members traded with outsiders for the few necessities they lacked, such as salt and iron. A few local Hindu craftsmen might provide such items as cooking utensils. The twentieth century, however, has seen far-reaching changes in the relationship between tribals in India and the larger society and, by extension, traditional tribal economies. Improved transportation and communications have brought ever deeper intrusions into tribal lands; merchants and a variety of government policies have involved tribal peoples more thoroughly in the cash economy, although by no means on the most favorable of terms. Large areas fell into the hands of non tribals around 1900, when many regions were opened by the government to homestead-style settlement. Immigrants received free land in return for cultivating it. Tribal people, too, could apply for land titles, although even title to the portion of land they happened to be planting that season could not guarantee their ability to continue swidden cultivation. More important, the notion of permanent, individual ownership of land was foreign to most tribals. Land, if seen in terms of ownership at all, was viewed as a communal resource, free to whoever needed it. By the time tribals accepted the necessity of obtaining formal land titles, they had lost the opportunity to lay claim to lands that might rightfully have been considered theirs. Generally, tribals were severely disadvantaged in dealing with government officials who granted land titles. Albeit belatedly, the colonial regime realized the necessity of protecting tribals of India from the predications of outsiders and prohibited the sale of tribal lands. Although an important loophole in the form of land leases was left open, tribes made some gains in the mid-twentieth century. Despite considerable obstruction by local police and land officials, who were slow to delineate tribal holdings and slower still to offer police protection, some land was returned to tribal peoples.

In the 1970s, the gains tribal peoples had made in earlier decades were eroded in many regions, especially in central India. Migration into tribal lands increased dramatically, and the deadly combination of constabulary and revenue officers uninterested in tribal welfare and sophisticated non tribals willing and able to bribe local officials was sufficient to deprive many tribals of their landholdings. The means of subverting protective legislation were legion: local officials could be persuaded to ignore land acquisition by non tribal people, alter land registry records, lease plots of land for short periods and then simply refuse to relinquish them, or induce tribal members to become indebted and attach their lands. Whatever the means, the result was that many tribal members became landless laborers in the 1960s and 1970s, and regions that a few years earlier had been the exclusive domain of tribes had an increasingly heterogeneous population. Unlike previous eras in which tribal people were shunted into more remote forests, by the 1960s relatively little unoccupied land was available. Government efforts to evict non tribal members from illegal occupation have proceeded slowly, when evictions occur at all, those ejected are usually members of poors, lower castes. In a 1985 publication, anthropologist Christoph von Fürer-Haimendorf describes this process in Andhra Pradesh: "on average only 25 to 33 percent of the tribal families in such villages had managed to keep even a portion of their holdings. Outsiders had paid about 5 percent of the market value of the lands they took."

Improved communications, roads with motorized traffic, and more frequent government intervention figured in the increased contact that tribal peoples had with outsiders. Tribes fared best where there was little to induce non tribals to settle; cash crops and commercial highways frequently signaled the dismemberment of the tribes. Merchants have long been a link to the outside world, but in the past they were generally petty traders, and the contact they had with tribal people was transient. By the 1960s and 1970s, the resident non tribal shopkeeper was a permanent feature of many villages. Shopkeepers often sold liquor on credit, enticing tribal members into debt and into mortgaging their land. In the past, tribes made up shortages before harvest by foraging from the surrounding forest. More recently shopkeepers have offered ready credit—with the proviso that loans be repaid in kind with 50 to 100 percent interest after harvest. Repaying one bag of millet with two bags has set up a cycle of indebtedness from which many have been unable to break loose.

The possibility of cultivators growing a profitable cash crop, such as cotton or castor-oil plants, continues to draw merchants into tribal areas. Non tribal traders frequently establish an extensive network of relatives and associates.as shopkeepers to serve as agents in a number of villages. Cultivators who grow a cash crop often sell to the same merchants, who provide consumption credit throughout the year. The credit carries a high-interest price tag, whereas the tribal peoples' crops are bought at a fraction of the market rate. Cash crops offer a further disadvantage in that they decrease the supply of available foodstuffs and increase tribal dependence on economic forces beyond their control. This transformation has meant a decline in both the tribes' security and their standard of living.

In the previous generations, families might have purchased silver jewelry as a form of security; contemporary tribal people are more likely to buy minor consumer goods. Whereas jewelry could serve as collateral in critical emergencies, current purchases simply increase indebtedness. In areas where gathering forest products is remunerative, merchants exchange their products for tribal labor. Indebtedness is so extensive that although such transactions are illegal, traders sometimes "sell" their debtors to other merchants, much like indentured servants.

In some instances, tribes have managed to hold their own in contacts with outsiders. Some Chenchus, a hunting and gathering tribe of the central hill regions of Andhra Pradesh, have continued to specialize in collecting forest products for sale. Caste Hindus living among them rent land from the Chenchus and pay a portion of the harvest. The Chenchus themselves have responded unenthusiastically to government efforts to induce them to take up farming. Their relationship to non tribal people has been one of symbiosis, although there were indications in the early 1980s that other groups were beginning to compete with the Chenchus in gathering forest products. A large paper mill was cutting bamboo in their territory in a manner that did not allow regeneration, and two groups had begun to collect for sale the same products the Chenchus sell. Dalits settled among them with the help of the Chenchus and learned agriculture from them. The nomadic Banjara herders who graze their cattle in the forest also have been allotted land there. The Chenchus have a certain advantage in dealing with caste Hindus; because of their long association with Hindu hermits and their refusal to eat beef, they are considered an unpolluted caste. Other tribes, particularly in South India, have cultural practices that are offensive to Hindus and, when they are assimilated, are often considered Dalits.

The final blow for some tribes has come when non tribals, through political jockeying, have managed to gain legal tribal status, that is, to be listed as a Scheduled Tribe. The Gonds of Andhra Pradesh effectively lost their only advantage in trying to protect their lands when the Banjaras, a group that had been settling in Gond territory, were classified as a Scheduled Tribe in 1977. Their newly acquired tribal status made the Banjaras eligible to acquire Gond land "legally" and to compete with Gonds for reserved political seats, places in education institutions, and other benefits. Because the Banjaras are not scheduled in neighboring Maharashtra, there has been an influx of Banjara emigrants from that state into Andhra Pradesh in search of better opportunities.

Tribes in the Himalayan foothills have not been as hard-pressed by the intrusions of non tribals. Historically, their political status was always distinct from the rest of India. Until the British colonial period, there was little effective control by any of the empires centered in peninsular India; the region was populated by autonomous feuding tribes. The British, in efforts to protect the sensitive northeast frontier, followed a policies dubbed the "Inner Line"; non tribal people were allowed into the areas only with special permission. Post independence governments have continued the policies, protecting the Himalayan tribes as part of the strategy to secure the border with China.

This policies has generally saved the northern tribes from the kind of exploitation that those elsewhere in South Asia have suffered. In Arunachal Pradesh (formerly part of the North-East Frontier Agency), for example, tribal members control commerce and most lower-level administrative posts. Government construction projects in the region have provided tribes with a significant source of cash—both for setting up businesses and for providing paying customers. Some tribes have made rapid progress through the education system. Instruction was begun in Assamese but was eventually changed to Hindi; by the early 1980s, English was taught at most levels. Both education and the increase in ready cash from government spending have permitted tribal people a significant measure of social mobility. The role of early missionaries in providing education was also crucial in Assam.

Government policies on forest reserves have affected tribal peoples profoundly. Wherever the state has chosen to exploit forests, it has seriously undermined the tribes' way of life. Government efforts to reserve forests have precipitated armed (if futile) resistance on the part of the tribal peoples involved. Intensive exploitation of forests has often meant allowing outsiders to cut large areas of trees (while the original tribal inhabitants were restricted from cutting), and ultimately replacing mixed forests capable of sustaining tribal life with single-product plantations. Where forests are reserved, non tribals have proved far more sophisticated than their forest counterparts at bribing the necessary local officials to secure effective (if extralegal) use of forestlands. The system of bribing local officials charged with enforcing the reserves is so well established that the rates of bribery are reasonably fixed (by the number of plows a farmer uses or the amount of grain harvested). Tribal people often end up doing unpaid work for Hindus simply because a caste Hindu, who has paid the requisite bribe, can at least ensure a tribal member that he or she will not be evicted from forestlands. The final irony, notes von Fürer-Haimendorf, is that the swidden cultivation many tribes practiced had maintained South Asia's forests, whereas the intensive cultivating and commercial interests that replaced the tribal way of life have destroyed the forests.

Extending the system of primary education into tribal areas and reserving places for tribal children in middle and high schools and higher education institutions are central to government policies, but efforts to improve a tribe's educational status have had mixed results (see Education, ch. 2). Recruitment of qualified teachers and determination of the appropriate language of instruction also remain troublesome. Commission after commission on the "language question" has called for instruction, at least at the primary level, in the students' native tongue. In some regions, tribal children entering school must begin by learning the official regional language, often one completely unrelated to their tribal tongue. The experiences of the Gonds of Andhra Pradesh provide an example. Primary schooling began there in the 1940s and 1950s. The government selected a group of Gonds who had managed to become semiliterate in Telugu and taught them the basics of written script. These individuals became teachers who taught in Gondi, and their efforts enjoyed a measure of success until the 1970s, when state policies demanded instruction in Telugu. The switch in the language of instruction both made the Gond teachers superfluous because they could not teach in Telugu and also presented the government with the problem of finding reasonably qualified teachers willing to teach in outlying tribal schools.

The commitment of tribes to acquiring a formal education for their children varies considerably. Tribes differ in the extent to which they view education positively. Gonds and Pardhans, two groups in the central hill region, are a case in point. The Gonds are cultivators, and they frequently are reluctant to send their children to school, needing them, they say, to work in the fields. The Pardhans were traditionally bards and ritual specialists, and they have taken to education with enthusiasm. The effectiveness of educational policies likewise varies by region. In those parts of the northeast where tribes have generally been spared the wholesale onslaught of outsiders, schooling has helped tribal people to secure political and economic benefits. The education system there has provided a corps of highly trained tribal members in the professions and high-ranking administrative posts.

Many tribal schools are plagued by high dropout rates. Children attend for the first three to four years of primary school and gain a smattering of knowledge, only to lapse into illiteracy later. Few who enter continue up to the tenth grade; of those who do, few manage to finish high school. Therefore, very few are eligible to attend institutions of higher education.

2

Excluded and Isolated Section: Scheduled Tribe Experiences of Karnataka

Culture, Civilization and Natives

The Indian cultural heritage comprises of a wide variety of complex cultures as well as simple folklore found among the tribals living in the forest, clad mountains and hilly tracts of India. More than 300 major communities of tribals are distributed from Himalayas down to Indian Ocean and from the Arabian Sea to Bay of Bengal and Eastern frontiers. The original settlement patterns, their inter relations with other communities are lost in the mist of antiquity. But the oral traditions mythologies, folklore historical evidences partly reveal their glorious past. Adivasi traditions and practices pervade all aspects of Indian culture and civilization, yet this awareness is often lacking in popular consciousness, and the extent and import of Adivasi contributions to Indian philosophy, language and custom have often gone unrecognized or been underrated by historians and social scientists. Adivasi society was built on a foundation of equality with respect for all life forms including plants and trees. There was a deep recognition of mutual dependence in nature and human society. People were given respect and status according to their contribution to social needs but only while they were performing that particular function. It was the simplicity, the love of nature, the absence of coveting the goods and wealth of others, and the social harmony of tribal society that attracted

Gautam Buddha, and had a profound impact on the ethical core of his teachings. Tribal societies were under constant pressure as the money economy grew and made traditional forms of barter less difficult to sustain.

The extension of commerce, military incursions on tribal land, and the resettling of Brahmins amidst tribal populations had an impact, as did ideological coercion or persuasion to attract key members of the tribe into "mainstream" Hindu society. Unfortunately, even sixty years after independence, Adivasis have benefited least from the advent of freedom. Although independence has brought widespread gains for the vast majority of the Indian population, Adivasis have often been left out, and new problems have arisen for the nation's Adivasi populations. With the tripling of the population since1947, pressures on land resources, especially demands on forested tracks, mines and water resources have played havoc on the lives of the Adivasis. A disproportionate number of Adivasis have been displaced from their traditional lands while many have seen access to traditional resources undercut by forest mafias and corrupt officials who have signed irregular commercial leases that conflict with rights granted to the Adivasis by the Indian constitution.

India is one of the few countries in the world having the largest tribal concentration. The tribals of this country are having fascinating rich cultural heritage and played a significant role in enrichment of composite culture. The objective and comparative studies of pre-literate societies and their contribution to great indigenous culture of India is essential before they are totally eclipsed in the fast changing cultural canvass of India. Such in-depth, comparative and analytical studies may throw light and provide missing cultural links in understanding complex Indian heritage. Santal culture may provide certain clues for decoding the scripts on the seals of Indus Valley Civilization. The study of the process of indigenization of alien culture is essential in order to bring about harmonious integration of tribal societies. A national cultural policies of tribal communities is also necessary to promote sustainable development, on the lines of their own genius. One has to love tribal culture in India to understand the uniqueness of their culture. Warm hospitality, simple ways of living and sincere judgment of the opinions are some of the traits that mark the tribal cultures of India. Their custom depicts their belief in simplicity. Most of the tribes in India have their own gods and goddesses that reflect the dependence of Tribal people on nature. Except for the few most of the tribes in India is sociable, hospitable, and fun loving along with strong community bonds. Some of the tribes shares patriarchal cultural ties and some of the tribal societies are women oriented. They have their own festivals and celebrations. The tribal people are clinging to their identity despite of the external influences that threatened the tribal culture especially after their post independence turbulent period. However it is seen that Christianity has bought change that can be termed as a total transformation in the tribal lifestyle and out look particularly in the North Eastern states of India. Of late it has been discovered that the efforts of the missionaries were not at directed in changing the basic customs of the tribal society.

Definition

The term 'tribe' is nowhere defined in our and in fact there in no satisfactory definition anywhere to the ordinary. The words suggest simple folk living in the hills and forests; to the people who are a little better informed, it signifies colourful folk famous for their dance and song; to an administrator it means a group of citizens who are the special responsibilities of the president of India to an anthropologist it indicates a special field the study of social phenomena. At present the 'term' tribe, according to western writers, generally, means an ethnic group, geographically isolated or semi-isolated, identified with one particular territory and having distinct social, economic and cultural traditions and practices. In the Indian context the term has undergone further change, particularly in post Independence period. A tribe as a collection of individuals shares a common culture. The conception and of the tribe as its social correlate coincides very closely with actual anthropological usage as this has developed through several consensus rather than explicit definition. So the tribal is a society having a clear linguistic boundary and generally a well defined political boundary. In tribal societies the relations of production are homogenous what ever the mode of production followed whether hunting, gathering or primitive agriculture there is no conspicuous separation of social categories on the basis of their production. Tribal societies are uncertified. Again a tribe has been described as a kinship group that constitutes a society (Rajasekar, 2007)

The total population of scheduled tribes in the country is 8.65 crore and they constitute 8.2 per cent of the total population as per 2001census reports. The popular names of these tribal groups in India are Vanya Jathi castes of forest, Vanavasi-inhabitants of forest, Pahari-hill dwellers, Adimajathi-primitive people, Anusuchit Janajathi – scheduled tribe and so on. Among all these terms Adivasiis known most extensively and Anusuchit Janajathi or scheduled tribe is the constitutional name covering all of them. The smallest numerical strength tribal community is Andamanese. There are 553 tribes (with many overlapping types in more than one state) as per notified Schedule under Article 342 of the Constitution of India in different States and Union Territories of the country with the largest number of 62 being in the State of Orissa. Tribal development has been given one of the major attention by all the Governments in India during all five years plan on account of the socioeconomic backwardness of the tribals. Also a lot of provisions have been brought in to the constitution to safeguard their basic interests. A study team remarked that tribal welfare should aim at the prospective within reasonable time. Advancement of the social and economic life of the tribes with a view to their gradual integration with the rest of country on a footing of equality. It is noted that Scheduled Tribe (ST) population of India constitutes about 8.08 percent of the total as per the 1991 census. Out of this more than 62 percent tribes are spread only in Five states of the country. However, the total number of such ST is 635 (Singh, 1992). All ST groups are entitled to have many benefits directly from the Governament, with reservations for them in many sectors of the development. The total number of tribal communities recognized by the Government of India as Scheduled Tribes is 572 in number. Scheduled Tribes have been listed so by the President of India in keeping with Articles 341 and 342 of the Constitution. These tribal communities mainly live in Scheduled areas, or those underlying areas, which during the British times did not come under the direct purview of civil, criminal and revenue administration.

Tribals are at the bottom of social and political ladder in India. Development projects have not only bypassed them, but have often harmed them by taking away their lands and other resources on which their livelihood was based. Unless the processes which result in their proletararianization are identified and corrective action taken to prevent it, chances are that new programmes will continue to ignore their interests as in the past. Articulation of such processes will not only lead to appropriate solutions but it also helps in sensitizing field officers who in the past often held a negative stereotype about tribals. From the viewpoint of policies, it is important to understand that tribal communities are vulnerable not only because they are poor, assetless and illiterate compared to the general population; often their distinct vulnerability arises from their inability to negotiate and cope with the consequences of their forced integration with the mainstream economy, society, cultural and political system, from which they were historically protected as the result of their relative isolation.

Primitive Tribal Groups (PTG)

The first attempt was made in 1931 to identify the PTG in the country. That group of tribals who have following characteristic features can be classified in to primitive tribal groups 1) still practicing pre-agricultural level of technology 2) extremely low level of literacy3) near stagnant or diminishing populations[1]. Till today 75 groups have been identified so far in

16 states and UTs. The problems of Indian tribals can be classified into two types.1 problems of major tribes and 2 problems of primitive tribes. But in India both of them are mixed up together and that's why no significant achievement could be made in solving the problems of primitive tribles. Now a days they are facing some serious problems like lack of basic facilities viz; no good houses, acute shortage of food, drinking water, power, medical facilities, unreachable to NGO's, lack of essential agricultural technology etc. In the resent past planning commission had issued some guide lines to the states that tribal development plan should be emphasizing on the following points 1 elimination of expatiation of all form 2 rapid social and economic development 3 improving their organizational capabilities and narrowing down the gap between the levels of development of the tribals and other are. Also commission suggested with ITDP an integrated area development plan fousing on the specific problems of the tribal people must be implemented.

Jenu kuruba and Koraga tribes have been identified as PTGs in the Karnataka State. Jenu kuruba tribe is concentrated around Mysore, Chmarajanager and Kodagu districts that are more or less 200 Km away from the Bangalore the capital city of Karnataka State. Total population of this tribe is 24654 and the literacy rate is 18.35 per cent. Male population has constituted 13.23 percent and female 5.12 per cent of literacy rate. Usually they are living in hamlet made out of bamboo and huts with there own judicial system. They believe in magic, sorcery and witchcraft. Neither polygamy nor polyandry is practiced. Besides Working with Raton and bamboo, collection of minor forest products like herb, honey, roots fruits etc as their major occupations. Poverty exists more in this group.

Koraga is a very primitive tribe in the Karnataka State. Mostly they are concentrated in Dakshina Kannada and some part of the Udupi district, which is around 450 Km away from the Silicon City-Bangalore. They very much believe in magic and witchcraft and local medicine men. The total population is 19784(2001Cencus). This tribal group has a literacy rate of 19.23

percent. Male constitute 13.11 percent and female constitute 6.3 percent of literacy rate. Neither polygamy nor polyandry is observed. They have their own rich culture and traditional heritage. Their traditional occupation is basket making. Few percentage of the population lives in semi urban areas.

Post-independence, requirements of planned development brought them the spectra of dams, mines, industries and roads on tribal lands. With these came the concomitant processes of displacement, both literal and metaphorical — as tribal institutions and practices were forced into uneasy existence with or gave way to market or formal state institutions (most significantly, in the legal sphere), tribal people found themselves at a profound disadvantage with respect to the influx of better-equipped outsiders into tribal areas. The repercussions for the already fragile socio-economic livelihood base of the tribals were devastating — ranging from loss of livelihoods, land alienation on a vast scale, to hereditary bondage. As tribal people in India perilously, sometimes hopelessly, grapple with these tragic consequences, the small clutch of bureaucratic programmes have done little to assist the precipitous pauperisation, exploitation and disintegration of tribal communities. Tribal people respond occasionally with anger and assertion, but often also in anomie and despair. However that too is branded as a typical 'law and order' problem, ignoring its socio-economic dimensions.

Scheduled Tribe in India are more like the "indigeneous" or "native people" in other parts of the world. The population of Scheduled Tribes in India according to 2001census is 8.43 crore. There is no definition of a tribe in the Constitution but one may distinguish some characteristics that are generally accepted: self-identification, language, distinctive social and cultural organisation, economic under-development, geographic location and initially, isolation, which has been steadily, and in some cases, traumatically, eroded. Many tribes still live in hilly and/or forested areas, somewhat remote from settlements. Many stereotypes flourish about the tribal persona and tribal society. Many of the tribal people are undeniably economically under-developed, and the process of their marginalisation can be traced to the intrusion of British colonialism, which quickly detected in the forest that was home to tribals, great potential for appropriation of resources. Exploitation of forest-lands by both the British and the zamindarsresulted in the clearing of huge tracts for commercial crops such as tea, coffee and rubber and allowing contractors to fell trees in the very heart of the forest. These actions deprived the tribal people of their livelihoods because many of them were hunters and gatherers of forest produce. The interaction with the outside world brought the tribal people face to face with problems they were not equipped to cope with, such as alcoholism and sexually transmitted diseases. In the post-Independence period, while the Constitution protected the rights of the Scheduled Tribes and accorded them reservation in the legislature, educational institutions and government jobs, other 'development' activities, such as the construction of large dams or the sale of timber, led to the further marginalisation of some tribes. The scenario is therefore a mixed one. It may be necessary to use natural resources to improve the living conditions of the people of the state, but it must be done in a manner that is sensitive to ensuring the protection of the environment, which provides a livelihood to tribal people. The Tenth Plan of the Central Government observes that these vulnerable communities have experienced a 'decline in their sustenance base and the resultant food insecurity, malnutrition and ill-health has forced them to live in the most fragile living conditions and some of them are even under the threat of getting extinct'. In Karnataka, the Koragas of Dakshina Kannada district and the Jenu Kurubas who are concentrated in the districts of Mysore, Chamarajnagar and Kodagu are classified as 'primitive tribes'.

Population: The tribal population of Karnataka increased to 34.64 lakh in 2001 from 19.16 lakh in 1991.The decadal growth rate during this period is a high 80.8 per cent, caused not by a spurt in fertility rates but by the addition of several new tribes to the Scheduled Tribes (ST) category. The decadal growth rate is higher for females (81.9 per cent) than for males (79.8 per cent).The highest decadal growth rate occurred in Mysore district (around 328.0 per cent), Bagalkot (261.6 per cent), Dharwad (201.1 per cent) and Belgaum (193.0 per cent).The decadal growth rate is negative in Dakshina Kannada (-2.9 per cent).Raichur (18.1 per cent) has the highest percentage of ST population followed by Bellary (18.0 per cent), while Chitradurga (17.5 per cent), which had the highest percentage of ST population in 1991 came down to third place in 2001 on account of its bifurcation.The reverse is true of Raichur.Bellary has the highest population of Scheduled Tribes as a percentage of the ST population in the state (10.6). The tribal population of Karnataka increased to 34.64 lakh in 2001 from 19.16 lakh in 1991.The decadal growth rate during this period is a high 80.8 per cent, caused not by a spurt in fertility rates but by the addition of several new tribes to the Scheduled Tribes category.

The Scheduled Tribes who constitute the weakest sections of our society have been subjected to economic exploitation and social discrimination for ages. This unfortunate situation has been largely responsible for their abject poverty, illiteracy and overall backwardness. Due to social disabilities arising from the practice of untouchability against the Scheduled Castes and geographical isolation in the case of the Scheduled Tribes, they have been alienated from the rest of the community as a result of which they have been forced to lead a life of economic and social subjugation. An idea of the enormity of the problems facing SC and ST can be gathered from the demographic profile which indicates that these two unprivileged groups constitute about one-fourth of the total population of the country. The 1991 Census of India revealed that the population of SC and ST was 13.82 crores and 6.78 crores respectively accounting for 16.48% and 8.08% of the total population of the country. Further, the census data also revealed that SC and ST children between the ages of 0-6 years constituted 19.63% and 20.18% respectively of the total SC and ST population. This means that about one-fifth of their population belongs to this vulnerable and formative age group. It may, therefore, be adivasis able for the planners to focus their attention particularly on this age-group and provide for larger investments in the areas of education, nutrition, health, etc., in order to prepare them better to face challenges in the subsequent years as a part of the mainstream Indians.

Despite the increased pace of urbanisation, India continues to be predominantly rural in character especially in the context of SC and ST. Out of the total SC and ST population of the country, as much as 81.28% and 92.61% respectively live in rural areas. Considering the fact that a majority of the SC and ST population live in rural areas where incidence of poverty is more acute, the thrust of planning should be directed towards this significant rural section of their population.

According to the 1991 Census 77.11% and 90.03% SC and ST workers were engaged in the primary sector of the economy, 9.83% and 3.85% respectively in the secondary sector and 13.06% and 6.12% respectively in the tertiary sector. In terms of work participation rate, the SC and ST compare favorably with the total population. However, considering the extent of poverty amongst SC and ST, it becomes imperative that the occupations in which they are engaged generate insufficient income. The other conspicuous feature with relation to the occupational classification is that 49.06% of the main workers among SC and 32.69% among ST were engaged as agricultural labourers. Another interesting fact comes to light on analyzing the data relating to distribution of working population by sex. While the work participation rates of male SC and ST workers are higher (51.48% for SC and 54.74% for ST) compared to female participation rates (25.98% for SC and 43.71% for ST), the SC and ST female participation rates are significantly higher than that of their counterpart in the total population. This difference is even more conspicuous in respect of ST female workers. This only confirms that the SC and ST women have to work in greater numbers because of economic compulsions.

Eradication of poverty and raising the standard of living of SC and ST persons have been the most important objectives of the countries economic planning. In the initial years of our planning it wont presumed that the economic growth to be realised through planned efforts would by itself ensure that benefits would reach the poorer sections of the population which is commonly known as the 'trickling down' or percolation theory. However, this was not to be and from experience the planners realised that unless specific plans/programmes/schemes were formulated in respect of the poorer sections of the society, especially SC and ST the main objective of eradication of poverty through economic planning would not be achieved. It was also realised that mere economic growth need not lead to better standard of living for all sections of the population, especially SC and ST, which constitute the bulk of the poorer sections of our population.

Tribal Sub-Plan

Against the background of the above realization by the planners the Tribal Sub-Plan was formulated in the context of welfare and development of ST and the strategy was adopted during the Fifth Five Year Plan. The Plan basically aimed at not only the economic development of ST but also their protection from various kinds of exploitation. At present the Tribal Sub-Plan is being implemented in 18 States and two Union Territories, viz., Andhra Pradesh, Assam, Bihar, Gujarat, Himachal Pradesh, Jammu and Kashmir, Karnataka, Kerala, Madhya Pradesh, Maharashtra, Manipur, Orissa, Rajasthan, Sikkim, Tamil Nadu, Tripura, Uttar Pra- desh, West Bengal, Andaman and Nicobar Islands and Daman and Diu. Keeping in view the fact that the ST are by and large concentrated in pockets, the strategy of the TSP was implementing the plan by identifying such pockets of tribal concentrations. Presently 194 Integrated Tribal Development Projects (ITDPs) have been launched and each of these has a contiguous geographical area of a Block or Tahsil where more than half of the population belong to the ST. In addition to this, 250 Modified Area Development Approach

(MADA) pockets have been selected in the country in which population in a contiguous area is at least 10,000 and 50% of them are tribals. Seventy five Primitive Tribal Groups (PTGs) have also been identified for the purpose of their al-around development.

One of the positive gains since the adoption of the TSP strategy has been that it has ensured separate financial outlays for utilisation' on schemes and programmes which exclusively benefit the ST. The earmarking of funds has also contributed significantly to increasing the size of the plan in terms of financial resources. The achievements can be appreciated from the fact that while during the Fifth Plan period the size of the TSP of the States imple- menting them was Rs.759.33 crores accounting for only 4.29% of the total State Plan, it increased to Rs.3019.74 crores in 1992-93 (about four fold) and represents 12.27% of the total State Plan size.

Sex ratio

The sex ratio for Scheduled Tribes (972) is higher than the all-India average (964) for STs as well as the state average (965) according to the 2001 census. There has been a perceptible improvement in the sex ratio of STs since 1991 when it was 9Among the southern states, Kerala performs well with 1,021 followed by Tamil Nadu (980). Andhra Pradesh is below Karnataka with 971.The child sex ratio for the 0–6 age group is also higher (960) than the state average of 946. Culturally, there is greater gender equity among the Scheduled Tribes compared with the general population, which is largely shaped and driven by a male-dominated discourse that prioritises son preference.Across districts, one impressive finding is that Udupi (1023) has a sex ratio higher than Kerala's followed by Kodagu and Bagalkot (996) while Bangalore Urban, typically, has the lowest sex ratio (913) followed by Haveri (941), Dharwad and Bijapur (944) and Bidar (950). In Bellary, which has the highest proportion of ST population to the state's ST population, the sex ratio is 985 while Raichur, which has the highest percentage of

ST population to the total population, is in fourth place with 993 (Appendix Tables: Series 10).

Literacy

It is a well-accepted fact that access to knowledge is crucial to improving the human development status of people. Improvements in literacy levels have positive spin-off effects, such as better health indicators and an increase in productivity, which can increase the income levels of poor people significantly. The literacy rate of STs in Karnataka is a cause for concern, as it has consistently been lower than that of the total population. The literacy rate among Scheduled Tribes, which was 36.0 per cent in 1991, increased to 48.3 per cent in 2001,while the state average moved up from 56.04 to 66.64 per cent. The gap between the literacy rate of the total population and the ST population is very wide, although there has been a marginal decline of about 1.6 percentage points in the last decade. The decennial literacy rate of the ST population has increased at a faster pace (12.3 per cent) than the rate for the total population (10.6 per cent). The literacy rate of urban STs (64.6 per cent) is higher than the overall literacy rate of STs and compares quite favorably with the state average. The female literacy rate among STs in 1991 was 23.6 per cent and it increased to 36.6 per cent in 2001.While it has increased at a faster pace than the male literacy rate (the increase during the decade was 13.0 percentage points for females and 11.8 percentage points for males) the gap between the ST male and female literacy rate declined only marginally, from 24.3 in 1991 to 23.1 in 2001, which is slightly higher than the gap between the male and female literacy rates for the total population (22.92 in 1991 and 19.22 in 2001).The literacy rate for ST women is the lowest in the state in comparison with all women as well as Scheduled Caste women. The literacy rate for rural ST women is a low 33.3 per cent compared with 56.9 per cent for men (Table 10.1).Overall, the Scheduled Tribes in the state have markedly lower literacy rates than other groups.

The fact that they are above the all-India average in respect of men and women is, of course, an indicator that Karnataka has performed better than many other states in this respect. However, the literacy status of the STs in Karnataka, which is in marked contrast to the improvements in literacy of other social groups, is a matter of concern and needs strong policies initiatives to push up literacy levels significantly. Dakshina Kannada district (72.95 per cent) has the highest literacy rate followed by Bangalore Urban (72.83 per cent), Udupi (69.62 per cent),Uttara Kannada (62.74 per cent), Shimoga (62.11 per cent), Tumkur (59.69 per cent) and Chikmaglur (58.84 per cent).The literacy rate is the lowest in Raichur (29.01 per cent), followed by Gulbarga (32.40 per cent) and Kodagu (40.37 per cent).While the literacy rate of Scheduled Tribes has improved in the decade 1991-2001, they still have a long way to go before they catch up with the rest of the population. The literacy rate of STs in Karnataka is a cause for concern, as it has consistently been lower than that of the total population.(48.3 per cent) was even lower than the literacy rate of the total population in 1991 (56.04 per cent), placing them more than a decade behind in literacy levels. Though the literacy rate for women has increased at a faster pace than for males, it is still problematic because it is so much lower than the literacy rate for all women in 2001. Districts that have high literacy rates have also done well with regard to STs with the exception of Kodagu. This is clear when we look at the statistics of districts with low literacy rates, such as Raichur (48.81) and Gulbarga (50.01),where the literacy for STs is also poor (29.01 and 32.40 respectively).The low literacy level suggests that the programmes of the Education Department have not had the desired effect on this very vulnerable sub-population. More concerted efforts are required to bring STs' literacy on par with the state average, at the very least. Culture-specific curricula would be a step in the right direction. Since illiteracy and poverty are factors that play off one another to create a cycle of deprivation, ensuring greater cohesion at the gram panchayat level between anti-poverty programmes and school enrolment/retention drives would provide the poor with viable ways to access education. Education Low literacy rates are matched by less than satisfactory educational attainments across all levels of primary, secondary and tertiary education. Many schools in tribal areas suffer from high dropout rates. Children either never enroll or attend for the first three to four years of primary school, only to lapse into illiteracy later. The attrition rate is quite strong at various levels of the educational system thereafter. The first step in the education ladder is enrolment, where performance is high for most social groups, except STs. For instance, the gross enrolment ratio (GER) in 2001, for STs for Classes I–VIII (90.12) was significantly lower than the GER for all students (98.81) and SCs (104.57).This inequality is heightened even more by the gap between the GER for south Karnataka (110.62) and north Karnataka (74.21). The GER for girls (103.64) is also much better in the southern districts than in north Karnataka (70.22). In that respect, the GER of the Scheduled Tribes in south Karnataka more closely approximates the overall GER of other social groups. The northern districts are caught up in a cycle of deprivation: they have the highest levels of ST population and also have poor human development indicators. Among districts, Bangalore Urban (319.10) and Bijapur (270.65) had high GERs, but then, the proportion of ST population in these districts is not significantly high. Districts with high ST populations did not perform well. Bellary (76.47), Raichur (58.21) and Bidar (48.76) are well below the state average. Kodagu has the lowest (73.41) GER in south Karnataka, followed by Davangere (76.23), Chamarajnagar (86.02) and Chitradurga (87.03). It is noteworthy that the ST population of Chitradurga and Davangere forms a significant percentage of the state's total ST population.

Since illiteracy and poverty are factors that play off one another to create a cycle of deprivation, ensuring greater cohesion at the gram panchayat level between anti-poverty programmes and school enrolment/retention drives would provide the poor with viable ways to access education. Unequal access to schooling is further exacerbated by the fact that ST children stay in school for the least amount of time, as indicated by the mean years of schooling. Scheduled Tribe children have the lowest levels of achievement (4.166 years) compared with SC (4.235 years) and non-SC/ST (4.458 years) children. Not surprisingly, in this context, then, ST children also constitute the highest percentage of out-of-school children (2.42), compared with the state average of 1.54 per cent. The percentage of out-of-school ST girls (2.67) is the highest across all categories. The Sample Survey of ST households conducted by the Department of Economics and Statistics in 2004,which elicited responses from persons in the age group 9–35 years, found that the principal reasons for females dropping out of school were (i) to work at home and (ii) their parents could not afford to pay for their education. The reasons are identical to the ones adduced to SC girls and indicate that the poor cannot afford the high opportunity costs of education. Girls are the first to be pulled out of school to work at home and take care of siblings to enable their mothers to work. In such cases, families do not find the many incentives offered by the government such as free uniforms, text books and even scholarships, an adequate compensation for lost wages. For boys, family work is the main reason for dropping out. Akshara Dasoha, the recently introduced midday meals programme for school children, will have a more sustained impact on ensuring enrolment and retention hereafter. Enrolment in secondary education is lower than in primary education. This is part of a pattern of attrition, which increases with levels of education and occurs across all social groups.The GER, in Classes I–X, in 2000-01, was 81.17, which was considerably lower than the GER for SCs (94.31) and all students (89.95).The differential between boys (85.59) and girls (76.51) was also higher than for SCs and all students. As with primary education, there is a marked disparity between the GER for south Karnataka (100.10) and north Karnataka (66.03).While a similar regional trend exists for all students and SCs, the disparity is not as high as it is with STs; Gulbarga (32.86), Bidar (43.06) and Chitradurga (77.93) were all below the state average. GER for Bellary and Raichur (61.89 and 43.89), which have the highest proportion of

ST population, is very poor. What are the outcomes for students who overcome the barriers of poverty and gender and stay the course? Surprisingly good, if performance in school examinations is taken as an indicator of educational attainment. Scheduled Tribe students performed well in the Class VII examinations in 2002, with a pass percentage of 88.25, which was higher than the pass percentage of all students (87.31) and SC students (87.87). Girls (89.41) had an edge over boys (87.39) as in all social groups. The inference is that girls will perform well academically, if they are enabled to overcome the socio-economic constraints that keep them out of school. This is apparent when we look at the percentage of students who passed the S.S.L.C examinations from 2001–2005 where ST girls have outperformed ST boys, SC boys and SC girls. In 2005, ST girls had a pass percentage of 55.18,which is higher than the percentage of ST and SC boys and SC girls. This outcome only serves to support the earlier finding that the performance of girl students in general, and ST girl students in particular, is exemplary, once they make it past the roadblocks. As the Sample Survey (DES: 2004A) found, the dropouts rate increased with levels of education. In the sample surveyed, there were only 0.18 per cent women graduates and 1.40 per cent male graduates, and only 0.02 per cent ST women were post-graduates. Scheduled Tribe students, in general tertiary education, cluster primarily in government .

Unequal access to schooling is further exacerbated by the fact that ST children stay in school for the least amount of time, as indicated by the mean years of schooling. In 2003-04, STs constituted 4.46 per cent of students in government colleges and 2.80 per cent in private aided colleges. There is a marked disparity in the enrolment of boys (3,209) and girls (1,652). This gap in male and female enrolment in general degree courses is uniform across government and private aided colleges. The percentage of ST students in engineering colleges averaged 0.1 per cent from 1996 to 2000 and went up to 1.7 per cent in 2002-03. Scheduled Tribes enrolment in engineering diploma courses is a minimal 0.2 per cent (Annual Reports, DTE; Annual Report

VTU 2002-03).This places young ST graduates in a disadvantageous position when they seek jobs in a market that wants trained technical professionals. They are ill-equipped to take advantage of the IT-fuelled boom in jobs in Karnataka. Economic status Historically, the tribal economy was based on subsistence agriculture and/or hunting and gathering. However, since the tribal people treated land as a common resource, they rarely had land titles, and thus, lost their lands to outsiders when exploitation of forest resources began to take place on a significant scale. This ensured that a majority ended up as small and marginal landholders. The 2001 Census data reveals that around half the ST population is in the workforce. Women constitute about 41.7 per cent of the workforce. More than 85 per cent of the working population is in rural areas. The distribution of main workers (76.4 per cent) is concentrated in the rural parts of the state where a high 51.5 per cent work. Bellary has the highest percentage of main workers (11.5 per cent) followed by Raichur (7.8 per cent).The highest percentage of ST marginal workers lives in Raichur (11.7), which also has the highest proportion of the ST population to the total population, clearly indicating their highly precarious livelihood status. Land holdings The data analysed in this section shows that STs largely own low-productivity assets: the principal asset being their own labour. This scenario is exacerbated by their low literacy and lack of vocational skills, which pushes them into jobs with poor remuneration, where men, women and children, between them, earn insufficient wages, as represented by their monthly per capita expenditure. Urban STs are slightly better placed than their rural counterparts. According to the 2001 Census, 7.65 per cent of STs are cultivators,11.86 per cent are agricultural labourers and 4.70 are in household industry. The largest percentages of ST women are in household industries (58.80) and agricultural labour (57.90). Only 29.89 per cent of ST cultivators are women here, but ST ownership of medium and large holdings is a low 7.9 and 1.0 per cent respectively. The majority of STs have small units with low productivity, which are so economically unviable that landholders are compelled to work as wage labour to survive.

Sources of income

The NSS (1999-2000) data shows that the largest percentage of rural ST households (12.8) reported rent as a source of income, followed by wages/salaried employment (9.7), cultivation (7.7), fishing and other agricultural enterprises (6.7). In Andhra Pradesh, which has a significant tribal population, 11.4 per cent derived income from fishing and other agricultural activities and 8.9 per cent from cultivation. An analysis of the income levels of STs in the Sample Survey (DES: 2004A) reveals a wide gap of more than 100 per cent between STs in urban areas and their rural counterparts. The annual per capita income of rural STs is Rs.4,768, as compared with Rs.10,987 for urban STs. The percentage of families below the poverty line in the rural ST population is 40 while it is 25 for the urban ST population. Rural Scheduled Tribes had the lowest monthly per capita expenditure (MPCE) of Rs.404, compared with Rs.419 for all social groups and much lower than the average MPCE of Rs.500 for all rural groups. In urban Karnataka, the MPCE for STs was Rs.634, which was again below the state average MPCE of Rs.911. Not surprisingly, the MPCE of STs is the lowest in rural areas given their concentration in rural areas and their dependence

The Sample Survey shows that while 57.39 per cent of rural ST households owned agricultural land, a high 74.35 per cent of it was not irrigated. The percentage of total area irrigated in the state to gross area sown was 21 per cent (2002-03).The Karnataka Agricultural Census 2001 established that STs hold 30.9 per cent of small and 19.4 per cent of semi-medium holdings. There is not much difference between STs and Ownership of land holdings by size. Rural Scheduled Tribes had the lowest monthly per capita expenditure of Rs.404, compared with Rs.419 for all social groups and much lower than the average MPCE of

Source : Agricultural Census 2004.
Directorate of Economics & Statistics 2006.

Rs.500 for all rural groups subsistence agriculture and agricultural labour (NSSO 55th round, 1999-2000). Report shows the MPCE for the southern states and Madhya Pradesh, which has a significant tribal population. Report shows an increase in the MPCE of urban households but a perceptible decline in the expenditure of rural households since 1999-2000.The decline in rural expenditure is disturbing and could be the effect of the increasing casualisation of labour. Healthcare Data on health, except for NFHS surveys, does not contain information disaggregated by social groups on a regular basis. Lack of data is a constraint when it comes to tracking the health indicators of the ST population. This section uses data from the NFHS surveys and the Sample Survey to develop a profile of the health and nutritional status of STs in the state. The Sample Survey estimated the crude birth rate (CBR) at 22.79, which is marginally higher than the state average of 21.8.The crude death rate (CDR) is estimated at 8.50 which is again higher than 7.50 for the general population. The CDR is lower for STs than SCs (9.12) in the state. Most of the health indicators show deterioration in the health of women and children. The health status of the tribal population is not on par with the rest of the state's population. The infant mortality rate (IMR) of STs (64.37) is much higher than the state average (52.0); the IMR for STs is marginally lower than the IMR for SCs (64.74) and there is a marked difference between male (75.84) and female IMR (54.48). The Sample Survey found that the principal causes of death among infants are diseases of the circulatory system (49.06 per cent) and respiratory system (23.45). Disturbingly enough, NFHS data for 1992-93 and 1998-99 shows regressive trends with the total fertility rate increasing to 2.38 from 2.15, the post-neonatal mortality rates to 21.9 from 18.0, the child mortality rate to 38.9 from 38.0 and the under-five mortality rate to 120.6 from 120.3. Only the neonatal mortality rate fell to 63.2 from 67.6.

National Family Health Survey-2 Karnataka 1998-99, IIPS, Mumbai, (November 2001) presents a grim picture of the health status of ST women and children. There are many reasons for infant and maternal deaths; the mother's age at the time of delivery, her nutritional status, access to antenatal care (ANC) and postpartum healthcare are all significant factors that determine whether women and their infants will survive the challenges posed by pregnancy and childbirth. The Sample Survey reveals that the most reproductive age group among STs in Karnataka is 20–29 years, which accounts for about 71.0 per cent of births. Given this data, the age of the mother is probably a lesser contributory factor than under nutrition and lack of access to healthcare services. *Antenatal Care*: Here too, women's access to antenatal care has either worsened or remained static. The percentage of tribal women receiving no antenatal care has increased to 28.2 per cent from 21.4 per cent during the period 1993-98.Pregnant women receiving antenatal care from registered medical practitioners also showed a decline from 53.6 per cent to 48.5 per cent during the same period. While the percentage of women not getting tetanus toxoid vaccinations at any time showed only a negligible increase from 33.0 per cent to 33.4 per cent, those receiving iron and folic acid showed a slight increase from 61.6 per cent to 63.3 per cent. This leaves a very large number outside the purview of antenatal care and the protection it affords to the mother and her infant. Institutional deliveries ensures that women receive professional care during childbirth and in the postpartum period will greatly reduce infant and maternal deaths caused by prolonged or complicated labour, eclampsia, haemorrhage, infections, etc. The NFHS data indicates that there was a marginal increase in institutional deliveries from 26.8 per cent in 1992-93 to 31 per cent in 1998-99.The Sample Survey (DES: 2004A) suggests that the situation has improved significantly with the percentage of births receiving some kind of professional care being a high 63.36 per cent, with another 24.08 per cent attended by trained dais. While this is a good development, the outcomes in terms of lowered IMR and MMR are yet to become visible. The inaccessibility of ST habitations, combined with high absenteeism of medical staff in primary healthcare centres, further contribute to the difficulties that tribal people have in availing basic health facilities. Genetic and other diseases There are also certain genetic disorders and deficiency diseases specific to tribal areas such as GEPD and sickle cell anaemia. Malaria, tuberculosis and sexually transmitted diseases are other areas of concern. Cases of HIV/AIDS too have made their appearance among the tribal

Karnataka Human Development Report 2001 (Health Issues)

Karnataka has 52 different tribal population. Given the isolation of some tribes, their traditional healing systems should be allowed to complement modern medical care practices. Many ST habitations are located in remote areas in the forest where immediate attention by trained medical staff is rarely available when it is most needed, so traditional healthcare can fill this breach. Nutrition The nutritional status of an individual depends partly on income but also on awareness of the importance of the nutritional content of food. The diet of ST women is likely to be low in terms of consumption of fruit (39.8 per cent), eggs (49.4 per cent) and chicken, meat, fish (26.6 per cent). Their consumption of milk/curd is higher than that of SCs, but less than OBCs and others, and contains some amount of pulses, beans, green leafy vegetables and other vegetables. If this is juxtaposed with data relating to the consumption patterns of (i) poor women whose consumption of milk, curd, fruit and vegetables is less than that of high income women and (ii) rural women whose consumption of milk, curd, fruit and meat is below that of urban women, then it is not surprising that ST women have very poor nutritional levels (NFHS-2,1998-99).Malnutrition is of many kinds. There is protein-energy malnutrition and micronutrient malnutrition caused by inadequate dietary intake, as well as intake of food insufficient in protein and micronutrients. Mal- and under-nutrition are reflected in the statistics relating to height and body mass. Among rural women, 9.4 per cent were below the mean height (which is on par with OBCs and others and less than SCs) and 49.0 per cent were below the body mass index (BMI), which is much worse than for all social groups. At the all-India level, 13.5 per cent were below the mean height and a high 46.3 per cent were below the BMI, which is poorer than SCs (42.1), OBCs (35.8) and others (30.5) (see Table 9.21,chapter 9).Given their poverty levels, ST women have very high levels of under-nutrition. Tribal children also suffer from sharp levels of under-nutrition. Policies directed at reducing under-nutrition among children and women must also target the dietary intake of adolescent girls in addition to focusing on pregnant and nursing mothers. Government programmes include ICDS, for children in the age group 0–6, pregnant women and nursing mothers, the public distribution system (PDS), which provides 10 kg of rice and wheat at Rs.3.0 per kg to the poor and midday meals for school children. The midday meals scheme is a big step in the right direction but, unfortunately, it does not address the nutrition needs of out-of-school children, many of whom are girls. Another cause of poor nutrition could be the declining access of the tribal people to forest areas, which had earlier provided them with food rich in protein and micro nutrients. Nutrition security through kitchen gardens is an intervention that would pay rich dividends. Family planning Awareness of birth control methods is relatively high among ST married males (48.0 per cent) and married females (45.0 per cent). Permanent forms of birth control appear to be the preferred mode, with 26.30 per cent women and a low Another cause of poor nutrition could be the declining access of the tribal people to forest areas, which had earlier provided them with food rich in protein and micro nutrients.

The brunt of family planning is borne by women, possibly because they have a higher stake in not becoming pregnant frequently and because men are not prepared to take equal responsibility for birth control, or possibly, because healthcare providers find it easier to target women. Sanitation: An unsanitary environment contributes to the proliferation of disease, leading to high morbidity rates, which reduces productivity and affects the earning capacity of individuals. The poor sanitary condition of ST households is highlighted by the 2001 Census data, which shows that 79.71 per cent of households do not have latrines and 61 per cent do not have any kind of drainage facilities. A high 90.3 per cent of rural ST households and 41.7 per cent of urban households do not have latrines, although it must be noted that the rest of the population is not well situated either, since the state averages are 82.5 per cent for rural and 24.8 per cent for urban areas. About 42 per cent ST households have a bathroom in the house, as against 58.9 per cent of the total population at the state level and 36.1 per cent at the all-India level. In Karnataka, STs have better sanitary facilities than their counterparts at the all-India level, but this is only a matter of degree. A low 11.18 per cent of ST settlements/villages have community latrines, about 30.5 per cent of households have open drains and only 8.6 of households have closed drainage. A high 58.0 per cent habitations lack storm water drains. Drinking water Tap water constitutes the main source of drinking water for 53.7 per cent ST households (58.39 for all households). Access to drinking water by tap within the premises is higher for all households (24.1) than for STs (12.7) and SCs (12.6). A slightly higher number of ST households have access to tap water near the premises (Census: 2001).Almost 89.0 per cent of ST villages surveyed have a drinking water facility within the village and the sources comprise bore-wells with hand pumps, mini water supply and piped water supply schemes. Three out of four villages have adequate drinking water supply during all seasons (Table 10.14).

Housing:The percentage of STs living in permanent houses (43.7 per cent) is lower than the corresponding figures for SCs (51.1) and all households (54.9) according to the 2001 Census. About 39 per cent dwell in semi-permanent houses compared with 35.6 per cent for all households and 36.6 per cent for SCs. A higher percentage of rural STs live in semi-permanent houses (43.4) than urban STs (23.1) who live predominantly in permanent houses (66.9). There is little difference between STs and all households, with reference to building material used. A high percentage of STs (84.4 per cent) owned their houses, compared with 78.5 per cent for all households. House ownership is highest in rural areas (91.9 per cent). This can be attributed to the very progressive state and Centrally-sponsored housing programmes (Ashraya, Ambedkar, Indira Awaas), which clearly have had visible outcomes. Almost 89.0 per cent of ST villages surveyed have drinking water facility within the village and the sources comprise bore-wells with hand pumps, mini water supply and piped water supply schemes. Three out of four villages have adequate drinking water supply during all seasons.

Electricity: Electrical connectivity is fairly high among ST households. According to the 2001 Census, a total 64.7 per cent of ST households in Karnataka had electricity as a source of lighting, compared with 78.5 per cent for all households and 68.5 per cent for SC households. In rural areas, STs depended on electricity (60.3 per cent) as well as kerosene (38.8), whereas urban ST households relied principally on electricity (80.6 per cent). These high levels of connectivity indicate that state policies to provide electrical connections to ST households have paid off handsomely.

State Policies: The Department of Tribal Welfare was formed specifically to address the needs of STs in Karnataka. Its budget is part of the budget of the Department of Social Welfare.Tribal Sub-PlanThe concept of the Tribal Sub-Plan (TSP) and its counterpart the Special Component Plan (SCP) emerged in the National Fifth Five-Year Plan. The Tribal Sub-Plan was first introduced in 1976-77 when it was implemented in fiveIntegrated Tribal Development Projects (ITDP) in the districts of Mysore,Chikmaglur, Kodagu and Dakshina Kannada (including Udupi). In 1992, it was extended to all districts in the state.The objectives of the TSP are poverty alleviation, protection of tribal culture, education, healthcare and providing basic minimum infrastructure. Poverty alleviation includes programmes in agriculture, animal husbandry, sericulture, horticulture, village and small industries as well as all employment-generating schemes such as Swarna Jayanthi Swarozgar Yojana(SJSY).Pooling TSP funds Under the TSP, departments earmark three per cent of their plan budget for expenditure on tribal development. However,as in the case of the Special Component Plan for Scheduled Castes, some departmental schemes were not particularly relevant or effective and ended up being symbolic gestures to the development of STs. The TSP funds were first pooled in 1991. In 'pooling', funds earmarked under TSP are partially or completely withdrawn from the department. The resultant corpus is then utilised to finance three strategic areas: housing, education (construction of hostels) and financing irrigation wells and The Department of Tribal Welfare was formed specifically to address the needs of STs in Karnataka.

Not surprisingly, a high 30.82 per cent of families failed to maintain their assets (Tribal Sub Plan-Asset Evaluation Study 2000-01).Income Generation: Apart from poverty reduction and income generating programmes such as SJSY, SGSY, Stree Shakti,there are also specific schemes to address the needs of the Scheduled Tribes who are landless or who have land that is not irrigated. The Karnataka Scheduled Castes and Scheduled Tribes Development Corporation implements various programmes for the economic development of the community, among which, the most important are: a. The land purchase scheme: This provides land to landless agricultural labourers by purchasing lands from non-SC/ST landholders at a unit cost of Rs.60,000 with a subsidy of 50 per cent. Self-employment programme: Under this, financial institutions provide assistance for setting up businesses. The corporation provides a subsidy of Rs.10,000 for a unit cost of Rs.1,00,000, and the remaining amount is a loan from financial institutions. Where the unit cost is above Rs.50,000,the corporation sanctions 20 per cent as 'margin money loan', with a ceiling of Rs. one lakh in each case, with an interest of four per cent, while 75 per cent is a loan from banks and NSFDC. The beneficiary must meet the remaining 5 per cent as his/her contribution. Ganga Kalayana : This comprises (i) the

Community Irrigation Scheme, under which, land owned by several ST families are provided bore-well irrigation. Depending upon the availability of water, two to three bore-wells are drilled and other expenses for installation of pump sets, energisation, storage tanks, pipelines are provided bythe corporation; (ii) the individual irrigation bore-well programme, where the corporation takes up construction of irrigation bore-wells and provides infrastructure at a unit cost of Rs.75,000 of which Rs.65,000 is subsidy and the rest is a loan from financial institutions. The land purchase scheme provides land to landless agricultural labourers by purchasing lands from non-SC/ST landholders at a unit cost of Rs.60,000 with a subsidy of 50 per cent.pump sets under the Ganga Kalyan scheme. Report provides information about the TSP outlay and the funds pooled since 2001-02. Review of programmes in this section: we look at programmes, which have been more successful than others in promoting tribal development. Collection of minor forest produce and tribal co-operatives: Tribal people living in hilly, forest areas depend heavily on minor forest produce (non-timber forest produce) for their livelihood. As much as 50 per cent of the income of the Soliga Tribe in Chamarajnagar district, for example, comes from the collection of minor forest produce (MFP).Large-scale Adivasi multi-purpose societies (LAMPS) were formed in the late 1970s, with tribal people as members, to market non-timber forest products (NTFP) procured from the forests by the tribal people. It also supplies essential food commodities and consumer items to its members. At present, there are 21 LAMP Societies in Karnataka with 42,182 tribal families in the jurisdiction. Only 25,504 out of 63,558 members, are active. LAMP Cooperatives, which were established to provide marketing tie-ups and ensure better prices for NTFP products procured by the tribals, have had mixed outcomes. One view is that they do not provide much scope for tribals in the price fixation mechanism for NTFP. While the NTFP selling rates have been registering a steady increase, the purchase price fixed for procuring the produce from the tribals has shown only a nominal increase. LAMPS should enhance rates so that the poor tribal people, who actually procure these items from within the deep jungle at some personal risk, can improve their economic conditions. Animal Husbandry : Unlike subsistence agriculture, animal husbandry is an important income-generating activity for the tribals, as it gives immediate returns. Unfortunately, the income from these activities is meagre due to tribals' inability to provide adequate fodder and water Sectors, which have direct and quantifiable benefits for the Scheduled Tribes, are classified as 'divisible' and the TSP allocation is limited to these sectors. 'Non-divisible' sectors include major and medium irrigation, energy, borrowings, etc.

Micro industries: The objective here is to utilise local skills for the promotion of micro industries like bee-keeping, minor forest produce, tribal crafts, sericulture, and carpentry. An investment varying from Rs.500 to Rs.25,000 generates an income of about Rs.30–40 per day. Self-help groups: Self-help groups (SHGs) have radically changed the micro-credit systems in rural areas. Tribals, who form a large percentage of rural agricultural labour, and subsistence farmers find it difficult to source credit from financial institutions and are likely to benefit from the SHG philosophy. Self-help groups promote savings and microfinance among members, but they also have other objectives such as social empowerment and gender equity. The Stree Shaktiprogramme of the department of Women and Child Development has 1,19,621 ST women members in 1,00,000 SHGs. The role of NGOs in tribal development There is growing realisation of the need to develop a healthy partnership between the government and the non-governmental organisations (NGOs). The role of NGOs in tribal welfare activities, though small, has been responsible for introducing qualitative changes in the lives of the people.Vivekananda Girijana Kalyana Kendra, Swami Vivekananda Youth Movement, DEED,FEDINA, CORD, Samagra Grameena Ashrama, Janashikshana Trust, Chintana Foundation, DUDI,Samvriddi/Krupa,Vanavasi Kalyana Ashrama are some of the NGOs involved in tribal development in Karnataka.Community based organisations. It is possible to make development works more effective and sustainable through an engagement with the local community, which has a better understanding than non-tribals, of its own socio-economic needs, traditions and culture. Their participation in programmes, funded by government and voluntary organisations builds confidence in the people to utilise the services thus offered and provides feedback for modification and re-orientation of programmes. In Chamarajnagar district, the tribal people's organisations are known as sanghas. They actively Under the IPP-9 project, the Health Department and NGOs trained tribal girls as Auxiliary Nurse and Midwives (ANM) and they were posted to sub centres in remote tribal areas. These ANMs are now providing good healthcare services to tribal women and children. The government-owned primary health centres at Gumballi and Thithimathi, were handed over to Karuna Trust and Vivekananda Foundation respectively and are run as model PHCs. In B.R. Hills, VGKK, an NGO, is promoting the traditional knowledge systems of tribals and has integrated traditional healthcare system with modern medicine. Tribal knowledge of herbal medicines is being promoted. Their participation in programmes such as sustainable harvesting of NTFP through participatory resource monitoring, value additions to the NTFP and conservation of bio-diversity has helped to reduce the exploitation of minor forest produce by outsiders. Concerns Some state programmes have been very successful in providing services to the Scheduled Tribes, e.g.free housing, drinking water supply and electrical connectivity to ST households. There is a gamut of programmes designed to address the problems of school dropouts (Ashram schools, scholarships, free text books and uniforms, midday meals) and income poverty through the many poverty reduction programmes. Unfortunately, the degree of effectiveness in terms of programme implementation that one sees in these sectors is not evident in the three critical areas of health, education and poverty reduction. The magnitude of the problem is so great that a large percentage of Scheduled Tribe families is still poor and lacks access to resources that would improve their education and health status. It can be said, based on some of the indicators discussed above and in chapter 2, that the human development status of the Scheduled Tribes is more than a decade behind the rest of the population of the state and they are the poorest and most deprived of all sub-populations in the state. The role of NGOs in tribal welfare activities, though small, has been responsible for introducing qualitative changes in the lives of the people. Tribal participation in programmes such as sustainable harvesting of NTFP through participatory resource monitoring, value additions to the NTFP and conservation of bio-diversity have helped to reduce the exploitation of minor forest produce by outsiders.

Their literacy rate is the lowest for all social groups and female literacy, which is a low 36.6 per cent when compared with the state average of 56.9, places ST women far behind a population that is, itself, disadvantaged to start with. There are disparities between ST students and others at every level and along all indicators of educational attainment: enrolment and retention in primary education and subsequent participation in secondary and tertiary education. One bright feature is the fact that girls perform well scholastically once they clear the hurdles to the deceptively simple acts of first enrolling and secondly, being allowed to stay on in school. The health of the tribal people has not improved significantly over the previous decade. Their IMR (64.37) is worryingly higher than that of the total population (52.0) of the state. This scenario can be partly attributed to the inadequacy of institutional support. Both antenatal and post-partum care by skilled attendants is not adequately available to the tribal people, especially those who live in remote or inaccessible habitations. State functionaries have not focused sufficiently on these vulnerable people to ensure a reduction in maternal and infant deaths. Under-nutrition levels among children are severe enough to lead to stunting. The occupational distribution shows that the majority of the tribal people are small and marginal farmers and agricultural labour. Their holdings are unirrigated and therefore economically unlivable. The Scheduled

Tribes also have very low monthly per capita expenditure compared with the rest of the population. Access to MFP and NTFP is critical to the survival of certain tribes, who live in or around forests, most of which are now classified as wildlife sanctuaries.

Recommendations

Develop a comprehensive policies on tribal development, which derives inputs from people at the grass root level to ensure sustainable development that is ecologically sound, people oriented, decentralised and culturally acceptable. Ensure the collection and collation of disaggregated data to enable benchmarking and monitoring. Conduct a rapid survey of the health status of the tribals and prepare region-specific and tribe-specific health plans. Relax norms for primary health centres and sub-centres in tribal areas and make allowances for geography and population. Select tribal girls for training as ANMs and post them to sub-centres located in predominantly tribal areas. They could also be trained in traditional medicine and health practices, thus encouraging and integrating traditional healing systems into modern medicine. Encourage nutrition security by promoting kitchen gardens. Focus on genetic diseases. Ensure 100 per cent antenatal care coverage and immunisation of women and children. Provide secondary and tertiary care, transport facilities for emergency services and obstetric care. Ensure greater access to education through convergence of the services of several departments: Education, Rural Development and Labour to monitor child labour, track dropouts and provide local employment to their parents. Include tribal culture, traditional knowledge systems, tribal history and vocational skills training in the school curriculum. Involve tribals in biodiversity conservation; encourage them to grow fruit trees on degraded forest-lands; allow sustainable harvesting of the non-forest produce for their livelihood, without endangering the biodiversity of the forest. Encourage need-based economic activities that use locally available raw materials and assist in marketing of finished goods. Provide more budgetary support to the land purchase scheme. Promote organic forming, conservation of traditional seed. Empower tribals at village level to participate effectively in Gram Sabhas, by promoting community based organisations. Develop a comprehensive policies on tribal development, which derives inputs from people at the grass-root level to ensure sustainable development that is ecologically sound, people oriented, decentralised and culturally acceptable. Include tribal culture, traditional knowledge systems, tribal history and vocational skills training in the school curriculum.

The Indian sub-continent has the largest population of tribal. They born and grows the children of the nature; but they are deprived of many civic facilities. They are spread across the country mainly in forest and hilly areas. Most of them are living below poverty –line. The absence of institutional schooling; distinctive customs regarding birth, marriage and death; a moral code different from that of Hindus and Muslims; specialties of religious beliefs and rituals etc. are the distinguishing features of tribal. In India- most of the tribal persons are suffering from illiteracy, unemployment, poverty, indebtedness, liquor habits, health problems and insufficient infrastructural facilities. In the given institutional set up, they have no access to the various economic social development programmes implemented by the Government. Due to some governmental efforts, considerable changes have taken place in the tribals. Yet, for more improvement of tribal conditions; their forest -rights should be protected, some employment generation programmes should be made, special health programmes must be promoted, number of primary schools in tribal areas should be increased and the infrastructural facilities should be improved.

The Chapter is based on various resources.

3

Tribals and Education: Few stylized facts

The total number of tribal communities recognized by the Government of India as Scheduled Tribes is 572 in number. Scheduled Tribes have been listed so by the President of India in keeping with Articles 341 and 342 of the Constitution. These tribal communities mainly live in Scheduled areas, or those underlying areas, which during the British times did not come under the direct purview of civil, criminal and revenue administration. Traditional tribal societies are undergoing a rapid change with the mainstream policy of the Indian Government. For the tribal communities the process of becoming a part of the mainstream has meant a declining control on their resources and erosion of their cultural heritage. The major issue affecting the tribals in India is displacement – not merely displacement by large projects but resource displacement, thus violating the basic survival rights of tribal communities. Tribal areas reveal a high degree of land alienation. Non-tribals have invaded tribal protected areas. Deforestation, mainly due to exploitation of forest for industrial purposes, is another manifestation of resource displacement. This has resulted in decreasing access to forest resources by tribal communities. With increasing globalization and privatization, the land rights of tribal areas is under greater threat since these are regions which have a high natural resource base and has tremendous potential to meet multiple market demands. Added to resource displacement is project displacement where development projects have threatened the livelihood needs of tribal communities. More than forty percent of displaced persons of all large development projects are tribals. Although there are protective laws governing tribal areas these laws are being circumvented or not implemented in spirit. The forestlaws and land acquisition laws also run counter to the landrights of tribal communities. The government programmes especially earmarked for tribal areas do not reach the people for whom they are meant due to ineffective implementation system.

Education has limited connotation. It is largely concerned with the existing formal structure of education and the institutionalized methodology of imparting knowledge to individuals. Within this very system exist many sub-groups of individuals with specific needs and tribals are one of them. In fact tribals form a large group of individuals in the Indian society. For several historical, economic and social reasons the scheduled groups have remained economically backward and socially retarded even to this day. The ST population accounts for 8.6% of the total population of the country. There are many constitutional provisions and legislative support available for safeguarding the welfare and the interests of S.Ts. In addition planned developmental efforts have also taken place through Five-Year plans. Despite the concern reflected in the Indian Constitution and the developmental efforts initiated for the welfare and the development of S.Ts. Their socio-economic and political development is still far below the others and therefore much more needs to be done in this direction, including their empowerment – educational, social, economic and political – with due regard to their special identity – culturally, habitation ally, traditionally – and in terms of the tribals' age-old rights and customs. The number of educational institutions in 1978, together with the number of pupils within the area covered by the plans for tribal development, is low. The students accommodated in hostels were also given special coaching. The number of teachers in ashram schools was 1,171, and the number of teachers employed in primary, upper primary and high schools was 1,821. The number of students in receipt of postmatric scholarships was 1,950. Further 468 tribal students were admitted to reputable private schools and public schools, and 90 students were enrolled in the special residential school for tribals.

Education for the marginlized people, as for anyone else in India, has today become a matter of great importance. Ever since India gained independence a considerable amount of money and resources have been spent so that the unprivileged, undeveloped and neglected marginlized people could get a fair deal. It has been generally recognized that India being a welfare state cannot afford to leave a particular section of the population behind in the field of education, as indeed in any other field. This would be against the principle of democratic development of the country there is hardly any necessity, therefore to emphasize the need and importance of education for these people. Everyone everywhere feels these needs. An earnest endeavor is being made by all concerned at all levels to bring these less privileged people, the scheduled tribes, on the same educational level as that attained by the more advanced community of India.

From 17.6% the literacy rate of the country has increased 67.7%. The total number of educated population has also increased by 204.67 million. The literacy rate of women also has been increased. The gender gap which was existed in the past has also been narrowing down. women are showing a all-round development in all sectors . Along with government private educational institutions in the country also growing.

According to the 1993 educational survey 93% of the total Indian rural people was served by primary schools and 81% of the habitations had primary schools. The most interesting aspect is student enrollment has gone up more than 6times particularly girls by 10.11 times. Further, the total number of student ratios in primary school has increased from 41.7% in 1951-52 to 93.1% in 2000-2001. Total enrollment for higher primary schools has gone from 11.3% to 56.63% from the independence till today.

These two data shows existence dropouts even in primary stage schooling. In case of teachers from 622,000 in 1951-52 has reached upto 3,243,000 in 2000-2001. In the same way percentage female teachers also increased. Incase of dropping out from primary until higher primary significant decline could be seen.

Indian Marginalized Group

No community can make their development without the spread of education. Development means all-round development, i.e., in the field of social, economic, cultural and above all the quality of life of human being. Whenever man uses the modern scientific devices for their progress in then, very much spread of education is badly needed. Education and development –these two terms are correlated. That is why, the developed countries give too much attention for the growth of education with a view to make their fast development in all aspects of their country. Thus, any micro or macro level study on education is very much relevant for the development studies of any country. Again, it has found that, a country that is more advanced and scientific in the field of education, the rate of growth is higher of that country and vice versa. Hence, to understand the nature and extent of development of a particular community, the study of the state of education of that community is very significant and important.

As a welfare state the governments of our country have taken a lot of developmental programmes with a view to make the all round development of the people. For the purpose of the overall development of the people the central as well as state governments have set up born macro and micro projects, development cells etc. Special emphasis is given among the grass root people and more particularly among the tribal people of the country.

Developmental Programmes

Both State and Central govt. have implemented many special programmes to uplift the these primitive group in the State, namely (1) promotion of developmental activities to raise level of living of tribals and (2) protection of their interests through legal and administrative support. Presently these programmes have covered more than 260 hamlets scattered in two few districts of Karnataka. These programmes are implemented through ITDP. Stae govt. has implemented several sub plans. This special sub-plans has been implemented the through financial resources drawn from1 State plan, 2 special assitences3 sectoral programmes 4 institutional programmes. Till now 4.67 crores of money have been spent on primitive tribal groups only. Department of health and family welfare has sent 22 lakh rupees to upgrade the primary health centers in the tribal area. State govt. has spent 1.34 crores rupees especially to provide basic infrastructure to these tribal hamlets and to give a commercial out look to the several items produced by these tribal group. Department of education has appointed some NGOs to improve the quality of the education in this tribal sector. Up lift ment of Ashram schools have got some importance in the state budget. Two marketing and service extension centers are being exclusively set up in tribal areas by the state govt. with the help of local NGOs for marketing tribal handicrafts. State agriculture department also implemented some programmes to improve the agriculture techniques of these tribals.

This author has had an intensive fieldwork in selected tribal areas where large concentration of the above mentioned tribals could have been found. The methodology included participant observation, micro and macro study, and focus group interview with tribal leaders, NGO's, local politicians, resources persons, and state officials.

Result and Discussion

Of course, Government has implemented various tribal welfare programmes through ITDP, but failed to show any interest in the feed back process. Success and failure of any polices and programmes depend on the participation of local people. Our study has shown that the non-tribal officials who don't have any first hand field experience about tribals are framing all these policies and programmes. Our study also reveled that agriculture, animal husbandry, cottage industries and forest development programmes have limited success so for because concerned policies do not have any scope for the peoples participation. Most odd thing we found those, even Governament officials did not have complete awareness about various tribal developmental schemes. Few NGO's working for the welfare of these tribals have suffering with many problems like lack of organizational programmes have limited success so for because concerned policies do not have any scope for the people participation. Most odd thing we found those even Governament officials did not have complete awareness about various tribal developmental schemes. Few NGO's working for the welfare of these tribals have suffering with many problems like lack of organizational efficiency, no trained Anthropologists and realising of fund/grants on time. Some NGO's said they have to pay bribe to the concerned officials for the release of the money in the form of commission. Only 9.32 per cent of tribal people aware about some of the Governament schemes for their self-development. It shows the acute rate of illiteracy among these tribles. More than 77.74 percent tribal people said medical felicities is beyond reachable to them. Also they said allopathic doctors are rarely visits to the primary health centers may be once/twice in a weak. During summer these people should walk many miles to get drinking water. Infectious diseases are most common among these tribles. Usually Attendance is very low in Ashram Schools. Teachers says that acute poverty, lack of interest in both parents and children, and superstitious believes are the most common reasons for the high rate of- drops out among tribal children. But on the other hand it is also true that most of the teachers are not showing any interest to teach tribal children. Many of them are working in these schools just for special remuneration by the Governament. Our study has shown that the sectional allocation of the tribal sub plan do not reflect the felt needs of the people and as such have not created the desired impact. More than that this study has revealed that there is no scope for a set planning for implementation, monitoring and evaluation of programmes in the tribal sub plan. Not only the PTG, even other tribal groups in the state have yet to seen the different faces of Basic Infrastructure. Governament has implemented many developmental schemes but the main problem seems to be that it has no any set channels to make reach these programmes to each and every tribal family. Our study has reveled that only more than 12-18 percent of these groups has got some of the facilities like housing, power and water. Governament has a plan to mapping new under ground water areas with the help of Geo Information System. Many houses constructed by the Governament agencies have become already ruined due to low quality of work. More than two third families don't have power facilities. Now Governament has a plan to provide new solar technologies to the some of the hamlets that are not so easily reachable. People have to walk 2-3 miles to get drinking water. Most of the families are using water from near by ponds and open wells. So these people are facing acute health problems. Good drainage and toilet facilities have become nightmare. Many tribal leaders told that they tried their level best to bring these problems to the notice of the concerned officials but the result is a big zero. Some of them told local political leaders visits only during election time. But politicians and other people's opinion are that these people don't like to receive any new technology/things in to their life. Many of the GRAM PANCHYATHS are absolutely inactive due to the lack of fund and political consciousness. Roads and other communication systems are more or less absent. During rainy season all links between these tribes and the rest of the world will be completely out of order. State Governament has a plan to shift some families of these tribes and rehabilitate in new places with assured basic infrastructure. Families are protesting against this decision saying that Governament provide every basic infra structure in the new habitat first. Then we will ready to move from here.

Shifting cultivation still prevalent in these two tribal groups. So policies makers should seriously think to providing new agricultural technologies emphasizing on integrated farming system.[3] Since these people does not shows any interest in using chemical fertilizers, sustaining agricultural through green manure can be promoted through field demonstrations. Now PTG are facing acute shortage of the food. Hence the best possible alleviative before the Govt. and local NGO's is introducing new eco-friendly technologies for rice and other crop cultivation's. Many tribal people are getting different types of help from co-operative societies like LAMPS but it is not working round the year. Due to this now a days they are not getting any good prices for their products. So, they are very eager to sell their products directly to the market but the main problem is involvement of middlemen, as they are exploiting uneducated tribes in different ways. More odd thing is that these middlemen have good relation ships with developmental officials at various levels. Also 33 to 40 percent tribal households have been affected by land alienation problem. Our study has revealed that about 77 percent of land were alienated by the non-tribles there, by cause indebtedness among the tribles. The effort made by the Governament to tackle this problem is not even partially succeed because, some invisible hands are effectively functioning between rich nontirbles and concerned Governament officials. This is the main hurdle in reaching all the schemes to the grass root level. In case of promote of cottage industry, Governament has established Tribal Cooperative Marketing Development Federation of India Limited. The main work of this limited is to provide commercial market to the tribal products. Also it helps to promote enterpriunrship among tribals by providing soft loans. Apart from this Governament has newly introduced a project called Tribal Women Empowerment Project. But the main draw back is no provision of imparting training to the local artesian to up grade their skills. Some time there will be no enough supply of raw materials to the cottage industries. Since Governament has brought a strict forest conservation rules backed by the recent Supreme Court verdict many tribal people says, they are not permitted to collect any minor forest products. Then how can we get raw materials for our traditional work? Many NGO's said Governament should revise its forest polices and connect to the tribal welfare programmes

The extent of education among tribal women is lamentably low. In most tribal societies, men and women enjoy equal status and work shoulder in home, field and the forest. Women are not segregated or confined behind the pardah. If men alone are educated it creates an imbalance among couples with the husband educated and the wife unlettered. There is emotional mal adjustment. Educational young men long for educated wives and if they are even prepared to change their faith. It should also be remembered that the education of a girl has a more lasting impact on society than that of a boy. When the educated girl becomes a mother and the mistress of a house, she will see to it that her children receive education even though it may mean some sacrifice and inconvenience for the family. Education of tribal girls would also provide a large number of women teachers for the primary schools. Nurses and women social welfare workers would also be available in large numbers. In many tribal areas, Ashram and Residential schools have proved very useful. Tribal education planning should enable the tribals to learn the way o f cooperation, acquire a sense of self-reliance and meet the new challenges of life. If the tribal education programmes were sincerely worked out it would definitely bring tremendous change in the economic structure of tribal areas. Special vocational education is to be imparted to tribal girls in crafts like tailoring, cutting, typewriting, embroidery, and other non-traditional skills like computer education. Tribal economic development is closely related to their educational development. Programmers of economic development and the spread of education should go side by side if both are to succeed. The approach to education should be flexible. Ashram shalas, Vikaswadis and non-formal conscientization programs are well suited to tribal areas.

Education cannot change in any fundamental way unless we change our basic patterns of thinking and interacting so that learning can become a way of life. Teachers, parents, administrators, district resource and community people are coming together throughout hundreds of school communities to learn how to revitalize their schools with a process known as "Tribes." Evaluation of Tribes Learning Community Schools has examined the impact of the Tribes process on student behavior, academic performance, school culture, and teacher collegiality. Studies have shown that: Tribes TLC has a positive impact on classroom environment, teachers report spending less time managing student behavior, students are significantly less likely to be referred for disciplinary problems, the Tribes process helps teachers address performance and content standards, students in well-implemented classrooms score significantly higher on standardized tests than students from comparison groups, teachers report increased staff collegiality and planning. "Responsive Education" is an essential pedagogy for academic achievement and school reform. It is the synthesis of artful teaching practices. It is based on understanding the critical developmental needs of a student age and cultural group. The Goal is to engage all teachers, administrators, students and families in working together as a learning community that is dedicated to caring and support, active participation and positive expectations for all students.

4

Development of Primitive Tribal Groups in Karnataka: Some Preliminary Observations

India is one of the major countries having larger concentration of tribal groups in the world. Among the tribals, primitive tribal groups are highly vulnerable. These groups are still isolated from the main stream of civilized society. They are small in number and having pre-agricultural technology. Literacy rate is extremely low. The different people are exploiting these primitive tribles group in different ways. Both Govt. and NGO's have implemented many polices and programmes for the up lift ment of these tribles. But result is not so significant and encouraging because of rigid traditional aspects of these tribals and more then that some time there dwelling places will be beyond reachable. Also the implementation machinery was faulty and development programmes could not be implemented properly. In this paper an attempt has been made to explore the different developmental aspects of two identified primitive tribals of Karnataka state I,e *jenu kuraba* and *koraga with* emphasizing on the crucial areas for an urgent action.

Introduction

Tribal development has been given one of the major attention by all the Governments in India during all five years plan on account of the socioeconomic backwardness of the tribles. Also a lot of provisions have been brought in to the constitution to safeguard their basic interests. A study team remarked that tribal welfare should aim at the prospective within reasonable time. Advancement of the social and economic life of the tribes with a view to their gradual integration with the rest of country on a footing of equality. It is noted that Scheduled Tribe (ST) population of India constitutes about 8.08 percent of the total as per the 1991 census. Out of this more than 62 percent tribes are spread only in Five states of the country. However, the total number of such ST is 635 (Singh, 1992). All ST groups are entitled to have many benefits directly from the Governament, with reservations for them in many sectors of the development.

Who are the Primitive Tribal Groups (PTG)?

The first attempt was made in 1931 to identify the PTG in the country. That group of tribals who have following characteristic features can be classified in to primitive tribal groups 1) still practicing pre-agricultural level of technology 2) extremely low level of literacy3) near stagnant or diminishing populations$_1$. Till today 75 groups have been identified so far in 16 states and UTs. The problems of Indian tribes can be classified in to two types.1 problems of major tribes and 2 problems of primitive tribes. But in India both of them are mixed up together and that's why no significant achievement could be made in solving the problems of primitive tribles. Now a days they are facing some serious problems like lack of basic facilities viz; no good houses, acute shortage of food, drinking water, power, medical facilities, unreachable to NGO's, lack of essential agricultural technology etc. In the resent past planning commission had issued some guide lines to the states that tribal development plan should be emphasizing on the following points 1 elimination of expatiation of all form 2 rapid social and economic development 3 improving their organizational capabilities and narrowing down the gap between the levels of development of the tribles and other are. Also commission suggested with ITDP an integrated area development plan fousing on the specific problems of the tribal people must be implemented.

Area of the study:

Jenu kuruba and Koraga tribes have been identified as PTGs in the Karnataka State. Jenu kuruba tribe is concentrated around Mysore, Chmarajanager and Kodagu districts that are more or less 200 Km away from the Bangalore. Total population of this tribe is 24654 and the literacy rate is 18.35 percent. Usually they are living in hamlet made out of bamboo and huts with their and judicial system. They believe in magic, sorcery and witchcraft. Neither polygamy nor polyandry is practiced. Besides Working with Raton and bamboo, collection of minor forest products like herb, honey, roots fruits etc as their major occupations.

Koraga is a very primitive tribe in the Karnataka State. Mostly they are concentrated in Dakshina Kannada and some part of the Udupi district, which is around 450 Km away from the Silicon City-Bangalore. They very much believe in magic and witchcraft and local medicine men. The total population is 19784(2001Cencus) with 19.23 percent of literacy. They have their own rich culture and traditional heritage. Their traditional occupation is basket making. Few percentage of the population lives in semi urban areas.

The author has had an intensive fieldwork in selected tribal areas where large concentration of the above mentioned tribes could have been found. The methodology included participant observation, micro and macro study, and focus group interview with tribal leaders, NGO's, local politicians, resources persons, and state officials.

Literacy Status of PTGs of Karnataka

Table-1

PTG	*Total Population*	*Total Literate*	*Male-Literates*	*Female Literates*	*Male*	*Female*	*Total*
Jenu kuruba	27597	4033	3172	2161	15.10	19.29	17.09
Koraga	11566	3543	1678	1865	27.82	29.38	28.06

(Source: Mohanty, 2002)

Result and Discussion

Of course, Government has implemented various tribal welfare programmes through ITDP, but failed to show any interest in the feed back process. Success and failure of any policies and programmes depend on the participation of local people. Our study has shown that the non-tribal officials(22%) who don't have any first hand field experience about tribals are framing all these policies and programmes. Our study also reveled that agriculture, animal husbandry, cottage industries and forest development programmes have limited success so for because concerned policies do not have any scope for the people participation. Most odd thing we found those, even Governament officials did not have complete awareness about various tribal developmental schemes. Few NGO's (12%) working for the welfare of these tribals have suffering with many problems like lack of organizational programmes have limited success so for because concerned policies do not have any scope for the people participation. Most odd thing we found that even Governament officials did not have complete awareness about various tribal developmental schemes. Few NGO's working for the welfare of these tribals have suffering with many problems like lack of organizational efficiency, no trained Anthropologists and fund/ grants on time. Some NGO's said they have to pay bribe to the concerned officials for the release of the money in the form of commission. Only 9.32 percent of tribal people aware about some of the Government schemes for their self-development. It shows the acute rate of illiteracy among these tribles. More than 77.74 per cent tribal people said medical facilities is beyond reachable to them. Also they said allopathic doctors are rarely visits to the primary health centers may be once/twice in a weak. During summer these people should walk many miles to get drinking water. Infectious diseases are most common among these tribles.

Attendance is very low in Ashram schools. Teachers says that acute poverty, lack of interest in both parents and children and superstitious believes are the most common reasons for the high rate of- drops out among tribal children. But on the other hand it is also true that most of the teachers are not showing any interest to teach tribal children. Many of them are working in these schools just for special remuneration by the

Governament. Our study has shown that the sectional allocation of the tribal sub plan do not reflect the felt needs of the people and as such have not created the desired impact. More than that this study has revealed that there is no scope for a set planning for implementation, monitoring and evaluation of programmes in the tribal sub plan. Not only the PTG, even other tribal groups in the state have yet to seen the different faces of Basic Infrastructure. Governament has implemented many developmental schemes but the main problem seems to be that it has no any set channels to make reach these programmes to each and every tribal family. Our study has reveled that only more than 12-18 per cent of these groups has got some of the facilities like housing, power and water. Governament has a plan to mapping new under ground water areas with the help of Geo Information System. Many houses constructed by the Government agencies have become already ruined due to low quality of work. More than two third (71%) families don't have power facilities. Now Governament has a plan to provide new solar technologies to the some of the hamlets that are not so easily reachable. People have to walk 2-3 miles to get drinking water. Most of the families are using water from near by ponds and open wells. So these people are facing acute health problems. Good drainage and toilet facilities have become nightmare. Many tribal leaders (21%) told that they tried their level best to bring these problems to the notice of the concerned officials but the result is a big zero. Some of them told local political leaders visits only during election time. But politicians and other people's opinion are that these people don't like to receive any new technology/things in to their life. Many of the gram panchyaths (31%) are absolutely inactive due to the lack of fund and political consciousness. Roads and other communication systems are more or less absent. During rainy season all links between these tribes and the rest of the world will be completely out of order. State Governament has a plan to shift some families of these tribes and rehabilitate in new places with assured basic infrastructure. Families are protesting against this decision saying that Governament provide every basic infra structure in the new habitat first. Then we will ready to move from here.

Shifting cultivation still prevalent in these two tribal groups. So policies makers should seriously think to providing new agricultural technologies emphasizing on integrated forming system.[3] Since these people do not shows any interest in using chemical fertilizers, sustaining agricultural through green manure can be promoted through field demonstrations. Now these PTG are facing acute shortage of the food. Hence the best probable alleviative before the Govt. and local NGO's is introducing new eco-friendly technologies for rice and other crop cultivation's. Many tribal people are getting different types of help from co-operative societies like LAMPS but it is not working round the year. Due to this now a days they are not getting any good prices for their products. So, they are very eager to sell their products directly to the market but the main problem is involvement of middlemen, as they are exploiting uneducated tribes in different ways. More odd thing is that these middlemen have good relation ships with developmental officials at various levels. Also 33 to 40 per cent tribal households have been affected by land alienation problem. Our study has revealed that about 77 per cent of land were alienated by the non-tribles there, by cause indebtedness among the tribles. The effort made by the Governament to tackle this problem is not even partially succeed because, some invisible hands are effectively functioning between rich non-tirbles and concerned Governament officials. This is the main hurdle in reaching all the schemes to the grass root level.[5] In case of promote of cottage industry, Governament has established Tribal Cooperative Marketing Development Federation of India Limited. The main work of this limited is to provide commercial market to the tribal products. Also it helps to promote enterpriunrship among tribals by providing soft loans. Apart from this Governament has newly introduced a project called Tribal Women Empowerment Project. But the main draw back is no provision of imparting training to the local artesian to up grade their skills. Some time there will be no enough supply of raw materials to the cottage industries. Since Governament has brought a strict forest conservation rules backed by the recent Supreme Court verdict many tribal people says, they are not permitted to collect any minor forest products. Then how can we get raw materials for our traditional work? Many NGO's said Governament should revise its forest polices and connect to the tribal welfare programmes

Crucial Areas for Urgent Action

Economic Deprivation

Now-a- days most of these tribal families are living on the edge because of weakening of the subsistence based economy. Basically their basic economies are depended on land, water and minor forest products. But recent restriction on the collection of minor forest products by the Governament has made an adverse effect on their self-sufficiency and high threatening their very existence. Also few of these tribal families are still practicing the hunting and gathering mode of economy. Due to the recent ban on collecting minor forest product for the commercial purpose by administration has made them their life still worst. The problem of food shortage has been gradually increasing. Shortage of raw materials has made cottage industry dead and local artisan as bonded laborers to rich non-tribal people. New forms of exploitation were super imposed older once. This is the time of the administration to think seriously about family based alternative income generation programme wherever the present occupation is dwindling and application of science and technology for manpower development.

Land –Alienation.

More than 90 per cent these two tribal groups are dependent on agriculture and allied activities. More are less their economy is primarily agro based. The major percent of Jenu kuruba and 31.21per cent of Koragas have become absolutely land less labourers. This study has revealed that in many cases these tribles are the official landlords and the non-tribals are its virtual owners. Also it is noted that in certain cases certain type of land is owned by recognized village community and here land alienation is less. So the administration think more seriously about this problem by ceiling loopholes in the legal provision and immediate action should be taken to identify alienated land and restoring it to the tribals with delivery of possession. Also we observe that the rigid implementation of the forest conservation act without any regard of the local situation has worsened the relationship between forest dwellers and the officials. More than that, linked up with the alienation of land is the problem of indebtedness among the tribals, who have placed their lands with the local moneylenders. Our study has revealed that 61.32 percent of jenukuruba and 59.21 percent of koraga tribal people are severely suffering from indebtedness. Also study has shown that apart from poverty, ignorance of equitable price system, spending lot of money for various rituals, and remitting fines as set by their own local panchyanths or judicial system are other major problems of these tribals. It is necessary to have first hand knowledge of the causes of poverty and indebtedness of these tribal people and Governament immediately must take proper action to remove indebtedness among tribal people.

Problem of shifting cultivation.

Despite, banning on the shifting cultivation still most of the families of these group are practicing shifting cultivation. This kind of cultivation is most common among the families who are living in hilly areas like Kodagu and Mangalore district of Karnataka State. The practice of shifting cultivation is done for two or there years regularly and, thereafter, that piece of land is left. Absence of wells irrigation faculties, fertilizer, and loose of soil fertility and damage by the wild animals, further deteriorates the agricultural yield and they're by increasing nutritional problems in these tribals.

Migration and Unemployment.

This problem is not so common in above-mentioned tribals but due to drought and other reasons few families who are living very next to the border of the urban areas migrates in searching of jobs. Usually Jenu Kuraba tribes migrates to other places during harvesting (Coffee plantations) season for the employment. Koraga tribes migrates to the near by urban areas to work as wage labourers. Our study has revealed that most of these tribes are migrating in search of employment and whose descendants are hardly return to their home land. Since these tribes are hard workers they are very much exploited by the middlemen.

A Reconsideration of role of Panchyaths

73rd amendment panchyaths have more legal provisions to implement well fare programmes at gross root level. They can ensure effective participation of tribal people in to the process of planning, implementing and monitoring the various schemes. They can play a vital role during the framing of polices at higher level. To strengthen good relation ship between forest ant forest dwellers joint forest management system can be more effective under the supervision of the panchyaths. There by panchyaths can help tribal people to improve socio economic conditions. The proper management of forest produces could alleviate poverty, generate employment opportunities and improve quality of life. Some time primitive tribes are victims of the regional imbalance too. So panchyaths should act as a central monitoring agencies to check this problem by advising both the Governments as and when required and they should have qualified technical manpower to implement programmes more effectively. Also, together with local NGO's they can initiate more meaning full role in sustainable development of tribes. Panchyaths should take action to provide essential services such as road, drinking water, primary health centers etc to all tribal hamlets. Only 13 per cent of jenukuruba and 17.34 per cent of koraga have some awareness about the existences of panchyaths in their respective areas. Panchyaths officials say these tribes are not ready to come out of rigid traditional thinking and they are not interested in politics. Now a days jenu kuraba tribes are showing some interest in political consigns also.

Displacement of tribal groups

The Karnataka Government has a plan to shift jenu kurbas to some other new places but these tribes are not interested in shifting to new places as lack of proper basic infrastructures. These tribes are not satisfied with new packages. Because most of tribal leader says, we are not ready to believe the Government and compensate money is not enough to live in urban/semi urban areas. Previous examples shows tribles, displaced by the various reasons are become unemployed, debt bondage and destitute. They are not ready to loose their traditional resources of lively hood.

Conclusion and Policy Implication

We should always keep in our mind that the problems of the tribals are basically different in different region of the country. Before implementing any polices and programmes the executive agencies should identify the area of minimum and maximum resistance to innovations in their culture[2] Also it should be followed recognizing vital linkages in their cultural fabrics. Even though the Government is spending a lot of money under various tribal sub plans the result is not encouraging because these schemes are not geographically/ culturally specific and not need based one. Since the problems of both major tribals and primitive tribals are entirely different micro level analysis of the problem is most essential. Understanding of tribal organization and value through sustained scientific studies is most essential now a days. The tribals can avail of the welfare and development programmes only if the anti-exploitative measures are effectively tackled. The fundamental lacuna in all tribal sub plan is framing of polices with out involving any tribal members in the panel and not even at implementation stage. Next many of these programmes don't have any scope for identifying the integrative forces in tribal life. They are treating as just receiver of benefits. Before taking any decision on tribal development administration should consult local NGO's who are working at grass root level[6]. The so called primitive tribes who are usually less vocal than other major tribals have little or no contact with the administration and planners as a result of which they remain out side the pale of the developmental benefits. As much as possible new tribal sub plan should involve lot scope for self-management, ecological disequilibrium conscious efforts should be made to prepare the people psychologically to accept the change in environment. Our study has shown that how they would fail in mobilizing their local resources if they are completely depend on either, Governament/NGO's. The present situation demands a revitalizing of existing development. Owing to their numerical inferiority, the so-called primitive tribals are not so competent too resist the atrocities, and are not capable of creating a mechanism of self-defense except that of retreat to further remote are, which are not easily accessible. But more vigorous step has to be taken to bring them into the main stream of the Nation. Public participation in each and every policies and programmes is highly essential. While implementing the tribal development plans, care should be taken that the cultural traits of primitive tribes are not disturbed with in the process of their interaction with the mainstream of nation life. More over watch on the trends set in motion, which should not destroy the social solidarity of the tribles and kill their zest for life should be the part and parcel of every tribal developmental policies. Also there should be a lot of scope for prioritizing their needs, solving their own problems and raising their own resources to meet their urgent needs in all schemes. On the basis of allocation of funds, area specific and people specific tribal plan should be formulated. The so-called primitive tribes, particularly those, who depend on forest resources for their livelihood, have often had their way of life disrupted by a drastic change in the ecology. Formulation of welfare plans with a view to accommodating tribal needs with regional and national interest is most importent. Thus integration not assimilation, should be the leading principal behind and tribal development policies. Finally, it is difficult to conceive of a trained mind, other than an Anthropologist, who can effectively tackle this problem with greater insight. Also it very essential to orienting the administrator to tribal life and culture in all aspects considered above and giving them special training for the tasks they have to undertake among the tribes.

5

Tribal Education: What we Know and What we Dont Know?

The Scheduled Tribes represents one of the most economically impoverished and marginalized groups in India. Karnataka has a high proportion of the tribal population. According to 2001 Census the population of Scheduled Tribes in Karnataka is 26.51 Lakhs, which constitutes1.04% of the total population. The Scheduled Tribes female population is 3.22 lakhs which constitutes 50% of the total Scheduled Tribe population. Education of tribal women is recognized as indispensable for their growth and development. The education of tribal women according to 2001 census, the Scheduled Tribe female literacy is 8.07%as compared to the male literacy of 12.68% in Karnataka. So long as there is disparity between male and female in education levels the difference between the position of men and women would continue to exist. The tribal women's access to education in the country is inadequate and discriminating because of ignorance, lack of motivation, etc.. Thus education is the key catalyst to the development of human resources. Lack of education is largely responsible for the exploitation and pitiable plight of the tribal women. For the tribal, education disseminates knowledge, knowledge give inner strength, which is very essential for the tribal for attaining freedom from exploitation and poverty. So due to ignorance arising out of illiteracy, the tribal have not been able to take advantage of new economic opportunities. Empowerment of women covers aspects such as education, economic status etc. Abolition of gender based discrimination in all institutions and structures of society and participation of women in policy and decision process at domestic and public level are sew dimension of women empowerment.

Unity in diversity is our main strength. Our land is cradle for various traditions, religious, ethnic, cultural, customs and linguistic groups. We can say it is more or less a plural society. Hence the researchers can get plenty of data to study cross-cultural aspects of the country. Even though India has diverse groups only few percentage has eating fruit of main stream development and a lager section of the under privileged of the society has remained near the periphery or long away from the so-called development.

One of the weakest link in the chain is strong existence of caste system in the Indian society. Caste is a foundation stone of the Indian society. Without understanding the caste no one can properly understood the Hindu society and social institutions. Experts of the opinion that Varnas are the basic reasons for the existence of complex caste system in India. Brahmins have got first place in the social stratification of the Hindu law and Sudras have got a last place. These people have now recognized as SC under the Indian constitution. They represent 17.5 per cent of the total population of India

Anthropologically speaking a tribe is a social group (Jha,2001).The tribal people constitute an out caste group (Mishra,1999).The members of these groups live in common ritory, using common dilated posses cultural homogeneity. Experts of the opinion that as per these characteristics it is not very easy to locate many tribal groups in India who posses all these outstanding characteristics Further many tribal group have been recognized as scheduled tribal in our fifth schedule of the constitution.

Literary speaking these people are commonly called Adivasi. It means original inhabitants, or tribal peoples comprise a substantial indigenous minority of the population of India. Tribal people are particular numerous in the Indian states of Orisa, Bihar, Jarkalnd and in other northeastern part of the country.

The scheduled tribe lie mostly in isolated, and mostly inaccessible hilly areas. These regions are relatively underdeveloped and poorly integrated with the rest of the regions. They have not much cultural contact with the rest of population and have thus remained closed static societies. They have also thus maintained their characteristic way of living.

The government of India have taken –up in right earnest the duty of educating the 25 million Adibasis of the country, with the object of helping them to become absorbed in the larger Indian society. This is a very difficult but a very necessary task. The difficulty is partly due to the differences in the cultural levels of the various tribes, and partly due to the intra tribal social solidarity which can be an obstacle to the integration of the Adibasis with the Indian society. The Adibasis cannot therefore be expected to rise to the full stature of citizenship immediately. Neither would any large-scale and sweeping legislation bring about the desired end. It can be done only by a gradual process of adjustment for which a suitable type of education has to be planned and carried out.

As per the 1991census, the scheduled tribes (ST) account for 67.76 million representing 8.08percent of the country's population. Of this, 1.32 million (1.95%) belong to primitive tribal groups (PTG) who are marginalised than the ST population. The ST population is estimated to have reached 88.8 million in 2001which is 8.6% of the country's total population in 2001. The scheduled tribes are spread across the country and reside mainly in forest and hilly regions. The proportion of scheduled tribes within general population varies across states/union territories and indicates heavy concentration n certain parts such as mizoram (94.7%), Lakshawadeep (93.2%), Meghalaya (85.5%), Dadra and Nagar Haveli (78.9%). States of Kerala (1.1%), Tamilnadu (1%), and Uttar Pradesh (0.2%) have low percentage of scheduled tribe popul,ation in comparison to the general population. Since Independence, the percentage of ST population has steadily increased following the growth in general population.

Truly speaking the problems of the Indian tribals can be classified in to two main groups; 1. problems of the major tribes and 2. problems of the minor tribes. One of the main hurdles of our tribal administrations is mixing up together. Out of many major problems like land alienation, poverty, shifting cultivation and migration the problem of solid education system has blacken their entire way towards empowerment and entry to the main stream of the sustainable development. It not only deprives them of the opportunity in the new ventures but also alienates them from their resource base.

Constitution and STs

Constitution provides various safeguards in favour of the scheduled tribes. These may be broadly divided into two parts viz., (a) protection and (b) development. Protection of interest of scheduled tribes is very essential for their development. The protective provisions are contained in articles 15(4), 16(4), 19(5), 23,29, 46, 164, 330, 332, 334, 335, 336, 339(1), 371(a), 371(b), 371(c), fifth schedule and sixth schedule. Articles 16(4) and 19(5) are exceptions to the fundamental rights, rights of equality and freedom guaranteed under part lll of the constitution. Provisions relating to development of scheduled tribes are contained mainly in article 271(1) first provision and 339(2).

Problems of Education

After the independence of India in 1947, sincere efforts were made by the government to improve the economic and social life of the tribals through the spreading of education. In fact, education has occupied an important place in the Tribal sub-plan. Some of the steps taken for this purpose were- (1) opening of schools, Balwadis, and Angan Kedras in tribal areas; (2) establishing community centers; and (3) granting financial assistance to tribal children. Soon it was realised that these measures are not sufficient for the progress of tribal education for the following reasons;

(1) problem of providing free and compulsory education to all 6to 13 year old tribal children by establishing sufficient number of schools in the remote tribal areas; (2) problems regarding the unfavorable negative attitude of the tribal parents towards the education of their children. The formal education, given to the tribal children in the schools, does not bring any immediate return. It is therefore natural that the parents develop a negative attitude towards it which indirectly lead to high drop out rates. Besides these, some of the major problems regarding tribal education are

(1) the problem of getting educated men and women teacher from the same tribal group;
(2) the problem of the medium of instruction;
(3) the problem of supervision and inspection;
(4) the problem of evaluation and examination;
(5) the problem of linking education with life;
(6) the problem of providing technical schools;
(7) the problem of providing physical facilities and amenities;
(8) the problem of providing residential schools;
(9) the problem of preparing text books;
(10) the problem of girl's education etc.

Policy Suggestions

(Access, Retention, Achievement and Capacity Building)

Under access, alternatives to formal schooling like NFE and Ashram schools should be encouraged. A good amount of hope should be placed on the outcomes of interventions like effective awareness campaigns, and community outreach programmes. Under retention and achievement, the it is suggested a review of relevance of national curriculum, MLL* measure used in tribal schools, development of textbooks in tribal dialect incorporating tribal history and culture, setting up of residential schools specially for migratory tribes. Under capacity building, there is a need for a national level group that would oversee coordination and

* MLL - Minimum Level of Learning

convergence of services at all levels, Besides forming VECs/ PTAs in tribal villages, reorienting and empowering these bodies, construction of more ashram schools should also be undertaken as a vital part of capacity building. The importance of socio-cultural aspects of tribal education was emphasised by Prof. K.L. Sharma. According to him, the educational calendar must take into account the working cycle of tribal child renamed their festivals. Generally it was observed that the schools are open during the season when they are busy and are closed when they are free. This step might play a crucial role in retaining the tribal children in schools as well as improving their learning achievements. Reviewing the vital role that the incentives play in retaining the tribal children in school, It is suggested that DPEP should also have intervention programme with regard to incentives. It is also emphasized the role of incentives in motivating the teachers in tribal schools. Expert felt that only those teachers who have positive attitude towards tribals and who volunteer to work in tribal areas should be selected. Besides, a special orientation training should also be given to the beginning of their service. He also suggested that the national component should formulate some guidelines with regard to their selection process and prepare training modules for teachers in tribal areas. Experts have threw light on the "Linguistic Aspects of Tribal Education". According to them the child can be taught in his mother tongue in critical stages with provision for gradual transfer in the regional school languages. The science subject can be taught in their mother tongue while subjects like humanities can be taught in regional languages. It is necessary to focus on the economic aspects of the tribal education and pleaded for providing compensation to tribal parents who have to loose the labour if their children go to school. Experts also spoke on the absence of relevance of present school education for tribal children which makes them aliens in their own community. Thus there is an urgent need to contextualise the primary education. The increasing role of NGOs in creating a demand for education among tribals so that it becomes need based and is not thrust upon tribles should be emphasised. According to the many writers national strategy under DPEP can use NGOs as an entry-point to help make inroads into the more difficult tribal groups so that their children come for education. Besides, the NGOs can assist in providing local based training, environment building, help in giving feed-back about teaching-learning that can be developing material using local knowledge and local language.

Empowering the community by entrusting the key role of sustaining and monitoring to bodies like VECs was found essential by Haredia, However, he maintained that monitoring of the project including accountability and transparency must be systematized. It is suggested that National Component should provide full expert support in developing material in different languages, provide help in finalizing bridge languages dictionaries and also conduct impact studies. The research findings as well as the success and failure stories must be documented and disseminated under material strategies for circulation. According to Dr. Sujatha, during pre-appraisal of district and State proposals under DPEP, it was realized that there are common broad issues and inadequate capacities at district and State level for effective intervention to tackle those issues. This necessitated national support and intervention for tribal education. Evolving National Component for Tribal Education, the national component for tribal education was discussed in two parts. The first part comprised the broad issues and constraints of tribal education and identified the gap areas which require national support to improve the education of tribals. The second part covered the action plan for the identified areas along with work plan for coming years. The issues which were raised by the many State teams as well as the Resource Parsons are basically in the area of access, pedagogy, capacity building and policies framing and planning. Access can also be a planning process. Establishment of schools within 1.5 Kms radius to tribal habitations is not the only option. Moreover, this is also not available option for the geographically difficult terrain. Other alternatives to formal schooling like NFE and outreach schools should be tried. In order to make education sustainable, involvement of the community(VEC/VLCs/PTAs etc.), government and NGO sectors is also needed. Relaxing the norms of school mapping, managing incentives, revising the curriculum and re-writing them in tribal language etc. are other major issues which need to be tackled by both state and national components in order to make education accessible and contextual to the tribal children. Besides, a large number of issues related to capacity building at State/district/ block/ cluster level had been raised by the State teams as well as the Resource Parsons where there is a need for the national component to develop it's own strategies to guide and counsel the State strategies. The district education officers are found to be lacking training in disaggregated areas and group specific micro-level planning, which is the back-bone of DPEP strategy for tribal education. These administrators also lack orientation as well as knowledge about tribal specific culture. The disparities between the literacy rates of tribal males and tribal females is alarmingly high, much higher than the disparity level between generally category males and females. However, the State strategies for tribal education under DPEP lack gender dimension. Even though most of the existing incentives and special measures are developed to tackle the economic problems of tribals and a significant amount of money has been diverted to meet these programme needs, the planning and management mechanism of these incentives remained weak at all levels leading to delay in supply, poor quality and doubtful relevance. Even though the number of beneficiaries increased over the years, no corresponding change was found in resource allocation in planning and management. Improving Access Even though it was increasingly realised that in tribal pockets, more number of NFE and outreach schools need to be tried, the states/districts are facing problems in school mapping in the tribal areas, basically because there is almost no expertise available in the State in school mapping especially in relation to tribal areas. Programmes like community mobilisation, strengthening VECs/PTAs/MTAs and involving NGOs to reach out of school tribal children would need to be re-visualised in a more tribal specific context. Keeping in mind the poor socio-economic background of tribal children, a re-assessment is required on how free the primary education is for the tribal child and what further measures are required to be taken to make their education totally free.

Capacity Building: at all level as expressed by the State teams, there is a need for training and orientation to administrators, resource persons, teacher-trainers on different aspects of tribal education. However it would be wrong to say that there is a dearth of experts at State/district level. Rather, what is required at present is that the State resource persons should be identified and trained by the national core group in developing separate training modules for administrators, teacher-trainers and teachers. It was recognised that the teachers working in tribal are as required special pedagogical training to tackle the special needs and problems of tribal children, especially as the present pre-service and the in-service training modules are found to be devoid of any special component of tribal education. Even though it was realised that a more powerful and demanding VECs/PTAs/MTs would exercise indirect control over school functioning (e.g. regulating effectively the incentive schemes etc.), the State nodal persons were lacking any directives regarding how to make these bodies more powerful. All the State strategies have included community awareness campaign. But the community awareness modules developed by the State or district components were not found effective. A fundamental error was pointed out in conceptualising the awareness campaign. It was assumed that the tribal parents are not aware of the free primary education being provided by the Government. But as revealed by the State nodal persons, the tribal parents are aware of it but they are not convinced of the relevance of this education for their children. Thus, emphasis should be placed on convincing these parents about the relevance of primary education for their children. However, pedagogical revolution, backed by adequate compensation of the tribal parents for their labour loss, and a suitable academic calendar would convince the parents of the utility of primary education for their children. Although it was long back decided to have adequate representation of tribal parents in VECs as well as PTAs, not much has been achieved in this regard. Besides, many of the tribal villages do not have either VECs or PTAs. Relevance of Pedagogy: The tribal cultural and tribal life styles are not considered while either setting the academic calendar or in deciding the relevance of education. The tribal children are lovers of free nature and independence. The rigid and discipline oriented schooling process is found to create conflict and resistance among the children leading to lack of interest, high dropout and poor performance. The group oriented tribal child finds the present education system more individualistic in nature and thus irrelevant. Not much has been achieved with regard to incorporating the relevant curriculum containing the tribal experiences and introducing the tribal dialects and bi-lingual primers in the first two grades. However, all the DPEP States teams revealed that they cannot proceed much in this context without getting any expert help from National Componentry Karnataka seemed to have proceeded a step or two ahead of other States in having included tribal groups specific plans in developing relevant pedagogy. The capabilities at State and district levels are not developed for responding effectively to flexible group specific pedagogic needs.

*** (This portion has been extracted from the proceedings of National Level Workshop on Tribal Education)

6

Tribal Education and Associated Factors: A Review

Education of Scheduled Tribe children is considered important, not only because of the Constitutional obligation but also as a crucial input for total development of tribal communities and also for the economic development of a country. One of the challenges in providing education to tribal children is to setting up school facilities in small, scattered and remote tribal habitations. The majority of the Scheduled Tribes live in sparsely populated habitations in the interior and in inaccessible hilly and forest areas of our country. So an attempt is made by the researchers to discuss and analyze the problems of tribal children's education in India since tribal children are neither culturally inferior nor cognitively less competent than the children of other groups. Education has limited connotation. It is largely concerned with the existing formal structure of education and the institutionalized methodology of imparting knowledge to individuals. Within this very system exist many sub-groups of individuals with specific needs and tribals are one of them. In fact tribals form a large group of individuals in the Indian society. For several historical, economic and social reasons the scheduled groups have remained economically backward and socially retarded even to this day. The ST population accounts for 8.6% of the total population of the country. There are many constitutional provisions and legislative support available for safeguarding the welfare and the interests of S.Ts. In addition planned developmental efforts have also taken place through

Five-Year plans. Despite the concern reflected in the Indian Constitution and the developmental efforts initiated for the welfare and the development of STs., their socio-economic and political development is still far below the others and therefore much more needs to be done in this direction, including their empowerment – educational, social, economic and political – with due regard to their special identity – culturally, habitation ally, traditionally – and in terms of the tribals.

Education refers to the method by which a society attempts to direct and accelerate the learning process of its individuals. In spite of efforts made by the constitution, the position of tribal education is still poor in India. The present paper examines the social and economic factors which lead to educational deprivation among the tribes. As most of their education is informal, the tribes find the formal type of education disinteresting. Poverty, the changing economy and lack of knowledge affect the educational development among the tribes. They are not aware of the educational facilities and the function and value of education. The attitude of teachers towards the tribal students is not healthy. The medium of instruction is not in their mother-tongues, the matter in the textbooks has no relevance to their culture and needs, as they have rich oral tradition they are sensitive to print. They are basically not interested in education so they have low motivation and aspirations. All these lead to educational deprivation among the tribes. Hence educational programmes could not make much progress due to their ignorance and illiteracy. So education among the tribes should be viewed against their background of economy and society.

In the wider sense education is a universal phenomenon of socialization of the younger generation by the elder generation. It plays an important role in personality development in breaking social boundaries, raising the standard of life and in inculcating modern values in social, economic, political and cultural fields. Thus it is a cultural process in which inculcation of values, norms, morals and skills the members of a society, ensures continuity in each generation with regard to various aspects of society.

Margaret Mead (1943) defines" education as the cultural process, the way in which each reborn human infant is transformed into a full member of a specific human society".

India has the largest concentration of tribal population. Indian history reveals that historical general backwardness of the tribal along with isolation and subsistence economy has kept these tribal backward for many centuries. To improve their condition much attention has been given to their education, but it has made little progress among the tribal. In spite of efforts made by the constitution to equalize educational opportunities, more and more educational schemes are being implemented by the state and central Government for the educational development of tribal unfortunately the position of tribal position education is still poor in India.

The literacy rate among the scheduled tribe population recorded during 1961, 1971, 1981 and 1991 census was 18.53%, 11.30%, 16.35% and 29.60% respectively (Excluding population of age group 0-6). These figures are much lower than the corresponding figures for total population of India. It is observed that tribal literacy percentage in 1961 census was quite high than the succeeding censuses Since education has an inherent relation with culture, economy and society the need for an anthropological approach to education in tribal areas is needed. The scenario of education among the tribes who are considered backward needs to be examined.

National Scenario of tribal literacy during, 1991 census as compared to the general population is as follows:-

Literacy Rate among Scheduled Tribes during 1991 Census

Sr. No.	*Name of States/UTS*	*General*	*Tribal*
1	2	3	4
1.	Andhra Pradesh	44.09	17.16
2.	Arunachal Pradesh	41.59	24.45
3.	Assam	52.89	49.16
4.	Bihar	38.48	26.78
5.	Goa	75.51	42.91
6.	Gujarat	61.29	36.45
7.	Haryana	55.85	—

8.	Himachal Pradesh	63.86	47.09
9.	Karnataka	56.04	36.01
10.	Kerala	89.81	57.22
11.	Madhya Pradesh	44.20	21.54
12.	Maharashtra	64.87	36.79
13.	Manipur	59.89	53.63
14.	Mizoram	49.10	46.71
(Included in Assam)			
15.	Nagaland	82.87	60.59
16.	Orissa	61.65	22.31
17.	Punjab	49.09	—
18.	Rajasthan	58.51	19.44
19.	Sikkim	38.58	59.01
20.	Tamil Nadu	56.94	27.89
21.	Tripura	62.66	40.37
22.	Uttar Pradesh	60.44	35.70
23.	West Bengal	57.70	35.70
Union Territories			
1.	Andaman & Nicobar Islands	73.02	56.62
2.	Dadra Nagar Haveli	40.71	28.21
3.	Lakshadweep	81.78	80.58
4.	Daman & Diu	71.20	52.91
	All India	52.21	29.60

Excluding population of age group 0-6
Source: Census of India 1991

The present paper focuses on socio-economic factors such as poverty, changing economy, desire, aspiration, motivation and attitude towards education, socio-economic aspects of the family, and awareness about educational facilities, gender and education, which affect the educational development of the tribes.

Economic Aspect of Tribal Education:-

It is an accepted fact that the economic and socio-cultural aspects of a family affect the education of children in all societies in India. Education is essential as it enables one to take up their rightful place in the economic, social and cultural life of modern India and at the same time to keep respect of one's own culture. The culture and environment in which one is born and brought up shapes the personality of an individual to a large extent. This way education is related to culture.

After independence as the socio-economic conditions of the tribes was backward as compared to the general population the constitution makers and planners decided to allot more money for development work in the tribal areas. Some were of the opinion that education was the only way to improve the condition of tribes while some believed that it was of no use educating the tribes when they didn't have enough to eat and that education would take care of itself once when the people's standard of living improved. But soon they came to realize that both education and economy are interdependent and complementary and the development of both could go on side by side. Economic development is a never-ending process and economic development without educational development does not have any sense because if people are not educated they cannot use the benefits of economic development in the best possible way. So adequate funds were released for education and economic development. In spite of facilities such as establishment of special schools, free schooling, scholarships etc the progress of tribal education has not been impressive.

Tribal societies are small in scale are restricted in the spatial and temporal range of their social, legal and political relations and possess a morality, a religion and worldview of corresponding dimensions. Characteristically too tribal languages are unwritten and hence the extent of communication both in time and space is inevitably narrow. At the same time tribal societies exhibit a remarkable economy of design and have a compactness and self-sufficiency lacking in modern society.

Majority tribes live under poverty line. The tribes follow many simple occupations based on simple technology. Most of the occupation falls into the primary occupations such as hunting, gathering, and agriculture. The technology they use for these purposes belong to the most primitive kind. There is no profit and surplus making in such economy. Hence there per capita income is very meager much lesser than the Indian average. Most of them live under abject poverty and are in debt in the hands of local moneylenders and Zamindars. In order to repay the debt they often mortgage or sell their land to the moneylenders. Indebtedness is almost inevitable since heavy interest is to be paid to these moneylenders.

For ages tribals are considered primitive segment of Indian society. They lived in forests and hills without any contact with civilizations. During British rule they consolidated their position and their political aspirations and administrative need necessitated to open up the entire country. The British introduced the system of Land ownership and revenue. Annual tax was trebled which was beyond the pay in capacity of tribal cultivators. Many non tribals began to settle in the tribal areas offering credit facilities. Initially it provided relief to tribals but gradually the system became exploitative.

The economic causes leading to educational deprivation among tribes are:

1) Poverty:

Since most of tribal people are living under subsistence economy, life is very hard for them. Even the tribes who practice agriculture lead a hand to mouth existence. In agricultural families both male and female contribute to the economic activities of the house. Even among the non-agricultural tribes every member of the family goes to the forests to collect fruits, to dig roots and for hunting. Boys in the family take the cattle for grazing, help on the fields while girls are engaged in collecting firewood, helping the mother's in household activities, take care of the younger siblings. Thus sending children to schools means losing two healthy hands in the struggle for survival. Thus each child is an economic asset. If the child is sent to school, the parents have to feed him out of their meager income which puts a burden on the family economy. Save (1945) wrote "In case of people who hardly get bread twice a day, literacy is a tall talk". Verrier Elvin (1963) very appropriately sums up the situation in this way. "For a tribal family, to send it's grown up girl or boy to school, is essentially a matter of economies, and entails dislocation in the traditional pattern of division of labor. Many parents cannot just afford to send their children to school". Similarly Chitnis (1974) reported that a high proportion of ST students came from poor homes and belonged to rural occupations. Berdie (1954) observed that there is a very strong positive relationship between educational aspirations and income-levels. B.A. Deshmukh (2004) reported in his study that the Kokna tribe's school age boys and girls are engaged in agricultural and household work. He also found that economic cause as not only the factor for educational backwardness of Kokna tribe but social factors were also equally responsible. Another important reason for their poverty is, they spend their earnings lavishly on rituals and ceremonies. They spend much on liquor which is a part of their socio-religious life.

2) Low agricultural Returns:

Their agricultural return is very low and hardly enough for their subsistence. R.S. Mann (1978) in his study on the tribes of Rajasthan observed that the low agricultural productivity is due to lack of irrigation facilities and also because the tribes do not use fertilizers and other modern techniques of agriculture. One can find a marked difference between the farmers of tribes and non-tribes. It is also seen that the tribes themseives are not enthusiastic towards increasing their agricultural production, they feel satisfied with whatever they get. In this connection R.S. Mann (1978; 76) has rightly said "Most of the Bhils still express that they are satisfied with whatever they practice. That means the hangover of traditionalism is not over. A Bhil will still not be ready to do any labour if he has food provision for a few days in his house. He shirks hard work and remains sitting idle". Of late many industries have started working in the tribal areas but they do not employ the tribal youths as they do not have the desirable qualifications. So it would be worthwhile to open industrial training schools and give vocational guidance to the tribal students.

3) Changing Economy:

Changing economy affects the education and educational development affects the economic pattern. Due to the industrial growth in some places there is seasonal migration in search of labor which affects the education. There has been a sudden change in the economy and the corresponding change in education has not kept pace with it. Change in education is a slow process and therefore the tribals are not fully prepared to take the advantage of the sudden change in economy. Also the introduction of formal education has resulted in a change from agriculture and forest economy to service and wage earning economy. Many of the tribals are now working in the public and private sectors and government offices. This has created a fear in the minds of the traditional tribal that an educated boy will leave his family for he will be attracted to the city life in search of a job and would settle there. Ambasht (1970) observed in his study on the tribes of Ranchi district in Bihar that there are a good number of families who are losing grounds as farmers in tribal society and there is practically no one to look after the agriculture in the family and they fight over the the paternal property.

4) Lack of Knowledge:

In tribal as well as other areas of the country various programmes have been taken up for economic development under the Community Development programme. But it is seen that these programmes have not succeeded as expected. Even to take advantage of these schemes, a certain degree of awareness, progress and education is necessary. N.K. Singhi (1979:4) says even to take advancement of these development schemes and obtaining modern jobs, education is necessary. Socio-economic development and expansion of education are thus closely interlinked and inter-dependent process. For e.g. the profit gained from the paddy crop, produced by the Japanese method of paddy cultivation was wasted on drinks and petty things. They didn't know that the income has to be used as revolving capital for the next season. Sometimes it so happens that the crop comes up very well but they get cheated of their money by crooks, money-lenders, Govt. employees and contractors. According to B.A. Deshmukh (2004) observed that the bulk of schemes in mixed tribal areas go to non-tribal people, the tribal people do not come forward to take up schemes as they have no trust in government agencies. This indifference is born out of ignorance and this is due to lack of education. Even if the economic programmes have succeeded, it is not seen in their standard of living as they have been cheated of their money by crooks.

5) School Timings:

The school timings are clashing with the agricultural hours. Ambasht (1970) noticed that during the agricultural season the attendance in the schools goes down while in the slack agricultural season the attendance goes up. This was seen in the tribal areas of Ranchi. Education suffers on account of the fact that the tribal boy or girl is an economic asset. Here too economy determines the number of pupils, the length of time of their stay at school. Here the form of education and the nature of schools do not conform to the economic circumstances. Education therefore should conform to agricultural season. Then only the economic need and educational activities could go together without clashing with each other.

Social Aspect of Tribal education:

The social aspect of a community deals with the social customs, beliefs, attitudes and practices of man. It involves methods of grouping and grading people for the effective conduct of the various activities for common existence by sharing common activities under bonds of relationship. As the tribals form a small community they have their own tradition and culture, their own territory and their relations are direct and intimate. Some of the prevailing attitudes, customs, beliefs and practices among them lead to their educational deprivation.

As the tribe who practice hunting and are food-gatherers in India is very low the educational problems faced by them needs a special study. As most of the tribes are agricultural, artisan tribes, their lack of interest in education may be due to some other causes. Many studies have shown that economic cause is not only the factor for educational backwardness but social factors are also equally responsible.

The social factors leading to educational deprivation among the tribals are:

1) Desire for Education:

The urge for education has to be created among the tribal parents. They should be made aware and convinced that education will bring a change for their material well-being, and then only they will realize the value of education. For example Shaileshwar Prasad (1980) observed "In villages having Christian and non-Christian population, it has been noticed that most of the Christian parents send their children to school, whereas most of the non-Christian do not send their children to school because the utility of education has been well impressed on the minds of the Christian tribal parents". Among Christian tribes this awareness is so strong that the children are forced to go to school. B.A. Deshmukh (2004) reported that in Bihar Christian and Non-Christian tribesmen stay side by side. It is seen that one brother who is a Christian sends his children both male and female to school, while the other who is not a Christian is satisfied with his traditional way of life although both the brothers have same resources. An awareness of the importance of education has to be created by the social workers working in the tribal areas. Rathnaiah (1977),Shyamlal(1987), Das(1993), Shah(1992) and Patel(1984) studies indicate that the tribal parents themselves are not basically interested in the education of their children as they gave priority to economic pursuits over schooling, even if they are favorable towards education they do not actively participate in the process of education.

2) Awareness about education and educational facilities:

It is found that fairly a large number of tribes are still unaware of the facilities and programmes for education. For example Shah and Patel's (1985) study covering 64 villages in Gujarat tribal areas shows that only about one-fourth of the respondents knew about industrial training institutes, about one-half of them know about colleges and hostels Similarly about one-fourth of them know about preferences given to tribes for admission to educational institutions, reservation of seats in engineering and medical colleges, reservation of jobs in government and semi government organizations. It is seen that there is a positive and significant relationship between the level of awareness of the household heads, family's socio-economic status, the educational level of parents and family size on the educational attainment of their children. Rathnaiah (1977) study indicates that there is a strong and positive co-relation between adult literacy and child enrolment. Several studies like Ambasht (1970), Rathnaiah (1977), and Shah and Patel (1985) indicate that parental education assumes greater importance in schooling of their children and further continuance of the education from primary to secondary level. Regarding family size Shyamlal (1987), T.B. Naik (1969) observed that the enrolment of children increases as the size of the household increases as they may be able to spare a child for school as his job in the house could be taken over by some other member of the family. When asked why they were so selective they said "We have earmarked one child for education and the others to look after the cultivation" This indicates their typical attitude towards education.

The aspects of tribal education will vary from area to area and nothing should be spared in understanding the problems which arise in different context as different tribal people are at varying stages of economic and cultural development.

3) Low Level of Motivation

It has been also observed that limitations in the spread of education among the tribes are due to their low level of motivation and aspirations. It is seen that the gap between aspiration and achievement also restrict and is responsible for the success of any programme of social development. Shyamlal (1987) found that among the Bhils the parents had low motivation and low aspiration, but the students had high motivation for study to secure better employment. Rathnaiah (1977) also found in his study on the tribes of Adilabad district that the parents and children have low motivation and low educational aspirations, most would like to study up to matric level only and only a few wanted to go to college. The prime motive to study was to get 'some employment'. But as some tribal youths with moderate level of education could not secure paid employment and this is developing frustration among them. B.A. Deshmukh (2004) found that among the Koknas tribe in Maharashtra that the parents of the tribal children had low motivation which was seen from their low educational aspirations.

4) Medium of Instruction:

The basic drawback of the education system for the tribals is that the language that is being taught is alien to the tribal. Shyamlal (1987) reported that a major proportion of students felt problem in learning English and mathematics while a few students blamed the teacher for their low quality teaching. Basu (1993) has also discussed the importance of mother tongue as the medium of instruction. . Singh (1997) found that "majority of the scheduled tribe students felt problems in learning English and Mathematics

In brief, it can be said that all the findings emphasize that the best medium of educating them would be their own language at least up to primary level and then it can be changed over to the regional language.The little spread of education among some of the tribes is mainly because of no provision has been made to teach them in their mother tongues

5) Content of Textbooks:

Kundu (1980) points out that the 'textbook families' are urban upper middle class families whose customs, traditions, dress and food appear alien to the tribal learner. So they create a negative attitude towards their own culture. If the school and the curriculum are based on the culture of the learners, then they feel at home and then the school is just an extension of home for them. Education makes a person fit to face the problems of life with courage. Education in tribal areas therefore should have direct relevance to their needs.

6) Oral Tradition:

influence of tradition on education is marked in all societies. Tribals have long oral tradition. Their history, myths and customs, folklore are orally handed down from generation to generation. This is well expressed through a santhan proverb "Purthi reak khon, thuti reak sorsa" (Memory is superior to books). Therefore they are sensitive to print and are poor in reading skills. So formal education for them is disinteresting. Moreover the tribes have rich history, literature, folk-lore, song, dance, music but the schools do not seem to have any provision to teach these aspects of tribal culture. So education for them should be made pleasurable by making use of the material of informal education like tribal plays, recitation, riddles, story-telling, fables, proverbs, etc. in their teaching.

7) Existence of Ethnic stereotypes:

A student's performance depends on the teacher's expectation which is often referred to as "Pygmalion Effect". If the teacher's expectation is low, the student tends to satisfy him by his poor performance. All these lead to culture conflict in the classroom. Kundu (1981) pointed out that negative stereotyping of tribals is very strong among non-tribals teachers. A survey of such stereotypes revealed that the non-tribal teachers have negative stereotypes of their non-tribal pupils such as 'they are genetically inferior in intelligence', their culture is inferior'. Desai and Patel (1981) reported that the attitude of teachers towards the tribal children was not healthy. Joshi (1981) also reported that the "heads of the tribal families expressed that the teachers did not show favorable attitude towards their children". Most of the teachers didn't have any training to work in backward areas. As they belonged to the upper castes they were prejudiced towards the tribal students. The tribal students are shy and submissive by nature and also due to the negative attitude of teachers they do not approach the teachers in case of difficulty resulting in poor results.

8) Sex and Enrolment:

It is seen that at the primary stage the girls are in large numbers, but in the middle standard the number is reduced. This is due to the differential conception of functional roles of girls in traditional societies. Early marriages are common among the tribals, so as soon as they attain the age of twelve or fourteen, they get married. In this context education is not considered necessary for girls.

K.Mann (1987) study on Bhil women of Rajasthan observed that the females are not allowed to attend school as the mother is deprived of her assistance in household and other works, school education is said by some, to spoil the girls, while some say sending females to schools is no use as they have to get married and it is a loss to the parents. This also explains the absenteeism and stagnation at schools.

Conclusion:

Economic condition of tribals creates a bottleneck in the education of children. The tribal students come from poor families; many of them have to assist their parents in agricultural and other economic pursuits, so sending a child to school means an economic burden for parents. Also the attitude of giving priority to economic pursuits over education and lack of interest for education leads to educational backwardness.

Their agricultural return is low as they do not follow the modern methods of agriculture. Industries have started coming up in tribal areas but they do not have the qualifications to join them. Due to the industrial growth they migrate to towns in search of labor seasonally which affects their education. Due to their lack of knowledge they do not take advantage of the government schemes and are cheated by the contractors and moneylenders. The school timings clash with the economic activities so the attendance is low in the agricultural season.

Moreover the desire, motivation and aspiration for education are found to be low as the parents and guardians of the tribal students are generally illiterate and therefore cannot give proper guidance to their children. And therefore the level of aspiration is not much higher among the tribal students. A positive relationship is seen between the socio-economic aspects of the family, the literacy level of parents, family size and the enrolment and educational aspirations of children.

Little or no education is imparted through tribal mother tongues. Lack of education through tribal languages is partly responsible for the tribal's poor performance in education. The content in the textbooks is not based on their culture so it appears alien to them. As they are used to oral tradition they are sensitive to print and poor in reading skills. Also as the teachers are mostly non-tribes they are prejudiced towards the tribal students and being shy the students do not approach them for any problem leading to poor performance. Another factor dampening the zeal for education is the lack of general consciousness about the function of education and also the unawareness about the facilities available for education.

As per their social norm the marriageable age is quite low and they leave schools in the middle or in the latter part of secondary education. This is wastage in education. In case of girls due to their functional roles in the house, early marriages, the attitude that girls education is loss to parents all these are responsible for large number of drop-out among girls.

Thus education, economy and society are closely linked. Change in one is bound to affect the other two. So the educational problems of the tribes have to be viewed against the background of their economy and society. Only then will the educational efforts be successful. B.A. Deshmukh (2004) aptly quotes "of all the items in the development programme for the tribes, education is the most important as it is both the means and the end of real progress".

7

Educational Status of Selected Native's of Karnataka: An Appraisal

The tribal people being kept both physically and socially away from the civilized people, the development was too slow, when compared to the development of the civilized society. The main reason is that the Geographical separation and also a cultural boundary from which the tribals don't want to come outside. Even though it was enjoyable to the tribals, laterally it became the major reason for the barrier for the welfare measures to reach them. Due to this the tribals are still experiencing the problems regarding social, cultural, economic and educational disabilities. Even though there are Constitutional measures for providing reservation and protecting them from Socio Economic exploitation and atrocities the results have been quite varied and not as per the desired goals.

Tribal education in India has reached a threshold point. The spread of education in a vast tribal belt of the country is still a challenging one. Many government have in the recent past followed the path of the trial and error method and have been able to identify special needs of the tribal children in the field of education. But the result is no encouraging one. This paper examines the present educational status among ST, reasons for low educational development and policies implications. Study is based on the fieldwork in the selected districts of Karnataka State and documentary methods. Since education for tribal children is quite different from other cultural groups of the Nation a culturally sensitive, ecologically valid and economically viable programmes of education will have to be evolved and implemented soon.

Introduction

To spread the education in case of highly marginalised section of our society has been a gigantic task to any Govt., especially to the tribal people. Among tribals education is the indigenous learning process which is the systematic influence of senior member of the family to junior member in dormitory where all young kids gather to get oral education from elder of the community.

The educational backwards of ST has its roots in the socioeconomic and cultural setting in which the tribal people live. In Inida they remained isolated for a long time and were confined to their traditional economic activated such as food gathering, shifting cultivation etc. The very primitive conditions of the tribal life, their vulnerability to exploitations and the existing socio psychological barriers develop through prolonged isolation, ha clear manifestation in the life they led.

Since independence of the nation, quite a large number of anthropological studies have been conducted on the different tribes of Karnataka. But very few studies have been made exclusively on the tribal education so for. Some o the anthropologist while studying the different aspects of a tribe concerned studied also its educational aspect. Reports, symposia and surveys conducted from time to time, relating to welfare activities of the tribals include various problems of tribal education(Rao,2001).

Modernization, privatization and globalization have done enormous positive and negative effect on the education of tribals. Hence education to the indigenous people has undergone a different phase. In spite of tall claim of Globalisation and its success in relation to boost up the economy, very seldom attempts are made to analyze the adverse outcome with regard to the tribals.

Traditional Education

Many tribes had their indigenous system of education and some of the tribles are still following them. As we known the tribal societies in the past have been mostly closed societies as for contacts or communications with distinct groups are concerned. Hence most of them did not develop any script for the language this mean that they had distinct grammars and language structure minus written form. To fulfill their educational needs many tribal commune in Karnataka had their traditional dormiritores and institutions. These institutions prepared the young to take off their socially useful work as members of the community. Further, these institutions. Further dormitories also impaired traditional education to boys and girls of adolescent age. Children were supposed to spend their nights in these dormiritores. They learn legends, folk, songs, mythic tales, music and dances they were also guide in adult responsibility. Group life was its main character (Mishraa,1993).

Modern Education

Truly speaking Missionaries were first to introduce the tribal to modern education. Some of the missioners have tried level best to education some of the tribals like Jenukuruba, Kaadu kuruba, Soliga an Koraga tribes of Karnataka. They also opened many informal learning centers for these tribals. Also these missionaries studied their language and prepared dictionaries and literature in a number of tribal dialects. The Indian education commission examined the problem in 1882 and found that the missioners were the most significant agents in spreading education among the ST (Mallik, 1997).

In the Directive Principal of State Policies also a number of schemes and programmes have been stipulated. Some of these schemes are; incentives, financial assistance, establishments of Ashram schools, hostels, etc. The education of tribal children has been engaging educational planners, as it is providing to be a hard core area in achieving universal elementary education.

The problem all the more is acute in the case of girls among the Tribes.

Methodology

We limited our study to selected major and minor tribals spread across The Karnataka State-south India. We selected few districts giving weightage for presence of patches of tribal to represent regional variations for analysis. For collection of data on the communities, I used the standard anthropological technique of intensive participant observation among selected tribals. Case study, Closed interview, Statistics are the other tools used on the basis of a broad research guidelines on Tribal Development. Our Secondary data were based on the various Govt. records an academic reports.

How is the Situation in Karnataka?

Karnataka is one of the major states in India having significant percentage of tribal people. According to the recent census (2001) there are 43 different tribes in the state. Out of these tribes Jenukuruba and korags are considered as primitive tribes. Soliga. Kuruba, Siddi and Nayka are major tribals living in different parts of the state. The major portion of the tribals is living in plain land while notable percentages of tribals are living in hilly areas like Coorg district.

According to the recent census (2001) the total rate of literacy among tribals is 13.45% against the general literacy rate 67.45% of the state. However, literacy rate of primitive tribals is very pathetic.

Enrolment of ST Students during 2004-2005

(numbers in lakh)

Sl.No	*Schools*	*Scheduled Tribes %*			*of STs to General Enrollment*		
		Boys	Girls	Total	Boys	Girls	Total
1	Primary School	0.37	0.31	0.68	2.68	1.56	4.24
2	Middle School	0.18	0.11	0.29	2.01	1.26	3.27
3	High School	0.11	0.06	0.17	1.45	0.44	1,89

4	Higher secondary	0.08	0.02	0.10	0.89	0.18	1.07
	Total	0.74	0.50	1.24	7.03	3,44	10.47

Source: Department of Education, Bangalore
Department of Labour, Bangalore

It is found that enrollment of students for primary education during 2004-2005 is 145.73 lakh. Out of this total enrollment only1.24 (0.95%) lakh children belong to the Scheduled Tribals. Out of this total only 0.37 lakh are boys and 0.31 lakh are girls. Out of total 0.29 lakh enrollment at middle school level 0.18 lakh are boys and 0.11lakh are girls. In case of High schools out of 0.17 lakh total enrollment 0.11 lakh are boys and 0.06 lakh are girls. Situation is still worst incase of Higher secondary schools 0.10 lakh 0.08 lakh are boys and 0.06 lakh are girls. From this data it is clear that negligible percentage of ST children have enrolled to the education at different levels.

Enrollment in Ashram Schools (2003-2004)

	Schools	*No.of Schools*	*Total no enrollment*
1	Primary Schools	97	28506
2	Middle Schools	18	11456
3	High Schools	08	3974
4	Higher Secondary Schools	03	2874
		126	46809

(Source: SC/ST Development Corporation, Bangalore)

This table gives a clear picture about enrolment of students in Ashram schools. In case of Karnataka totally 123+ Ashram schools are functioning. Out which more than 92% are primary schools in deep remote area of the tribal belt. Govt. has established only 8 High schools for tribal children. More interesting point here is why Govt. is not showing any interest in higher education of the tribal children. Since many high schools are quite for away from their hamlets majority of the parents don't send their children to schools. It very intensive in case of girls. This kind of disparity of schools will further detoriate the educational status of this children. More pathetic fact is that more than 98% schools don't have any permanent faculties and fundamental facilities are nightmare.

Discussion

Even after five decades of planned efforts and special provision in the constitution tribals in Karnataka lag much behind others in all fields. Our study has reveled about focusing attention on tracing the socioeconomic constraints, and poverty as a major reason for slow progress of education. Hardly, however, ther are any studies on internal aspects of school, quality of facilities and impact of education on occupational mobility of these tribals. Our study has shown that this kind of occupational mobility has increased affect the Supreme Court verdict on imposing ban on collect minor forest product. Also for all these years the tribals have been traced s a homogenous group in the macro level planning with uniform polices and programmes, though in reality the tribes and tribal areas are quite heterogeneous in terms of development due to their geographical locations, exposure to modernity and religion conversion (Kailash, 1993). The effectiveness of formal education in bringing about a change in the life of tribes, particularly in terms of occupational mobility, therefore may not be uniform across different areas and different groups in the state.

Education in tribal areas, despite being promoted on a war-foot manner by the various Govts., still struggles to survive. Increase in dropouts rate, decrease in enrolment rate. Lack of infra structural facilities, indifferent attitudes of teachers towards students and vague understanding of the benefits of education among the parents of tribal children are some of the major ills plaguing educational scenarios in tribal areas. More vital fact is that there are trends showing decline in sex ratio particularly in prosperous tribal belt where most children go to the primary schools are some of the major problems in case of Tribal education in Karnataka State. There is still much to do actualize the goal of universal education in Karnataka. More over on of the vital problem facing in spread of education in remote areas is the lack of transport and timely release of money from the State/Central Govt. By this study it is realized that the hamlet based education programme can sustain for-larger period of time if the village community is able to take over its running. Participation of local community in educational programmes in the tribal area not only ensures physical and human facilities at schools but also motivates the teaches to achieve kind of quality education. Also integrating an income generation component into the education programme may also help in a great manner (Verghese, 1993).

There is bad need to crate specially opportunities to respond to the educational needs of girl children Consequences of the development process are not neutral. They mitigate more against girl children than boys and hence end to result in grater negative effects in girl child education. Loss of access and control of resource in tribal areas tend to push women out of productive activities. This also affects adversely their status in the family and community as their participation in the economy decreases. The major strategy to address this issue is to educate and elect more women representatives at local self-govt.

The demand for education varies widely across the tribal households due to difference in religion, income, location and parental education. Only few tribes in the state who are living in semi urban areas are aware of value of education and the available facilities and they send ther children to schools. The cultural factors like polygamy also hinder the education of children. Drought, forest degradation, migration, displacement also hinder the education of these tribal children. Further, in case of many Ashram schools the midday meal programmes is not being implemented properly and corruption is rampant in managing the food Items by non-tribal urban teachers. It seems that few qualitative changes are required in the functioning of the Ashram Schools to make them truly functional. Moreover it is highly interesting to note that Govt. is not coming forward in establishing high schools and higher secondary schools unlike primary schools.

Tribal institutions of both primary and secondary level education are quite irrelevant and they are not succeeding in educating the children even after spending four years in schools. Probably the basic reason is that the content of text does not take into account their traditional knowledge system. More over these schools syllabus is for away from teaching about control of natural resources and recognition of their own identity as tribal communities. Also there is no scope in preset methodology of teaching to enhance their inherent learning capacities. Mainstream educational institutions tend to create an alienated group of youngsters with few opportunities to use their capacities. More specifically we need to campaign for a policies, which takes into consideration the learning needs of tribal youth dropouts the school and high school levels.

In the context of multiplicity of language scene in India ware the tribal children have learn 2-3 language in the schools it is needed to study the extent to which the concept of learning is affected, if learn in a language other than that of mother tongue. Further the long-range effects of bilingualism and multi-lingualism needs to be investigated. the effect of logistic structure, where language of different complexity exists, will be an existing of study. Unfortunately no studies have been undertaken so for to see the effect of sensory handicap mental retardation among disadvantaged tribal children. Similarly very little has been attempted to see the relationship between cultural traits ands cognitive development among tribal children (Maish,1998)

Conclusion

Several central Govts. have, in past, initiated various efforts to meet the challenge of educating particularly primary education in tribal areas. However, present Govt. is interested to give the primary education a massive thrust is discernible in its imposing a 2% cess on all the central taxes to mop up to least 7000 crore rupees to be used in universalisation of primary education. In India the educational efforts have to be continously meaningful and innovative to sustain over a long period of time. in our country where the society is facing various social and economic problems and indifferent attitude towards indigenous people and their education no uniform strategy can effetely work. If we are really committed about elimination prevalence of non schooling and living up to the constitutional directives of universal elementary education, our policies and programmes have to invest more resources while simultaneously staying open to multiple, context specific modes of meetings their objectives.

When an advanced technology is introduced into these regions a number of changes follow in various aspects of tribal culture and life. It is not simple replacement of old technology by the new one. Simultaneously the education system has to be changed because the labour force must now acquire more advanced technological skills. This leads on to changes in job ranking, wage structure and so on. And changes once set in motion must readjust themselves at some new level.

8

School Absence among Tribal Students (India): Where Rubber hits the Road?

Scheduled Tribe in India are more like the "indigeneous" or"native people" in other parts of the world. The population of Scheduled Tribes in India according to 2001census is 8.43 crore. Education of Scheduled Tribe children is considered important, not only because of the constitutional obligation, but also a crucial input for total development of tribal communities. The literacy levels of the Scheduled Tribes according to the 2001census is 47.10% as compared to overall literacy rate of the total population i.e., 65.38%,which shows a dismal picture of Scheduled Tribes education. So long as there is a gap between the literacy levels, the position of Scheduled Tribes will remain backward. Lack of education may lead to child exploitation, child labor, population explosion, etc., so the need of the hour is to bring quality education through 100% school enrolment and retention with more emphasis on the girl child education. We have given some policies suggestions for impart inequality education among the Scheduled Tribes in order to uplift themselves and to overcome the socio-economic problems.

Introduction

India is one of the few countries in the world having the largest tribal concentration. The tribals of this country are having fascinating rich cultural heritage and played a significant role in enrichment of composite culture. The objective and comparative studies of pre-literate societies and their contribution to great indigenous culture of India is essential before they are totally eclipsed in the fast changing cultural canvass of India. Such indepth, comparative and analytical studies may throw light and provide missing cultural links in understanding complex Indian heritage.

The spread of education among the weaker sections of our society is vital as education is a prime requisite for socio-economic development. The policies to promote educational interests of the weaker sections of the people, especially the Scheduled Castes and Scheduled Tribes, has been enshrined in our Constitution as a Directive Principle of State Policies. Therefore, the main thrust continues to be on education. The general level of literacy is very low and is lower still in the case of Backward Classes. To conclude in the words of Swami Vivekananda - "The Real India lives in the Villages. Unless we are able to uplift the Tribal and the backward classes, India faces to dark future. Along with their economic improvement they have to be raised culturally and spiritually."

The Scheduled Tribes represents one of the most economically impoverished and marginalized groups in India. Karnataka has a high proportion of the tribal population. Education of tribal women is recognized as indispensable for their growth and development. The education of tribal women according to 2001 census, the Scheduled Tribe female literacy is 8.07%as compared to the male literacy of 12.68% in Karnataka. So long as there is disparity between male and female in education levels the difference between the position of men and women would continue to exist. The tribal women's access to education in the country is inadequate and discriminating because of ignorance, lack of motivation etc. Thus education is the key catalyst to the development of human resources. Lack of education is largely responsible for the exploitation and pitiable plight of the tribal women. For the tribal, education disseminates knowledge, knowledge give inner strength, which is very essential for the tribal for attaining freedom from exploitation and poverty. Hence, due to ignorance arising out of illiteracy, the tribal have not been able to take advantage of new economic opportunities. Empowerment of women covers aspects such as education, economic status etc. Abolition of gender based discrimination in all institutions and structures of society and participation of women in policies and decision process at domestic and public level are sew dimension of women empowerment.

Ashram schools are residential schools for tribal children from a cluster of habitations. Based on the Gandhian philosophy of self-reliance, it was first experimented by Thakkar Bapa, a Gandhian in Panchamahal district of Gujarat in the pre-independence days (Ananda, 1994). Ashram schools were found effective as (i) it was not feasible to open full fledged schools in very small and scattered habitations (ii) it created congenial atmosphere for teaching learning as it is assumed that the tribal households do not have such an environment and (iii) it helped to develop the total personality of the child and impart vocational skills to improve employment opportunities.

Ashram schools generally provide admission to children from habitations at least 6-8 kms away from the school. If children from nearby villages are admitted, they are not provided with boarding. The curriculum of Ashram schools includes agriculture and other life skills in addition to general subjects. Many parents in Jharkhand, Orissa and Gujarat preferred Ashram schools as they provided free food, clothing and boarding. Some parents said that education of their wards in Ashram schools was not obstructed, when parents migrated for work.

Despite the significant progress that has been made the past 15 years in achieving universal primary education, approximately 115 million children do still not go to school. Especially in South Asia figures are alarming. Children who do not go to school in South Asia constitute more than one third of all children who are not enrolled in school around the world. If we look at the net primary school enrolment ratio (1998-2002) we see that in India only91% of the boys in the 6-10 age group were enrolled, for girls this figure was 76% (Bellary,2004). It is important to keep in mind that these figures relate to children who are officially enrolled in school, but who are not necessarily attending. Looking at the net primary school attendance these numbers go down to 80% for boys, and 73% for girls. However, the attendance lists kept by teachers are not always accurate, and the actual attendance figure might be even lower. When we then look at UNICEF's gross secondary school enrolment ratio (including all children, regardless of age) the figure is 56% for boys, and only 40% forgirls. Only a segment of the total number of children, which are not enrolled in school, can be found in the statistics of working children. There are thus a number of children that are excluded from these figures. These children can be classified as nowhere children, a termcoined by D.P. Chaudhri (1997). According to the Planning Commission of the Government of India, deriving their figures from the Census of India, incidence of tribals was 5.4 percent while incidence of nowhere children was 45.2 per cent in 199121. There has been a shift from the research-focus on tribals alone to the out-of school segment as a whole, which thus includes nowhere children. In order to design policies to also get these children in school, it is important to learn how they are spending their time. For this purpose IREWOC (NGO) initiated a project on nowhere children in four Indian states: Andhra Pradesh, Bihar, Chhattisgarh, and Karnataka. The results presented in this paper are derived from qualitative research that was conducted in three tribal areas in Karnataka between September and December 2006.

Methodology

This proposed research study consisted of three major components; in-depth schools studies, community norm study and an institutional ethnography. Data collected from five sources: household members, teachers, adults (18-25-age group) ashram schools students other community members and tribal welfare officials and NGOs.

Tools for data collection

Following types of data collection method have been used to

conduct this present study

1.Case Study 2.Interview 3.Participant observation 4.Ethnography 5.Unobsturive method 6.Content analysis

Analysis of data

Data analysis had incorporated both qualitative and quantitative data sets to insure triangulation of result. The qualitative data has been analyzed using *NUD*IST* database software and The quantitative data has been analyzed using SPSS software.

Result and Discussion

Karnataka is one of the largest state of India, with a total population that constitutes only 8.65% of India's population as a whole, is one of the most sparsely populated states. Being one of the driest regions, Karnataka is also among the poorest states of India. It is a predominantly rural state, with agriculture and animal husbandry as the most important sources of income. According to UNICEF for example, 14 % of all children aged 5-14 in India are engaged in tribals (Bellamy, 2004). According to the Census of India 2001, there are 342 million children. According to the Indian Ministry of Labour, 12.7 million children aged 5-14 are working, based on the Census 2001.

Karnataka is one of the least performing states in terms of tribal literacy. The state also has a tremendous gender gap in terms of both school enrolment and literacy.

Demand:

Household factors: Several factors are essential in identifying the reasons for absence of children in school. I will first give an overview of demand-factors such as livelihood strategies, poverty, gender, caste, family crises, which I found were crucial. Looking at livelihood strategies it appears that during seasons with a great demand for agricultural labour, such as the crop-cutting season, the attendance of children, especially girls, decreases. These children are not found in the field, but are required to stay home to take over household duties such as caring for siblings, so that the mother is able to go to the field to do wage work. Like the 10-year-old Rangi, oldest daughter of parents who are out in the field all day during the crop-cutting season, told me: "I have to be here to take care of my brothers, because who else is here to do this?" However, we cannot simply argue that children do not go to school only because parents have to do agricultural work. Similarly, where as many children can be found in the field looking after cattle, it is not the case that these children do not go to school, because they have to look after cattle. Often other factors are operational. In some cases parents might be aware of the importance to educate their children and try to send their children to school, but if the children are reluctant, the parents might lack the determination to make sure their children are indeed going to school. Here it is important to recognise the social capital of a child: if a child is surrounded by one or more educated relative who encourages him to go to school, it leads to increased motivation for the child to learn and to go to school regularly. The 12-year-old Syama explains: "But my uncle is literate, and he always encourages me to go to school. I want to continue the tradition of being literate in the family. I want to continue studying in the future and go outside the village to be a doctor". Likewise, if a child is not blessed with a learning environment at home, he or she is prone to fail and eventually to drop out of school. Migration occurs in various forms in the tribal areas. It can have both negative and positive consequences for the education of children. In some cases, especially with temporary migration of the whole household, the effects on the education of a child are negative, especially when the household leaves the village for a couple of months every year, and the child needs to leave school, and falls behind. However, temporary migration of only the father to the city in search of work could be positive, as it can also lead to increasing awareness about education for both boys and girls. Economical problems within the household do lead to absence of children in school. These may be a result of a crisis in the family, for example the illness or even death of a parent. This often results in the burden of working, in order to feed the household, falling on the shoulders of the child. Sons, suddenly the "man of the household", are required to tend animals, either their own or those of others in order to make money, and girls, especially the oldest daughter, have to stay home doing household chores, or are sent to the field to do agricultural work, especially during crop-cutting season. The 13-year-old Manchavva had to dropout of school when his father fell ill. His father complains: "I do not want this for my child, but if I die, Manchhva needs to know how to be the man of the household. He is the oldest, and thus the only one who can do this work". The sub caste system is still of significant importance among Karnataka tribes, especially in the northern areas. The traditional perception that tribals do not recognise the importance of education does not hold true anymore. Yet, there are still certain castes that, because of traditional work arrangements, do not send their children to school, and these include upper castes as well. For example, we found Soliga boys and girls expected to help out in the household of a socially higher ranking family member. Gender also plays a role. In general, there are more boys than girls attending school regularly. Of the total number of children enrolled in any school up to class V in the three tribal areas, 55% are boys. The difference is especially apparent on upper-primary level, where only 32% are girls 22%. For this there are various explanations. For example, it is often considered not safe for a girl, once she is a teenager and thus sexually vulnerable, to goout side the village for her education. Another reason given for keeping girls at home is related to household chores. In some cases it is a necessity for girls to stay home and, for example, take care of their younger siblings. This is often a result of economical crisis. In other cases household chores are looked upon as a good preparation for a girl's married life. Marriage then is another important reason behind gender discrimination. Quoting the seventeen-year-old Macha : "Education is useless for girls, because they are just living in our houses doing female chores. For us boys it is useful, so we can get a job". Some parents do not recognise how education can help their daughter in her future life, while others are reluctant to invest in her, since she is going to her husband's house after her marriage, like a father expresses: "But I cannot afford a good education for all my children, and in the future, the girls will be married off to another house, while the boys stay in my house". Thus, when a family has money for only one child's education, they will prefer to spend it on the boy. However, within some castes more and more people are interested in the amount of education the potential spouse of their child has received. Therefore, there is often overlap between the factors gender and caste mentality.

The supply-side of education

The next section will deal with supply-factors, since the quality of offered education is crucial when parents decide between sending their children to school, or keeping them at home. In all sampie tribal areas, all children, disregarding caste, have access to the same educational facilities. These facilities are within reach of the children. Government school buildings are often built just outside the village, whereas private school owners have been able to open their schools in buildings in the middle of the village. The location of the school influences the parents when deciding to which school they should send their children. Especially small children are more likely to be sent to a school that is nearby the house. This number only reflects on children who are attending school within their village, thus excluding the children who are attending a school outside the village. Also, keep in mind that these are enrolment figures and do not say anything about attendance along a busy road which has to be crossed by many people in order to reach the government school, a father wants to postpone sending his two youngest sons to school, "since they are too young and scared to cross the main road". In the three tribal areas that were included in the research, the general perception of villagers on the quality of education offered by the government is negative. Most villagers prefer the private school to government schools, but complain that they cannot bear the costs of private education. They believe that teachers are more committed and that children learn much more than children who are enrolled in a government school. In some schools, there are too few teachers appointed for too many children. Appointed teachers are usually present, and thus teacher absenteeism, a problem regularly mentioned in the literature, did not occur during my research, apart from the absence of teachers due to other government programmes, which they are required to attend. The fact that teachers reside outside the village and leave as soon as the school hours are over (or even earlier) makes communication between parents and teachers difficult. It thus would be better if teachers were appointed in their own village. Another issue is the lack of female teachers. There were only a few female teachers in the schools. This is unfortunate,since female teachers often serve as a role model for girls, as one of the teachers explained. The presence of female teachers could positively influence the enrolment and attendance of girls. The ten-year-old Radha told me she aspired to be a "madam in school". Among the children in all tribal areas, there is a fear of punishment by the teachers for skipping school, for not knowing the right answers or for not being clean or properly dressed. But children, as well as their parents and other villagers, also complained about the limited knowledge they actually gain after finishing a number of classes. When a parent asked a boy who studies in class ten to speak English to me, he replied (in Marwari, their local language):"If the headmaster does not even know how to speak English to her, then why should I?"Quoting a twenty-year-old from another village: "If you ask someone here who is enrolled in class V to read or write, he will not be able to do so, because he does not learn this in school". However, some parents did not blame the school: "My youngest daughter Sannavva is in class III, but cannot count until twenty. Radha is in class IV, and cannot even read a book properly. But my oldest daughter Pinki could do all these things when she was their age. As opposed to the other two girls, Pinki was very studious and always did her homework. She studied in the same school as

Radha and Kabita, and she is doing fine. So I do not blame the teachers". Both children and their parents mentioned the financial aspect of education as an obstacle. While primary education is supposed to be free, in all schools children were expected to pay fees. The fee structure however, is not transparent. Fees differ according to gender, caste, and class-level, and also per village. Furthermore, teachers and parents give different accounts on the exact amount that has to be paid for "admission" or "building maintenance". Boys of a general caste in class IV and V for example were expected to pay a yearly fee of Rs.60. Some households complained about having to pay the government school a yearly fee of Rs.151. In addition to these school fees, there are also the expenses for school uniforms (to have a uniform made is Rs.150-200) and stationary, which constitute a huge burden on the household's finances. Government schools were, however, still cheaper than private schools. These charged the children a monthly fee of Rs.30-70. In the three tribal areas an average wage is Rs.50 for one day of agricultural work or labour in a stone factory.

Conclusion

The problem of absence of children can unfortunately not be solved just by raising the quality of the offered education. Quality of education is not a sole reason for not sending children to school. But when the performance of school is inadequate, children may only be sent when their duties are not required elsewhere; for example, in the household or herding the cattle. For some, school attendance then becomes a residual activity. In other cases, when parents decide the money required for a child's education can better be spent on other basic requirements, children might drop out altogether. Dropping out might also be a result of failure in standards . And once dropped out, it is unlikely the child will find its way back into the education system. Explanations for this might be the reluctance to go over the same curriculum again, and often they find that they just get used to working. Closing remarks: When children who are out of school, for whatever reason, are not required to help out in the household, they can be found roaming around their house or in the village, and we might then consider them as nowhere children. It goes without saying, that these nowhere children also do some work to help their parents out in the household. But this work is not the reason that keeps them out of school. It is clear that the issue discussed here is a complex one. Overall, the awareness of the importance of education is present among all villagers, regardless of caste. We have seen that many factors can lead to the non-attendance of children in school, and more than often there is overlap. Both parents and children also seem to be convinced that the child will do the same work as their parents. Thus, the absence of a (government) job-perspective for children also leads to a preference to keep them at home and to prepare them for their future occupation as animal-herder, agricultural labourer, or in some cases shopkeeper.

Continue of the debate around quantity verses quality of education still is on. Before this, policy makers should note that quality and quantity are intertwined and cannot be separated. It is real sense of urgency. Differences expressed pertained to the placement of priorities for the achievement of universal education, and are in turn related to the broader views held on the nature of the challenges. If state is really interested in the eradication of tribal illiteracy or atlest mind to minimize the problem it must and should seriously think about the quality of primary education at present. Probably a new population policies may help in this regard. Resources need to be targeted at expanding provision if Govt. think providing alternative income generation programmes to the poor parents who would like to send children to work, then resource will have to diverted to making the curriculum relevant and of high quality. Given the manifest failure of the standard schooling system to include hard-to –reach children, special efforts need to be made in this area and particular attention should be given to first generation learners. Some noted that high rates could put off many aspiring to secondary and higher levels of education, thus eroding the incentive to send children regularly and consistently to school. Without providing of universal coverage and equivalent standards in terms of quality, it is not feasible or just to penalize parents who do not send children to school. Clearly, meaningful and genuine universal elementary education is associated not only with universal access to well-functioning schools but also with certain out-of –school initiatives. Children have varying capacities, apart from individual intelligence, depend on factors such as adequate nutrition good health and freedom to attend school regularly. It follows that thee prerequisite have to be ensured for effective and genuine universal education.

To conclude, how elementary education should be made universal is central to the concern for making it universal?. It is necessary to make sure that such education is effective. Apart from the need to scrutinize the education system, non-educational measures that prepare children for education and facilities the process of learning are also needed. India is one of the countries having largest number of tribals in the world, also country having highest percentage of dropouts at higher primary level. Poverty and overpopulation are intertwined with this problem (Sharma, 1998). At the same time, it has pioneered a number of different educational models for addressing the problems of hard to reach children, models which reflect a shared value given to the welfare of children and the need to ensure their right to education, but very different philosophies and modalities. If we seriously try with this model with some addition or subtraction suiting our culture and traditions which are more effective and under what circumstances, we believe that the experiences, of India will have made a major contribution to a long standing problem beyond boundaries.

The tribals of this country are having fascinating rich cultural heritage and played a significant role in enrichment of composite culture. The objective and comparative studies of pre-literate societies and their contribution to great indigenous culture of India is essential before they are totally eclipsed in the fast changing cultural canvass of India. Such indepth, comparative and analytical studies may throw light and provide missing cultural links in understanding complex Indian heritage.

9

Language and Schooling of Indigenous Children: Issues Related to Medium of Learning

Education is the out come of experiential learning of the human society. It is ingrained in the life and culture of the people. Concept of formal schooling is a modern phenomenon in which the life experience of mankind is fragmented in to different subjects and disciplines to understand the world in a systematic manner. The land, language and culture determine the learning of the people and through socialization the whole society learn from one generation to the other across time and space. The globe has many human society and many culture. Some of them have facilities of modern education and some have not. So even in 21st century, some have the facilities of information technology and some are still non-literate. Right and equity in education is still a dream in human society where half of the population is struggling for survival with out security.

Geography determines the life style of the people. This lead to a culture of difference and with the adaptation of nature, culture is created. People try to understand and interact with the nature and their life is shaped accordingly. They survive and sustain with struggling with many situations and get education and learn to live in a given situation. Personality and identity is shaped accordingly. The cultural symbols are created to signify the differences of one social group from the other. In course of history some become civilized where as some lag behind. Of course this distinction is the creation of the people who consider superior to the other in terms of achieving power, knowledge, property and service. They formulate the standard set of rules of development through which they measure the others standard of living. The disparity and dichotomy of cultural values makes some people in mainstream and some marginalized, though the latter have their own set of standard rules and practices, which cannot be compatible to the others. Albeit, people of mainstream culture try to impose their cultural values and hope for mainstream them. Being fascinated with the mainstream culture, people of marginalized group also mingle with them, forgetting their social values, and this result great cultural loss, which is irreparable. This happens when the cultural hegemony operates in the governance, society and mass.

Tribal people in the world have substantial contribution in shaping the human culture, more particularly in shaping the worldview of man nature relationship, interdependence of natural with supernatural. They believed in naturalistic worldview.

Their life is their experience, and their experience, collective memory and expression is their learning. Their work is their education. Their every action is associated with creative memory embedded with purpose and meaning. Their learning is not isolated from the life.

Concept of education is existent among the tribal / indigenous society is different from the formal education system. Concept of reading and writing letters was not found among them. Writing was existent in wall painting; complex creation was in the craft, weaving, and invention of technology. But these have not been thought of to be added in to education. Since the learning of all these aspects were in practice of the people, and were highly productive, expressive and generative. It was the part of informal learning.

Community as the creator and consumer of knowledge is ingrained in the tribal society. Diversity of culture in a society or in a State is the foundation of multiculturalism and multi-lingualism. This is not a threat to the National Integration, but to believe in co existence. People from different culture and different language live together for communal harmony. It is the duty of the State to provide equal opportunity and scope to safeguard the interest of the tribes.

Although research evidence has demonstrated the positive consequences of bilingual or multilingual schooling on cognitive development and social interaction processes, tribal children would require special programs to be able to cope. The Constitution of India allows the use of tribal dialect (mother tongue) as the medium of instruction if the population of the tribe is more than 100,000. Although the constitution on 1956 recognized the need for primary education in the mother tongue for linguistic minorities toady education still is being impaired primary in the 15 official languages and English. The denial of schooling in the mother tongue to children of tribal communities assumes significance in the context of their poor response to formal education and high attrition rates. An increasing number of researchers strongly advocate the use of the mother tongue or home language as medium of instruction in early stages of education. ST children face problems wherever teachers do not speak their dialect at all. Assam was the first state to prepare teacher training modules and separate teaching learning materials for the Bodo tribal language in 1995. A Growing body of research on language and education of ethnic minorities in western societies highlights at the crucial role played by home languages in early learning. This paper gives a platform to discuss some crucial issues relating to the instruction at t eh early state and reviews policies an practise relating to mother tongue education for tribal children in India.

Education of Scheduled Tribe children is considered important, not only because of the constitutional obligation, but also a crucial input for total development of tribal communities.

The spread of education among the weaker sections of our society is vital as education is a prime requisite for socio-economic development. The policies to promote educational interests of the weaker sections of the people, especially the Scheduled Castes and Scheduled Tribes, has been enshrined in our Constitution as a Directive Principle of State Policies. Therefore, the main thrust continues to be on education. The general level of literacy is very low and is lower still in the case of Backward Classes. There are 16 million ST children (10.87 million in 6-11 years and 5.12 million in 11-14 years) as on March 2001, out of the total child population of about 193 million in the age group of 6 to 14years in the country (Selected Educational Statistics – 2000-01). Realizing that Scheduled Tribes are one of the most deprived and marginalized groups with respect to education a host of programmes and measures were initiated ever since the Independence. Elementary education is a priority area in the Tribal sub-plans from the 5th Five Year Plan. Education of ST children is considered important, not only because of the Constitutional obligation but also as a crucial input for total development of tribal communities. Another important development in the policies towards education of tribals is the National Policies on Education (NPE), 1986 which specified among other things the following;

- Priority will be accorded to opening primary schools in tribal areas;
- There is need to develop curricula and devise instructional material in tribal language at the initial stages with arrangements for switchover to regional languages.

The Sixth All India Educational Survey (1993) showed that 78 per cent of the tribal population and 56 per cent of tribal habitations have been provided primary schools within the habitation. In addition, 11 per cent of the tribal population and 20 per cent of tribal habitations have schools within less than 1 km radius. About 65 per cent of rural habitations covering 86 per cent of the total rural population have primary schools within the habitation or within a distance of half a kilometer, as against

56 per cent of tribal habitations with 79 per cent of tribal population. Mizoram and Gujarat have the highest percentage of population and habitations covered by primary schools within the habitations. Up to 95 per cent of the tribal population and 85 to 90 per cent of the tribal habitations in the states are provided with schooling facilities within the habitation.

Quality improvement: Development of culturally relevant materials in local languages.

Most of the states recognize the need to address issues related to teachers' attitudes, medium of instruction, textbooks and materials, curriculum and pedagogy and teaching- learning process in tribal areas. An increasing number of researchers strongly advocate the use of the mother tongue or home language as medium of instruction in early stages of education. This assumes greater significance in the context of education of tribal children because their mother tongue is often quite distinct from the prominent languages in the state or regional languages. ST children face problems wherever teachers do not speak their dialect at all. From the perspective of language, it is desirable to have a local teacher from the same tribal community. Although research evidence has demonstrated the positive consequences of bilingual or multilingual schooling on cognitive development and social interaction processes, tribal children would require special programs to be able to cope. The Constitution of India allows the use of tribal dialect (mother tongue) as the medium of instruction if the population of the tribe is more than 100,000. Assam was the first state to prepare teacher training modules and separate teaching learning materials for the Bodo tribal language in 1995. Bodo is also a medium of instructions in some districts of Assam. The work on tribal language materials was undertaken through DIET staff and Block Resource Center / Cluster Resource Center coordinators who belonged to the tribal community. Resource material in Bodo language has been prepared and all workbooks at primary stage have been translated/adopted in Bodo language. In many districts, Garo medium workbook has been translated/adopted and distributed in the schools.

Most of the other States (Karnataka, Kerala, MP, UP, Bihar) have taken up activities for quality improvement of tribal area schools. One of the issues identified by the states was the problem faced by tribal children whose home language was very different from the regional language, which was the medium of instruction at the primary level. In Madhya Pradesh teachers' handbooks called Bridge Language Inventory (BLIs) have been prepared in 3 related tribal languages viz. Identified teachers were given training in using BLISs in their classrooms. The teaching-learning package called Dham Dhama Dham was translated into Gondi and supplementary reading material, Kopal, was developed for tribal children. The class I textbook Bharati has been translated into tribal languages. Supplementary TLM for tribal children has been developed in Jhabua district using local cultural form i.e. folk tales, songs, proverbs, riddles, to make the learning process interesting. In all, 450 teachers of 311 schools have been trained to use the supplementary materials. Researches have underlined the need to develop culturally sensitive programmes of school education that can ensure the dignity of tribal groups by providing them with economically viable options for life (Sinha and Mishra, 1997).

In many other states some attempts have been made for linking curriculum with the local needs of the communities. Such curriculum would make tribal children more sensitive to local contexts and sustain them in their respective environments instead of forcing them to move out in search of another life. In Karnataka a textbook for class I and II has been developed and introduced for Soliga language. A handbook has been developed for sensitization of teachers towards social and cultural specificities of tribal societies. In Maharashtra tribal language dictionaries have been developed. Language resource groups have been set up for Bhili, Pawara, Madia, Gondi, etc. Bridge material has been developed.

Kerala has developed bilingual language materials at district level in Kasarkode, Waynad, Malappuram and Palakkad. Orissa took the initiative to develop a comprehensive strategy for education of tribal children as earlyas 1997. The state has initiated a number of activities for addressing the quality improvement of tribal education. Andhra Pradesh has developed bilingual dictionaries and teacher training has been organised in Warangal and Vizianegarem districts. Research studies have also been undertaken on the issue of language and maths learning by tribal children. It has been decided to use the multi-level kits developed for tribal areas in Vishakapatnam district and also in other tribal areas. Gujarat has developed dictionaries in Dangi and Bhili dialects. A local word glossary in Dangi has been prepared and distributed in schools for class I-IV in Dang district. Similarly a local word glossary in Adivasi dialect has been prepared for class I-IV in Banaskantha district and distributed in schools. The Vidyasahayaks were given training on the use of these dictionaries. Gujarat has also initiated extensive work for preparation of TLM in tribal languages. The TLM developed include flash cards for different languages and also cards for mathematics. These have been supplied to all schools in tribal areas. A Bridge Language Inventory has also been introduced in Ho and Mundari languages in Ranchi district of Bihar. Use of Local teachers The acceptance of teachers by the community as one of them is critical for increasing schooling participation in tribal areas. An understanding of and respect for tribal cultures and practices and some amount of familiarity with the local language are important for teachers to gain this acceptance: The presence of tribal teachers, especially from the same community, has shown and improved school participation of ST children. Coming from the same community, it is believed that the teachers would understand and respect the culture and the ethos with much greater sensitivity. Studies suggest that teacher motivation contributes more to teaching – learning process than teacher competence (Vaidyanathan and Nair, 2001). Realising the importance of having teachers from the local community, many states have appointed community teachers or para teachers as they are popularly referred to. The deployment of community teachers was first experimented in the late Seventies in NFE and later in the formal school with the Volunteer Teacher Scheme of Himachal Pradesh (1984). Nineties saw spurt in the appointment of community teachers, who are from the local community and appointed by the gram panchayat or Village Education Committees. Different states have different schemes for appointing community teachers – Shiksha Karmi Scheme (Madhya Pradesh and Rajasthan), Shiksha Mitra Yojna (Uttar Pradesh), Lok Shikshak(Bihar), Andariki–Vidya Volunteer Scheme (Andhra Pradesh). Vidya Upasak Yojana (Himachal Pradesh), Shikshan Sevak (Maharashtra), Guruji (under EGS in Madhya Pradesh)Shikshak (under Basti Shala Scheme in Maharashtra) etc.

It is estimated that there are about 230,000 para teachers engaged in full time schools in the country (Ed.CIL, 2001). The issues relating to classroom transactions are difficult as they deal with well entrenched attitudes and prejudices of teachers as well as seemingly intractable problems of the huge difference between home and school languages. Attempts have been made to address the first issue through training programmes for teachers. However, more emphasis on attitudinal training of teachers on the lines of Orissa is required in most of the states. The second issue has been addressed mainly through the BLIs and primers in tribal languages. There may be a problem of acceptance of the tribal language as a medium of instruction in the tribal communities, therefore, adequate dialogue with tribal communities and their leaders is required to prepare them on this issue.

The constitution of India was framed in 1950with an objective to guarantee social, political and economic Justice to all irrespective of caste, creed and religion. It was well visualized that development in education along with other allied sectors would play a vital role to bring about desirable changes in the country. That means that backward sections of Indian population i.e. Scheduled Castes and Scheduled Tribes and other backward section must be provided opportunity in education to develop critical thinking and self determination and contribute to the progress of the country. These promises laid the foundation for the attempt of Universalization of Primary Education in India. In 1950, target was set to universalize primary education among the entire eligible category of children within the age group of 6-14 years of age within a span of 10 years. During that period a great deal of expansion in education facilities was achieved. However, universalisation was still a distant dream. National Policies of Education (NPE),1986 and its subsequent modification in 1992laid down clearly the following targets to achieve universalization of education at Primary stage.(i)Provision of universal Access to all eligible children by opening of formal or non-formal education Centres within a reasonable distance of one kilometer.(ii) Retention of all children in schooling centres and ensuring completion of 5 years of basic education.(iii) Provisions of Quality education where-by all children achieve minimum achievement level as per the standard. Karnataka is one of the 8th largest states in India, situated in the southern India.

The total population of the State is 5.670 crores as per 2001 census (provisional). The scheduled castes and scheduled tribes comprise 22.21 and 16.20percent respectively. The literacy percentage of the state is 63.61% (excluding 0-6population) in which male and female literacy stands as 75.95% and 50.97% respectively(Source census 2001, Provisional).If we consider the concentration of indigenous tribal communities, their highest concentration is found in the southern districts of Karnataka State. Chamaraja Nager (Karnataka) is one among these districts, which was formed carving out of earst- while district in 2000 in the process of expansion of districts in the State. The district lies between 29 degree to 80 degree in north latitude and 26 degree to 74 degree in the east longitude that occupies an area of 9580 square kilometers. The area is calculated to 7.9 per cent of the total area of the State. The district has a population of 923819 that is 3.24 percent of the total population of the State and rank 22nd in the State. The density of population is143 as against 101 in 1991 per square kilometer. The district has recorded an increase of 15.27percent over the last enumeration in 1991.(Source Census, 2001, Provisional). The district has been the dwell of a number of indigenous tribal communities some very marginal and some quite significant as far as their population is concerned. The Tribal population of the district is 573379. The male and female constitute 233120 and 340259 respectively of the total population with a percentage of 58.51 in the district. As per 2001 Census (provisional) the literacy rate of both the sexes stands as 32.61percent. The literacy rate of male is 45.35 percent while that of female is 21.31 percent. They have their own mother tongue having no written script except one tribe, Nayaka who have got a written script. All the languages belong to the Austric Speech family (Jha and Jhingran, 2002).

Kannada Language, Textbooks and Medium of Instruction:

A lot of attempts have been made to mainstream the tribal children in education process. Most importantly by providing access, reading writing materials, free textbooks and empowering village community to participate in management of school. Achievements are also quite significant in areas of provision of access by opening of new schools, hostels, enrolment of children and empowerment of teachers through mass teachers training on child centered approach. However, there seem to be lack of achievement in retention and achievement of students (on the basis of completion rates) in schools. The dropout rate is still quite high and achievement scores in subjects need significant increase.

DPEP, Karnataka Study conducted on 1353 schools, 22535 students joined in 1998-99.There are many reasons why the system fails particularly in the case of indigenous tribals. This paper will discuss in detail the problems and issues limited to the area of language, textbook and medium of instruction and other issues directly or indirectly related to that If we consider the case of tribal child and feature that motivate and de-motivate him in staying in school, we need to consider the background and inputs given to him as part of incentive to adopt the modern education successfully, some factors of importance maybe scrutinized. Language is a part parcel and vehicle of culture. It is the medium of expression. It can be symbolic or spoken. Language is learnt as part of the socialisation and enculturation process. It can not be taught in a sense that it is not merely sensible speech sounds rather typical cultural elements intrinsically linked and ingrained in it. Language can be learnt through interactions. The problem of providing free and compulsory education to all the children of the age group of 6-14 years by establishing sufficient numbers of schools in all areas in order to satisfy the directives of the constitution (article 45) poses many pertinent questions with at least one, for the education of indigenous tribal communities. Part-V of the constitution contains Directive Principles of State Policies contained in article36-51. These principles are ideals which the State should strive for and some directions to the state executive and legislature as to how their powers be used. Besides these are few other directives addressed to the State in other parts of the constitutions, which like the Directive Principles are also non-justifiable. Article 350- A directs the State to take steps to provide adequate facilities for instructions in the mother tongue at the primary stage of education and particularly to the children belonging to the linguistic minorities mainly with a view to preserve their language and facilitate better understanding among such children. A tribal child is relatively less exposed to other languages at the age of his entry to the school, because of the tribals have their own Eco-zone where they inhabit in relative isolation and therefore have lesser exposure to the outside world. Jenu Kuruba the major tribal communities in Karnataka are least mobile. Their movement as observed is limited to a maximum of 20 kilometers i.e. from home to work sites and to weekly local market not far away from the village. That means they hardly migrate to other part of the district and State unlike Nayaka's who although migrate to other part of the country seasonally in negligible numbers for daily wage laboring. The tribal child entering school for the first time sees a completely different environment. The building pattern with closed four walls, and sitting arrangement is alien to him. The teacher, his apparel and language - unseen and incomprehensive creates a sense of suspicion and fear in him initially. Subsequently the teachers' (mostly non-tribals) treatment makes impossible for him to continue in school. Here it's important to discuss the role of teacher in class room. It is often seen that teachers working in tribal areas have prejudices and biases towards tribal society and culture. They treat tribals as sub-human beings, who have a lot of blind beliefs and conservative ideas. To them the tribal language which has no written script does not qualify for a status of language and hence inferior. These senses of ethnocentrism are expressed in their dealings with tribal students in a classroom. He seldom inquires into the socio-cultural background of the tribal child. If one considers the case of a tribal child it is clear that he is no less competent even at a tender age. He acquires ability in learning songs at the age of 4-5 years. He learns beating of drums (Dhapa), dances memorizing short stories, proverbs, and riddles and often creates new songs of his own in impromptu exchange with peers at the age of 10. He is so close to his things that he dares, dreams, fantasizes, plays and interacts with an infinite thing, words, jargons which no one can even teach him in post-primary education. If we consider the scope of learning language, we will see that a tribal child gets plenty of contexts at home, where every thing is informal and friendly and language learning is spontaneous. However, in school, there is dearth of context and every thing is formal and structured and the language of the book is considered as the highest kind of knowledge. The child has no scope to interact with friends while the teacher is taking a class on monologue basis. The child can not concentrate because of communication failure and monotonous classroom process and instead chastised, beaten by the teacher for not being attentive, responsive and not doing wee in studies. The hostile and in-conducive school atmosphere leads to dropping-out and discontinuation of most of the students from school. Above all the tribal children are the first generation academic learners and have least scope of support and help from parents and relatives who are illiterate. The psychologists, educationist and linguists are of the opinion that a child exposed to multilingual situations in initial years has faster cognitive and intellectual development. But this opinion does not hold well in tribal areas because in urban areas, the child gets its formal education through state language as the medium of instructions, which is his own mother tongue and gradually exposed to other languages. But in tribal society, the child is directly introduced to the State language used in schools rather than his own mother tongue. Another reason is that in urban areas the child has relatively plenty of opportunity to interact with people coming from different linguistic areas. He is exposed to electronic media, Radio and T.V., which not only are the medium of entertainment but also are scope of learning and adopting traits and ideas. The tribal child has absolutely no scope where he gets exposed to other languages. There are many tribal language which has no script. Hence, preparation of suitable textbooks for such category children is a challenging task. In Karnataka, the textbooks are supplied free of cost to tribal and other categories of children.

The language of the textbooks is in standard state language for school students all over the state. It is believed that experts knowing tribal culture and language prepare these books. However, it is found that the books have contents of subjects which are reflective of dominant society. The books have few local specific contents and some time specters and description of animals, birds, trees, etc. alien to the tribal child which poses problem to comprehend. The colour of pictures is not realistic and lacks brightness. All the pictures are often bi-coloured. Overall the cover page, contents and contexts are not local specific and relate to the real life situations of the tribals for which the text book is not appreciated and adopted by the tribal children. The Paradox Considering the constitutional directives and actual implementation of educational scheme one would certainly find a gap or mis-match between what should have been done and what has been done so far. A country like India, where diverse linguistic groups are found, some quite significant and some negligible in number pose a great problem as to how to streamline them in the education process. As per the constitutional directives the basic education may be provided free of cost to indigenous tribal in their own mother tongue which seems to be a Herculean task for any state government. The indigenous tribal although have a definite territory, they have a number of sub-groups within it. Therefore, language varies in a limited geographical area and within a particular tribe. It also varies from sub-tribe to sub-tribe. Language of one sub-tribe is quite different from another within the limited geographical area due to impact of bordering community and their exposure to outside world. Such examples are innumerable in this district. One such example is that in Kollegal (as administrative division of the district) which has a sizeable number of Jenu Kuruba population and sub-sections like Soliga and Nayaka (relatively assimilated) who live close to each other. Although there are certain similarities in language and culture they differ a lot linguistically. Any textbook on either language could not solve the problem. Secondly, in case of multi-lingual situations in a classroom, whereby students come from different tribal or sub-tribal groups, the problem for the teachers is as to what should be the standard medium of instruction for all the children. This has been a feature of all residential schools running in the district by Schedule Caste and Schedule Tribe Department. The teacher knowing one tribal language finds it impossible to teach students coming from different ethnic and language background. Thirdly, the teachers, mostly non-tribals, do not have adequate knowledge of tribal language. There are tribal teachers (mostly Betta Kuruba and Jenu Kurubas), who can be useful for children. But there is no consideration of the above fact and a Soliga teacher posted in a Jenu Kuruba dominated village or school is as good as non-tribal teachers as they do not know the language of Jenu Kurubas. In the second case some of the non-tribal teachers who have been working reasonably for a long time at a particular tribal area have experience of tribal language where all the students belong to a particular tribal group. However due to a number of reasons, like health hazards (endemic malaria proneregion), lack of basic human facilities like shelter, market place and postal facilities, they get themselves transferred to other parts paving way for posting of a new teacher in his place. Fourthly, the problem could have been subsided with the engagement of sufficient number of local teachers from the community. But unfortunately there is dearth of qualified tribals who can be appointed as teachers in schools. The problems and issues in language, textbook and medium of instruction are very typical to the tribals of Karnataka as to any other region of the country where multi-ethnic and multi-lingual indigenous tribal groups are existing. Development in the education sphere can only be possible when the key issues are addressed properly. These are the issues and problems, which can fail the entire education system even before it is actually implemented unless addressed through strategic planning. Any generalized planning across the board for all category of children not only create an environment of education among tribals but also will delay and break the pace of spontaneous educational development. Therefore, careful and calculative measures must be taken keeping in view the educational need vis-a-vis the cultural orientation of the tribals.

Some indicative, if not exhaustive suggestions are given below. 1. Linguistic mapping should be done to assess the incidence and category of tribals before planning for their education. 2. The medium of instruction should be in the mother tongue by way of using bi-lingual primers prepared in a decentralized manner. That means it is not the state or district, it is the block where the teachers (tribal) with educated (although a few) tribal persons will prepare the text book for their own category of children. 3. The school environment should be attractive with gardens, plantations, and children friendly elements with cost effective locally available raw materials. The school must have play materials and self-learning materials for the children to create interest in them to attend school regularly.4. The teacher working in a tribal dominated school should be rightly informed about his role. He should be oriented on the richness of heritage and culture of the tribals. He should have enough patience to bear the tribal child in a classroom and act as a friend and facilitator rather than a master.5. The non-tribal teachers working for longtime inspite of various health hazards by knowing the tribal language should be identified and compensated with incentives and rewards as a token of commendations for their valuable services towards the education of tribals so that other non-tribal teachers will be interested to join the force.6. Tribal teachers should be identified by their category and be posted to schools where he can serve his community children better.7. The village community although illiterate, they are great assets as far as education onart and craft is concerned. Their resources should be used while topics related to agriculture, horticulture and material culture are transacted in the classroom.8. Innovation through research on various aspects of education must be conducted so as to identify problems and their solutions. The problems and issues identified at this juncture may seriously affect the future developments in the district. Hence, it is high time that appropriate strategies must be built up to find out ways and means not to subside but to mitigate the problems for the future.

Conclusion

The discussion presented above gives us two important lessons. One is that the cognitive qualities of tribal children have to be viewed and evaluated taking into consideration their ecological and cultural contexts that place very different demands on day-to-day life. Because of differences in the demands of tribal ecology, the patterning of their cognitive abilities shows considerable variation from those of other groups. A related and more important lesson is that tribal children are neither culturally inferior nor cognitively less competent than the children of other groups. Instead many of their skills and abilities are highly developed and extremely sophisticated. The implications of these findings for schooling of tribal children are clear. A programme of schooling, which does not pay attention to the ecological, cultural and psychological characteristics of tribal children is highly unlikely to make any significant impact. The educational system of the dominant non-tribal population is of very limited value in the tribal cultural milieu because it does not match with the lifestyle of individuals and the needs of the tribal community. Linking school education with life in general and the needs of the tribal communities in particular is a most important step that requires serious attention. The evidences suggests that tribal children do possess the basic cognitive abilities and psychological dispositions necessary for successful participation in school. Yet tribal children have very low levels of participation and success in school education programmes. This points to our failure to develop a sensitive model of education that is rooted in the psychological strengths of tribal children. Studies indicate that, in comparison to other groups, hunters and gatherers possess a high level of visual and tactual differentiation; they demonstrate capacity for fine judgment of shape and size of stimuli as well as spatial relations and they produce fine categorization of an array of objects (Mishra et al 1996). These abilities are required for success in science, art, music, dance, athletic activities, and vocations like carpentry, tailoring, wood and stone crafts. These skills need to be utilized not only for education of tribal children in schools, but also in the broader economic spheres of tribal life. Such attempts will be helpful in generating and promoting the sense of competence, self-efficacy, self-respect and positive self-image among tribal children in general. Such attempts are also highly likely to provide tribal children with a culturally meaningful, ecologically valid and economically viable alternative to life by reinforcing the dignity of their culture and identity. Ever increasing contact of tribals with the outside world over the years has introduced several changes in their culture and life. These changes are reflected in their psychological characteristics also. Studies (e.g. Mishra et al 1996) indicate that their ways of perceiving the world, categorizing objects, interpreting pictures, and strategies of learning and memory become more similar to those with whom they interact and negotiate their life in these changed circumstances. This suggests that tribal children can acquire all those skills that the members of other groups of the society possess. What is important on our part is to develop a positive frame of mind about tribal children. This is possible only through sensitivity to tribal culture and life, recognition of the cognitive strengths of tribal children, and appreciation of their personality qualities. Efforts in these directions will be very helpful in organizing the programme of tribal education as well as promoting economic and other aspects of tribal development.

Similarly a clear policies for language use in schools has to be developed. Research evidence suggests that significantly fewer students drop out of schools in which the language of tribal groups is used for instruction at the primary level. Development of primers in the tribal dialect involving content from the local context will go a long way in ensuring children's active participation in the learning process in school. While there is a general need for improvement in physical facilities in all schools in remote tribal regions, change in perceptions and outlooks of teachers about tribal children are equally important. Teachers must be sensitized to the cultural and behavioral strengths of tribal children and motivated to do their best for them in schools. Incentives should be initiated to attract effective teachers to work in tribal schools and to retain them there. Only such motivated teachers are likely to generate interest among tribal children towards schools education by attempting to link the contents of the curriculum with the existing realities of tribal communities through the use of innovative technologies.

10

Disparities and Dropouts: A Growing Constraint for Reforms of Tribal Education in Karnataka

Empowerment is about people - both women and men - taking control over their lives: becoming conscious of their own situation and position, setting their own agendas, creating space for themselves, gaining skills, building self-confidence, solving problems, and developing self-reliance. It is not only a social and political process, but an individual one as well - and it is not only a process but an outcome too. Realizing that Scheduled Tribes are one of the most deprived and marginalized groups with respect to education, a host of programmes and measures were initiated ever since the Independence. Elementary education is a priority area in the Tribal sub-plans from the 5thFive Year Plan. Education of ST children is considered important, not only because of the Constitutional obligation but also as a crucial input for total development of tribal communities. One of the super goals of SSA is to "bridge all gender and social category gaps at primary stage by 2007 and at elementary stage by 2010". The issues and challenges in tribal education can be categorized as external, internal, socio-economic and psychological. The external constraints are related to issues at levels of policies, planning and implementation while internal constraints are with respect to school system, content, curriculum, pedagogy, medium of instruction etc. The third set of problems relates to social economic and cultural background of tribals and psychological aspects of first generation learners. The literacy level of Scheduled Castes and Scheduled Tribes is very low compared to the general literacy rate. Recognizing that education provides opportunities for a permanent change in the socio-economic status of these people, this Government gives top priority to education. Hence out of a sum of Rs.448.91 crores provided in the Budget Estimate for 2004-2005 to this Department, more than70% is earmarked for schemes related to education. There is a need to evolve sensitive model of tribal education rooted in the psychological strengths of tribal children.

Scheduled Tribe in India are more like the "indigeneous" or"native people" in other parts of the world. The population of Scheduled Tribes in India according to 2001census is 8.43 crore. Education of Scheduled Tribe children is considered important, not only because of the constitutional obligation, but also a crucial input for total development of tribal communities. The literacy levels of the Scheduled Tribes according to the 2001census is 47.10% as compared to overall literacy rate of the total population i.e., 65.38%,which shows a dismal picture of Scheduled Tribes education. So long as there is a gap between the literacy levels, the position of Scheduled Tribes will remain backward. Lack of education may lead to child exploitation, child labor, population explosion, etc., so the need of the hour is to bring quality education through 100% school enrolment and retention with more emphasis on the girl child education. I have given some suggestions for imparting quality education among the Scheduled Tribes in order to uplift themselves and to overcome the socio-economic problems.

The Scheduled Tribes represents one of the most economically impoverished and marginalized groups in India. Karnataka has a high proportion of the tribal population. Education of tribal women is recognized as indispensable for their growth and development. The education of tribal women according to 2001 census, the Scheduled Tribe female literacy is 8.07%as compared to the male literacy of 12.68% in Karnataka. So long as there is disparity between male and female in education levels the difference between the position of men and women would continue to exist. The tribal women's access to education in the country is inadequate and discriminating because of ignorance, lack of motivation, etc.. Thus education is the key catalyst to the development of human resources. Lack of education is largely responsible for the exploitation and pitiable plight of the tribal women. For the tribal, education disseminates knowledge, knowledge give inner strength, which is very essential for the tribal for attaining freedom from exploitation and poverty. So due to ignorance arising out of illiteracy, the tribal have not been able to take advantage of new economic opportunities. Empowerment of women covers aspects such as education, economic status etc. Abolition of gender based discrimination in all institutions and structures of society and participation of women in policies and decision process at domestic and public level are sew dimension of women empowerment.

The National Policies of Education 1986 and Programme of Action 1992 envisaged for education of scheduled tribe and scheduled caste children and has specified objectives and strategies. The cultural variations and the gap of home language and school language, understanding space and time from tribal point of view and construction of knowledge from ones own cultural context are some of the points which determine the education of scheduled tribe children. Cultural plurality is the basis of contextual differences in primary education.

There are 16 million ST children (10.87 million in 6-11 years and 5.12 million in 11-14 years) as on March 2001, out of the total child population of about 193 million in the age group of 6 to 14years in the country (Selected Educational Statistics – 2000-01). Realizing that Scheduled Tribes are one of the most deprived and marginalized groups with respect to education, a lot of programmes and measures were initiated ever since the Independence. Elementary education is a priority area in the Tribal sub-plans from the 5thFiveYear Plan. Education of ST children is considered important, not only because of the Constitutional obligation but also as a crucial input for total development of tribal communities. Another important development in the policies towards education of tribals is the National Policies on Education (NPE), 1986 which specified among other things the following:• Priority will be accorded to opening primary schools in tribal areas.• There is need to develop curricula and devise instructional material in tribal language at the initial stages with arrangements for switchover to regional languages.• ST youths will be encouraged to take up teaching in tribal areas. Working group on Elementary and Adult Education for Xth Five Year Plan (2002-07) emphasized the need to improve the quality of education of tribal children and ensuring equity, besides further improving the access. S Ts and Literacy The literacy rate for S Ts has gone up from 8.5% (male – 13.8%, female – 3.2%) in 1961 to29.6% (male – 40.6%, female – 18.2%) in 1991 and to 40% (male – 59%, female – 37%) in1999-2000 as per the 55thRound of NSS.

Study has shown that one of the vital reasons for poor and difficulty in accessing school benefits in tribal areas before 1975s was the high norm on population, number of required children and radious for opening new schools. However, latter many states have relaxed these norms to enable setting up more Ashram Schools even in small tribal hamlets. For a first time, Andhra Pradesh has relaxed norms to set up schools in habitations even with 25 school-age children in each every nock and corner of the tribal belt of the state. Karnataka was not lagging behind in this regard. But, Karnataka govt. didn't show any interest in providing all basic amenities including subject and more over trained teacher's affect opening such lager number of schools. Followed by this move many other Indian states have decreased the conditional population size norm, especially for tribal areas. Today any one can open educational centers even for 15 children with the prior permission. In remote tribal habitations in hilly areas of States schools can be opened even with 10 children also 1993 Educational Survey has shown that 76 per cent of tribal population and 54per cent of tribal habitations have been provided Ashram schools within the habitation in general. Further it is found that 13 per cent of tribal population and 23 per cent of tribal habitations have schools with in less than 1 km radius. 'About 65 per cent of rural habitations covering 86 per cent of the total rural population have primary schools within the habitations or within a distance of half kilometer, as against 56 per cent of tribal habitations with 79 per cent of tribal population' (NIPEA, 2001). Mizoram and Gujarat have the highest percentage of population and habitations covered by primary schools within the habitations. In these states 95 per cent of tribal population and 85 to 90per cent of the tribal habitations in the States are provided with schooling facility within the habitation. Despite this effort, the same Sixth All India Educational Survey reports that there are about 186,700habitations without schooling facilities, mostly in tribal habitations and habitations of hardest to reach tribes. This problems is more prevalent in North eastern states. The situation regarding access has now improved substantially, thanks to these schemes like NFE/Education Guarantee Scheme and Alternative and Innovative Education (EGS and AIE), DPEP and Sarva Shiksha Abhiyan. More than 77,000 education guarantee centers and alternative schools were opened under the District Primary Education Programme (DPEP), EGS schemes and other programmes in the State over the last 10 years. In addition about 116,000 new primary and upper primary schools were opened since 1996-97 – as number of schools increased from 767,000 in 1995-96 to 883,000 in 2001-02 (Abstract of Educational Statistics 2001-02). Subsequent to this statistical report, SSA sanctioned in the last two years over 85,000new schools. In addition 300,000 EGS centers and equal number of alternative and innovative education centers were sanctioned to benefit more than 14 million never enrolled and out of school children. Many of these new schools, continuing educational centers and alternative schools have been sanctioned in the tribal habitations, improving the schooling access. As per the latest estimate (2003-04), there are about 81,000 unserved habitations in the country. The largest number of unserved habitations without primary schools is in Bihar (14200) followed by Orissa (13100), Assam (12300), Rajasthan (8000), West Bengal (6600) and Andhra Pradesh(4100). These unserved habitations are being covered under Sarva Shiksha Abhiyan (from various Resources)

Planning and Appraisal Planning process

At the outset, it is pertinent to mention that a solid database and clear visioning are essential for planning.SSA envisages the bottom-up approach of planning instead of the top-down approach in a decentralized manner, as it reflects the reality at the grassroots level. The planning process has to be participatory in nature as this type of planning not only creates a sense of ownership among the stakeholders, but also creates awareness and helps in the capacity building of personnel at various levels. The plans developed through consultative meetings and interaction with the community and target groups, at various levels, reflect local specificity. It is necessary that there be documentation of the process of the preparation of plan to evidence the fact that they have been prepared at the habitation level through participatory planning mode.

The following steps are an integral part of participatory planning. Interaction with community and target groups.

The bottom-up approach will not only help the planning team to acquaint themselves with various problems, but may also provide an insight to the possible solutions. The commonality of problems across such meetings will help the planning teams to propose interventions accordingly. Interaction with community and target groups has to be ensured by involvement of target groups and community leaders in the constitution of habitation, block and the district level teams on one hand and by mobilisation activities and extensive visits of planning teams to every habitation – ruraland urban (including slums) on the other. Such interactions not only provide an opportunity to be familiar with the problems of target groups and help in devising strategies to deal with these, but also mould the opinions of communities with the help ofthe good offices of community leaders.

Consultative meetings: The consultative meetings with the officials at block and district levels would facilitate the core teams in formulating strategies to address the problems. These meetings would also facilitate convergence among various schemes being implemented or proposed by different departments. As the responsibility of implementing the programme rests with the educational administration of the district, it is essential to involve them from the planning stage itself. Documentation of consultative meetings and community interaction would enable the persons at the district and state levels as well as the appraisal teams to know about planning processes.

Micro planning Exercises: Once the planning teams are in place and their capacity building has been undertaken, the micro-planning exercise should be undertaken after the collection of data from various sources. This data would be an indicator of the existing situation and reflect the position vis-à-vis the goals and targets of the programme. It may be ensured that this data is invariably used for planning purpose. This data would form the basis to identify district specific issues.

Identifications of issues and interventions

Once the consulting process has taken place at various levels highlighting the problems and issues, the next step is to identify the problems and needs in the light of educational and general information and studies that have been conducted earlier. The assessment of the educational situation will lead to the identification of problems, needs and constraints of elementary education in the district. The problems related to access, enrolment, retention and quality of education need to be identified and reflected in the District Elementary Education Plan.

Target setting: In order to meet the SSA goal of UEE, it is important to achieve the basic objectives of universal access, universal enrolment, universal retention and universal achievement within the stipulated time period. Various states are at various levels in the field of education. Thus, it may be possible for some states or districts to achieve the SSA goals before the target dates. It may, therefore, be essential for districts to set their own targets within the overall timeframe of the programme. The targets have to be set realistically in a phased manner. There is a need to set dis-aggregated targets (preferably block wise) for disadvantageous and other groups on the basis of gender. Targets can vary from district to district and within a district, from block to block.14 he Sub-Mission will review• the performance of states on education of disadvantaged groups including Girls,SC/ST/Minorities/Urban Deprived Children and Disabled Children as delineatedunder framework for implementation of Sarva Shiksha Abhiyan • suggest and facilitate capacity building exercises that may be state-specific or in the nature of cross-state sharing workshops to promote best practices. • facilitate Government and NGO partnership in promoting elementary education fordisadvantaged groups. • prepare a half yearly report that would be discussed in the Executive Committee ofthe National Mission for SSA.(ii)Tasks of the Sub-Mission (a) Inclusive Education• Suggest models of service delivery on inclusive education, which could be adopted by State SSA Mission Societies• Assist in providing a resource base on IE for states that require such assistance• Provide inputs on material available on inclusive education, which could be utililzed by State SSA Mission Societies. • Facilitate development of barrier free access in the schools for all kinds of CWSN• Identify good practices for documentation and dissemination • Monitor implementation of IE in States, in quantitative, qualitative and financial terms.

11

Tribals and Education in Karnataka: A Synopsis

In Karnataka, Schedule Tribes (ST) account for 6.55 percent (3.46 million) of the total State population, which comprises 4.11 percent of the total tribal population of the country. Bellary district has the highest concentration of STs in Karnataka. Thirteen of the Sector Development Project (SDP) districts1comprise approximately 60% of the total tribal population in the State. However, there are no concentrated tribal areas termed as Integrated Tribal Development Project in the SDP districts. There are 50 major tribes with 109 sub-tribes in the State (as of March 2005), according to the notified Schedule under Article 342 of the Constitution of India. From these, Central Government has identified (i) Jenu Kuruba; and (ii) Koraga tribes as primitive groups (PTGs). Jenu Kuruba tribes are originally from Mysore, Chamarajanagar and Kodagu districts and Koraba tribes are from Udupi and Dakshina Kannada districts. In Chamarajanagar district, only Kollegala Taluk hasPTG areas. PTGs constitute the most vulnerable among the all notified tribes. According to the surveys conducted by Department of Tribal Welfare, these tribes predominantly stay in districts where they originally belong to, however the possibility of tribal migration to neighbouring districts for better employment opportunities cannot be denied. Whether the migrated tribes have been mainstreamed into the society or still continue to live as primitive groups, statistics are unavailable. The SDP will finance investment in the sectors of

(i) water supply; (ii) sewerage and sanitation; (iii) urban drainage; (iv) roads and transportation; (v) poverty alleviation; (vi) non-municipal infrastructure inclusive of conservation of lakes, expansion of fire services and development of tourism facilities; (vii) institutional development; and (viii) investment programassistance. Potential impacts on indigenous peoples (IPs) were examined in sample subprojects. Discussions with Revenue and Gram (Village) Panchayat officials and a survey of Schedule Tribes show that Scheduled Tribes have been mainstreamed. The Sector Development Program (SDP) has a sector loan component. Thus it may include subprojects for which all or part of the impact area cannot be determined before the appraisal, owingto incipient technical designs, and/or the lack of clearly defined sites. Also, the possibility ofexpanding the current SDP area (i.e., addition of few more towns) cannot be excluded under a sectorloan approach, under which impacts on indigenous peoples (IPs) cannot be envisaged at this stage. Therefore, an Indigenous People's Development Framework (IPDF) has been developed. The Resettlement Framework also provides entitlements to IPs as vulnerable persons. The IPDF sets out the policies, principles and implementation mechanisms to address such impacts. During the course of the SDP identification and survey if any IPs are identified, the impacts (both positive and negative) of the subproject component on affected groups/ community will be addressed according to the IPDF. The IPDF will address the developmental needs of IPs as a distinct community through a process of sustainable development. The IPDF is a policies and procedural framework for Indigenous People Development Plans (IPDPs) that are developed for sub-projects and that are to be approved during Project implementation. Further, an IPDF sets out the indigenous people's policies together with the screening and planning procedures. The need for formulating an IPDP will be established if the subprojects to be funded under the SDP are screened as Category 'A' projects. Category 'A' projects envisage significant impacts on IPs Bagalkot, Belgaum, Bellary, Bidar, Bijapur,

Chamarajanagar, Davangere, Dharwad, Gadag, Gulbarga, Haveri, Koppal andRaichur. The ITDPs are generally contiguous areas of the size of a Block (Group of villages) or Taluka in which the ST population is 50 percent or more of the total population. Tribal groups are still at the most primitive stage. They continue to live in isolated areas and practice either primitive agriculture or no agricultural practice and most of them are still in food gathering stage with almost stagnating population. Covering the construction of the KUIDFC building in vacant government land. As per the ADB's F3/OP (13 May 2004), screening process categorizes projects by the significance of their impacts onIPs. It is recommended that for (i) Category 'A' projects: Impacts should be significant that require IPDP and/or IPDF; (ii)

Since the highest concentration of Schedule Tribes (STs) in Karnataka, thirteen NKUIDP districts comprise approximately 60 percent of the total tribal population in the State. Concentrated tribal areas termed as Integrated Tribal Development Project (ITDP) areas exist in districts of Mysore, Chickmagalur, Kodagu, Dakshina Kannada and Udupi (South and Coastal Karnataka), which do not overlap with the Project (NKUIDP) districts. There are 50 major tribes (Annex B) with 109 sub-tribes in the State (as of March 2005),according to the notified Schedule under Article 342 of the Constitution of India. From these, GoK has identified (i) Jenu Kuruba; and (ii) Koraga tribes as primitive groups (PTGs) 5. Jenu Kuruba tribesare originally from Mysore, Chamarajanagar and Kodagu districts and Koraba tribes are from Udupiand Dakshina Kannada districts (Map 1). In Chamarajanagar PTGs constitute the most vulnerable among the all notified tribes. According to the surveys conducted by Department of Tribal Welfare (DoTW), these tribes predominantly stay in districts where they originally belong to, however the possibility of tribal migration to neighbouring districts for better employment opportunities cannot be denied. Whether the migrated tribes have beenmainstreamed into the society or still continue to live as primitive groups, statistics are unavailable.

This again states a need for preparation of IPDF, to address the unforeseen impacts of sub-projects on indigenous people. Identification of tribes is a State subject. Constitution of India may classify these as Schedule Tribe (ST), Schedule Caste (SC), Other Backward Class (OBC) or General (Forward Class) category,taking into consideration the characteristics like (i) tribes' primitive traits; (ii) distinctive culture; (iii)shyness with the public at large; (iv) geographical isolation; and (v) social and economicbackwardness. This may vary based on the classification of particular tribe into any of the above stated category as per the status of that tribe in the respective State (for example, a Scheduled Tribe inKarnataka may be classified as a Scheduled Caste in Maharashtra). Therefore, tribes notified for Karnataka State are Schedule Tribes in Karnataka only and their category may vary in other States. Schedule Tribes in the State are covered by the Karnataka Land Reforms (KLR) Act, 1964, Karnataka Schedule Caste and Schedule Tribe (Prohibition of Transfer of Certain Lands - PTCL) Act, 1978, and Prevention of Atrocities Act, 1989. (i) Under the KLR Act, 1964, Scheduled Caste (SC) and Scheduled Tribe (ST) families are eligible for part of lands identified as surplus land in the State. (ii) The PTCL Act, 1978, was intended for restricting the transfer of land by members of Scheduled Tribes in the State, and for the restoration of lands alienated by such members. No Schedule Tribe can transfer allotted or granted lands without the permission of Government, if done, the new registration will be invalid. Further, nothing in this Act shall apply to the transfer of allotted/granted lands in favour of the Government or Central Government, a local authority or a bank either before or after the commencement of this Act. It is applicable in Bagalkot, Belgaum, Bellary, Bidar, Bijapur, Chamarajanagar, Davangere, Dharwad, Gadag, Gulbarga, Haveri, Koppal and Raichur districts. The ITDPs are generally contiguous areas of the size of a Block (Group of villages) or Taluka in which the ST population is 50 percent or more of the total population. Tribal groups are still at the most primitive stage. They continue to live in isolated areas and practice either primitive agriculture or no agricultural practice and most of them are still in food gathering stage with almost stagnating population. The Ministry of Tribal Affairs, Government of India (GoI), has instructed all States to consult the National Policies on Resettlement and Rehabilitation (dated 19thFebruary, 2004) prepared by the Ministry of Rural Development, GoI, in relation to any involuntary resettlement of tribes. The Policy provides guideline for the provision of minimum facilities and compensations towards resettlement and rehabilitation of persons displaced due to acquisition of land under public purposes. However, the National Policies on Resettlement and Rehabilitation falls short of the ADB's Indigenous Peoples Policies requirements of "the potential vulnerability of indigenous peoples" should be recognized, and "development interventional that affect indigenous peoples should ensure that they have opportunities to participate in and benefit equitably from the interventions" (1998 para 6). However, the recent directive from the National Commission on Schedule Castes and Schedule Tribes to establish Schedule Caste/Tribe Commission is a landmark in State level attention to indigenous peoples affairs and development needs. The above policies and legal instruments available in India and Karnataka are supplemented by ADB's Indigenous Peoples Policies (1998) for the implementation of NKUIDP. The Policies ensures equality of opportunity for indigenous peoples. It aims to ensure that any Bank-assisted development interventions which will have any impact on indigenous peoples will be consistent with the needs and aspirations of affected indigenous peoples and compatible in substance and structure with affected IP's culture and social and economic institutions.

An attempt has been made in this present research paper to analyse educational status of the tribal children in Karnataka. Data on completion rate, repetition rate, dropout rate, attendance rate, transition rate and enrolment rate for primary school children have been collected from the report of the Sarva Shiksha Abhiyan (SSA) during the year 2001 to 2005. Education is considered to be an important mechanism for economic development in India, especially for those who have been exploited viz. The scheduled castes (SCs) and scheduled tribes (STs). As these sections of our society were traditionally and historically deprived of their basic rights, education was far away from their reach (Wan khede, 2001).

Education is also the most powerful instrument for achieving an egalitarian type of the society. The framers of constitution, therefore, took a special care of the condition in which the people from these communities are provided several safeguards for the promotion of their educational and economic interests. No country or nation can become prosperous without achieving high literacy rate. The main reason for low literacy among the ST was due to the fact that they were profited from learning since time immemorialhowever the literacy rates for the STs is increasing at a very high rate after independence due to protective discrimination. The rate of literacy has gone up substantially for all social groups in 2001 as compared to 1991 in Karnataka. The rate of literacy was high among non-ST as compared to STs in Karnataka. There was a fluctuation in the rate of literacy by districts in Karnataka. The education status of urban population was high as compared to rural population. Further, the educational status of males was high as compared to females. The educational status has gone up for all social groups in 2001 as compared to 1991. The education status of Scheduled Tribes was low as compared to that of other social groups in Karnataka.

Factors Responsible for Dropouts

Construction of many schools and rentension of the children is quite a debatable and antagonistic issue today. Drops out among tribal children have become most common phenomenon in tribal schools. Construction of enough schools within the distance is purely related to the State. In the same way drops out of the children is purely related to 3 important aspects. 1 households related reasons,2 school related reasons and 3 teachers related reasons

Generally peaking, tribal education is Governed by the conventions of the National Policies of Education 1986, and the conventions that all Indian states have adopted for its implementation. As a result both state and central government have taken many more vital steps to construct primary and high schools in each every corner of the country. The total admission in India every year from class 1 to 8 is 12 crores and 60 lakh children and out of this the dropout is 65%(Subramanian,2005). In the same way the total admission of the tribal children will be between around 15 lakh and out of this dropouts is 67% . It is found that 52.4% tribal children were dropouts in MP and 64% at all India level.

Stopping dropouts remains a real challenge and continuing problem, and it is also feel a research has to be carried out to found outways and means to overcome this problem. Very few studies have been done so far in Karnataka state regarding dropouts among tribal children and it is found that they are not full fledged. This paper is based on the data collected in few selected patch of the tribal schools in Karnataka state.

12

Problems in Educating Indigenous Children: A Case Study of Paniya Tribe of Karnataka

India is a multi-racial country. Different parts have different cultural traits and levels of development. It is not uncommon to find that there are certain tribes, which are not yet touched even by the fringe of civilization. Aboriginal are examples of this. The word tribe is taken to denote a primary aggregate of people living under primitive or barbarous condition under a headman or chief. Tribe is a group of families living as a community under one or more chiefs, united by language and customs.

Strength of a society lies in the role of education in training, development and allocation of its manpower resources. Education has been conceived as training for better life and better social adjustment in a community or group. it is a phase of the social process which is fostered by society for life in group. It can be said that education is the complete development of individuality so that one can make an original contribution to human life according to one's best capacity.

It is clear that in an under developed tribal community, where the poor people form the majority, owing to sheer poverty, they could not avail of the educational opportunities. Thus, the educational development of the marginalized people is inter linked with their socio-economic condition. Hence prior to solving the problems associated with the educational backwardness of the tribals the problem of bread must be satisfied. Among the these people who hardly get meal twice a day, education is a tall talk, taking into account the predominant role played by socio-economic factors in determining the utilisation of facilities by the ST and SCs. (Das and Naidu, 2003:34).

No community can make their development without the spread of education. Development means all-round development, i.e., in the field of social, economic, cultural and above all the quality of life of human being. Whenever man uses the modern scientific devices for their progress in then, very much spread of education is badly needed. Education and development –these two terms are correlated. That is why, the developed countries give too much attention for the growth of education with a view to make their fast development in all aspects of their country. Thus, any micro or macro level study on education is very much relevant for the development studies of any country. Again, it has found that, a country that is more advanced and scientific in the field of education, the rate of growth is higher of that country and vice versa. So, to understand the nature and extent of development of a particular community, the study of the state of education of that community is very significant and important(Guptha,2001)

As a welfare state the government of our country has taken a lot of developmental programmes with a view to make the all round development of the people. For the purpose of the overall development of the people the central as well as state governments have set up born macro and micro projects, development cells etc. Special emphasis is given among the grass root people and more particularly among the tribal people of the country.

The spread of education among the weaker sections of our society is vital as education is a prime requisite for socio-economic development. The policy to promote educational interests of the weaker sections of the people, especially the Scheduled Castes and Scheduled Tribes, has been enshrined in our Constitution as a Directive Principle of State Policy. In the days of yore tribal people had a well-organised system of education. The child learnt at home and at 'dormitories' and this training related to various activities of tribal life. But with the advent of Christian missionaries modern schools came up in tribal areas.

Homogeneity is the main characteristic of a tribe; but this characteristic has been dealt a death-blow due to the impact of modernity. An implicit stratification system is emerging within the tribal society on the basis of education, income, status and power. On the one hand a few privileged people are reaping all the benefits and on the other the vast bulk of tribals is wallowing in poverty and privation. Moreover these educated elites, instead of trying to improve the lot of the underprivileged brethren, are ruthlessly exploiting them. This has led to a situation where the majority of the tribals look upon these educated 'babus' with distaste and distrust and thus it has evoked a negative attitude towards education. With modern education have come modern values, which have clashed with the age-old traditional values of tribal society; this has also led to the tribals being antagonistic to modern education.

Retarding factors

Lack of social mobility and the problem of inter-cultural communication are major retarding factors in tribal education. As the teacher and the taught in the tribal areas belong to different cultures the communication barrier becomes almost insurmountable. The late Humayun Kabir had rightly remarked that even the best system of education is bound to fail without an efficient and resourceful teacher. Most of the teachers appointed in tribal areas are a disinterested lot due to various problems faced by them such as lack of proper residential facility, good salary, communication facility and social distance from the tribal people(.

"Thus the teacher feels isolated and unhappy and a disgruntled teacher is, certainly, not the best communicator of modern ideas and messages to tribal children. So even though the government has come up in recent times with various plans and programmes to improve the educational lot of the tribals, there is not much result to show as there is lack of sincerity on the part of the officials charged with the implementation of these programmes. In fact a credibility gap has emerged between such officials and the tribal people. If all these problems are to be tackled successfully, the government has to bring about a change in the basic orientation in tribal education".

The government in its zeal to provide facilities to the tribals has constructed hostels for the tribal students, supplied textbooks, provided different types of scholarship, etc. But instead of bridging the gap it has widened the rift. The tribal students staying in separate hostels, availing themselves of separate scholarships, feel naturally ostracized. This should change and instead there might be some percentage reservation of seats for tribals in a general hostel and tribal students should be encouraged to take an active part in various college as well as hostel activities. Only then they could be brought into the mainstream.

It has also been proved that when a tribal child begins his education he starts with no linguistic information and conceptualisation whereas a non-tribal child starts with a few familiar concepts and linguistic associations. So preschool training programme for the tribal child is a prime requirement and the government should undertake such programmes if it means to put the tribal students on an equal footing with the non-tribal(Ambshet,1990)

As regards appointment of teachers, more and more appointments should be made from among the tribal population so that the teachers become 'accepted' and they deal with the tribal students by using a more permissive and motivational approach. The existing teachers should be provided with adequate facilities and they should be properly oriented. It should be a must for the teachers to learn the tribal language and there can also be attempts at writing textbooks in tribal languages.

Moreover the education of children has little functional importance to them. Even after secondary education there can be no gainful employment. Thus there is no incentive for education. So the existing curricula should be related to socio-economic and cultural life of the tribals. Emphasis must be on imparting skills and modern information on agriculture, poultry, forestry and carpentry, etc.

Only by providing better communication facilities, sanitary programmes, teaching materials and methods the government can hope to bring about an attitudinal change in the tribal population towards education. Otherwise with the present state of affairs the dream of our Constitution makers about tribal education would always(Sujatha,2001).

After India attained its Independence and Constitution framed in 1950, the universalisation of Primary education has become one of the priorities of development. Huge amount of money earmarked and spent on undertaking many schemes and programs that went begging with little success in areas of educational development. Analysis of the educational scenario of the country reveals that there is a huge gap between rural and urban literacy. Further going down the ladder, the educational attainment and literacy of Scheduled Castes and Scheduled tribes is far low and abnormal. Development practitioners and academia relates poverty and underdevelopment to lack of spread of education as the foremost reason. The Government at Center is always in pressure to revise policies and devise new strategies to curb the regional disparity that exists in educational development in the country.

Karnataka is the homeland of as many as 49 tribal communities who reside in nooks and corners of the State. Almost 2 such communities are declared as primitive, basing on their low educational achievement and economic practices. The "Paniyan" is declared as major tribe. They reside mostly in the Southern part of the State and known for their infamous human sacrifice during British colonization in India and even before that. They are mainly concentrated in the Kodagu hill ranges, They live in hill slopes surrounded by dense forests. They have a subsistence economy based mainly on shifting cultivation and hunting gathering. Besides by now they have become skilled horticulturists. The Paniyan once infamous for their pernicious practice of human sacrifice and female infanticide identified as early as August 1836 by Mr. Russell, a British official under Madras Presidency in British Colonization in India. It was of deep concern for the British Government to stamp out the barbarous practices to restore peace and order in the territory(Sridhar,2001).

The Paniyan is a marginal indigenous tribal community in the state having concentrated in the plateau of Malnadu hill range, which covers two blocks of Kodagu District -Karnataka. They live in hill ranges situated at a highest of 1000-4970 feet above sea level. Two Micro projects on Paniyan have been established. They cover 45 villages and hamlets and 678 families with a total population of 6085 as per the latest survey. The male and female ratio stands as 1000:898. There has been no enumeration of population by the State Government on Individual tribal communities since 1981.

The Paniyan villages and habitations are located in a tangle of thickly wooded hill ranges, which is determined by availability of perennial streams and sufficient land for shifting cultivation. The houses are generally mud-built and straw-thatched, although now a days, some brick-built straw-thatched houses are made by the Paniyan. The road communication network has not been developed much even after 50 years of independence of India. The dress and ornaments, which adore the Paniyan, are distinguishable from other sections of the tribe. Paniyan males put a narrow scarf wrapped around the waist will be seen tucked in the hair-knot at the back. Invariably all of them carry on axe on the shoulder and a knife is kept hanging from the waist belt. The women wear sarees. They use their chest with a small band of cotton cloth tied at the back. All the male and female members wear hair-clips on their head and often pierce their ears and love to wear as many earrings as they can. The women folk wear big neck rings made up of aluminum and iron.

Paniyan have a distinct skill of horticulture, which separates them from all other tribals in the state. They know their soil condition and grow many fruits of high commercial value. They grow pineapple, banana, jack-fruit, *and papaya* in plenty. They also grow high quality turmeric and ginger that has the highest demand in the state. Paniyan practise shifting or *podu* cultivation as it is called. They produce varieties of crops like maize, *ganja*, *ragi*, grams, etc. They also practice hunting and gathering. Some time they work as daily laborers in the coffee Eastates

Gathering of variety forest produce are made for daily domestic requirements. Folks drink liquor very often prepared from bark of some trees. Paniya rear pig, cattle, buffalo and goat. These animals and birds meet their nutritional protein requirement. But most importantly these animals and birds are sacrificed before the spirits and ghosts on the occasion of propitiation on account of family members falling sick. Sickness of any sort is attributed as the effect or wrath of spirits, ghosts due to breach of norms, known or unknown. The Paniya family is normally simple nuclear family consisting of father, mother and their unmarried children. Extended families are rare due to the fact that it needs big houses to accommodate all members which is a rare probability and often dangerous on a hill top with rugged level. The Paniya family is patrilocal and patrilineal.

Education

The Paniyan have their own dialect which has no script. Their culture is as strengthened as any one's with songs, riddles, proverbs, myths, legends, dances and full of literacy works which are generally transmitted orally from one generation to another. Each of these piece of literature are often based on and linked to tress, animals, birds, streams etc. in the forest which form the part of their ecology and environment. Therefore forest and tribal are in separable and forest plays the pivotal role in shaping their society and culture.

The tribal people are highly religious by the fact that their society and culture is totally governed by religious beliefs and practices. They see their world full of mysteries governed by deities, spirits, and ghosts; both benevolent and malevolent. Each and every natural object; animate or inanimate is attributed to be the abode of some sort of deities, spirits, ghosts; is worshipped and propitiated with prescribed norms. Deviation of any such norm by any member of society is dealt with impurity. The Paniya family is nuclear and polygynous. The woman is more diligent and hard working in comparison to their male counterparts. She does all sorts of household work ranging from fetching water from distant streams to prepare foods for family members, from taking care of brothers and sisters to working along with other male members in the field. Therefore, she is treated as an economic asset to the family. Due to this reason girl child is preferred over boy child in Paniya community. Further the prevailing marriage practice among the Paniya go in favor of women. The Paniya being conservative and educationally backward live in relative isolation from other people of the area. However due to various state development interventions like development in communication i.e. construction of Roads and Bridges, opening of offices for launching of various welfare schemes and programs by Government, they are relatively exposed to the outside world. These interventions effected in thinning down of forest base and deforestation due to indiscriminate cutting of trees by unscrupulous contractors. Wide spread deforestation has led to shrinking of their subsistence base, poverty and unemployment leaving their society exposed to widespread discrimination, exploitation by other people of the area (Rathniah,2000)

Education (Modern) does not seem to be the priority of Paniya community. They disvalue formal primary education because of lack of awareness and cultural orientation. Studies on their view of a happy life reveal they certainly prefer to have more of, forestlands where shifting cultivation can be practiced, fruit bearing trees for collection and consumption, wild animals and birds to hunt and more nos. of children to work for the household and run their progeny. It is worth describing their system of education here. In Paniya, the dormitory system is there to orient boys and girls to acquire skills and knowledge that is required to be a full phased member of their society. There are separate dormitories for boys and girls in each village. After returning from fields, they stay together in the dormitory and in an informal ways i.e. through songs, dance, riddles, proverbs, gossip etc. which are transmitted orally from generation to generation. The whole night in spent amidst dancing and singing, travelling to other dormitories and interacting with boys and girls over there. By the by when they turn to adulthood they master their arts, traditions and customs and command respect as a bonafide member of their community. Therefore sending children to school is a worthless investment for parents. Because, not only he/she is deprived of helping their parents in sibling care and household works and learning basic skills of their society but also the family looses an able hand from the household and by thus a lot of income.

If we consider the teacher and taught relationship, the teacher or instructor (most often non-tribal) is like a foreigner and looked suspiciously by the students and the community. His language, etiquette and manners are regarded as unusual and quite different from the tribal ways of life. The ethnocentric attitude of the teacher towards tribal society and culture also aggravates and worsen the situation. He does not have meetings and interactions with people around him to gain their confidence. He often creates fear psychosis among pupils by castigating and punishing them in classrooms using derogatory and sensitive comments about their life styles. That fear and inferiority complex created among student's cause massive scale dropouts among Paniyan students, specially the girls who are enrolled at an over-aged stage and close to the age of puberty. Therefore, at one end the school environment and attitude of teachers pushes them out of schools and all the other their love for freedom and forest based life pulls them out of the formal schooling environment (Singh,2003).

The situation is not better of or different where even a tribal teacher having a positive out look and dedicated approach is working. The tribal children have a year round season of forest based collection and festivals. Accompanying parents at tender ages to forest yield more forest collection of fruits, roots tubers and leaves, which in turn gives better economic property to family parental care is ample for children except sending children to school which has no tangible immediate gains for parents. There are few parents who have been mobilized and have got the conviction to educate their children. But in school the children find language as the greatest problem hence other curricular transactions meaningless. The standard language text book, its unfamiliar contents, contexts and picturisations depicts a whole range of foreignness and unfamiliarity for which the students lack interest and achieve nothing. The teacher centered monologue class room transactions throws the pupils into absolute poor achievement in tests fear or it is sea ore of and failure in examination is another most important reasons of dropouts from school among Paniya children. Above all, the students find the subjects, contents and contexts not linked to their real life experiences and extremely monotonous and boring. Those reasons are so strong that, even in residential schools run by Department of Welfare, Govt. of Karnataka, with all sorts facilities like free food, free reading- writing materials and other basic requirements like sitting mat, uniform, blankets, beds etc., the enrollment, attendance and achievement of students are far from satisfactory(Ganesh,2006).

The irony is that there is no supervision or monitoring of the works of Teachers and school management by the personnel who are supposed to be the decision-makers in the system. The lack of performance of the schooling system is always attributed to the lack of interest of the poverty and community for their children's education rather than the whole range of faulty planning and implementation by the Government.

Conclusion

The schooling facility must be provided on demand of community and community must be mobilized enough to spontaneously come forward to run and manage the school. The children should be provided text books in their own language in initial stages of their schooling and gradually they should be exposed to standard textbooks in state language at a later stage. The textbooks should be local specific contents, contexts and narration by which the children can relate their learning to their real life situation. The timing of the school should be as per the availability of children and holiday calendar as per the holiday pattern of the locality. The teacher belonging to the community should be posted if not a teacher having a positive attitude and some understanding about tribal community should be employed in the area. Moreover the education administrators should be more responsive and responsible to the education of the children with special needs close and continuous monitoring of schools (academic and administrative) would definitely render insights to the problem and it's solutions at the earliest.

13

Compulsory Education and Tribal Child labourers : A Paradox

Almost all out-of-school tribal children are in developing countries, especially in South Asia and sub-Saharan Africa where tribal child labour is a serious problem. While the number of child laborers decreased somewhat from 2000-2004, a huge number of out-of-school tribal children are child laborers, most of whom work out of poverty and various other cultural reasons. Recent studies have shown that tribal child labour depresses school enrollment rates, negatively affects school achievement, and decreases graduation rates. Given these realities, recent cash transfer programs have a comprehensive social protection approaches that encourage schooling by providing beneficiary compliance with requirement of schooling, vaccine, or other health-related conditions. These cash-transfer programs have tried to dismantle the intergenerational poverty cycle and thus have improved school attendance while reducing the number of child laborers. On educating its tribal children India remains so behind the rest of Asia that it will take a major infusion of resources and political leadership to catch up. Deep class and caste divisions have been barriers to the developmental of a national drive for mass education by those who have made it to the upper strata. As the economy opens and employment opportunities grow with the expansions of the countries consumer industries, the governing idle and upper middle class may recognizes that the country needs a more literate population and hence state must invest more in its tribal children. Only primary and sustained move to make a tangible amelioration in the life style of the downtrodden section of our society; supported by the spread of network of primary education can be expected to have a lasting impact on the elimination of tribal child labour. Recently India has brought compulsory education bill without having any agenda in improving the quality much needed at primary level. But it will take a major coalition of grass root organisations. This paper draws the attention of the educational policy makers and development agencies to reveal the nexus between compulsory primary education and the issue of tribal child labour in case of India.

Introduction

Those concerned about the growing number of tribal child laboureres, at present 23 million strong, may not find solace in the Supreme Court's recent ruling banning tribal children from being employed in hazardous industries. In their 36-page judgment, the judges directed the creation of a corpus fund with a contribution of Rs 20,000 for each child from the offending employer of the child's compulsory education. The court also reminded the government of its responsibility in implementing the Tribal child labour (Prohibition and Regulation) Act. The court added that the government must provide a job for one adult member of each child's family in lieu of the child's job.Certain pertinent questions, however, remain unanswered. Will the court order by itself ensure that an offending employer contributes to the fund? Who will ensure that a job is provided for an adult member of the child's family in lieu of the child's job? Again, even if a sufficient amount is collected from the offending employer, what is the guarantee the amount will be used for the child's compulsory education?

Whatever the answers, it is clear the battle against tribal child labour is yet to begin even after the ruling. On December 31, in Calcutta, some tribal children working in leather factories, car repair garages and roadside restaurants were sacked. This was because of a rumor that the police had picked up tribal children in some factories in Topsia and their employers asked to cough up Rs 20,000 per child as per Supreme Court orders. Although described as "epoch-making" the judgment is really a reiteration of article 24 of the Constitution. The article says: "No child below the age of 14 shall be employed in any factory or in any other hazardous employment." At most, the ruling can awaken consciousness. It can initiate consciousness. It can initiate some real action, regardless of the final outcome. The problem is not one of rulings, directives or laws. There are too many of those. The problem is that court directives by themselves will not do. What is needed is a vision which can link tribal child labour with the family's survival needs and the child's primary education .

Two years ago, the fifth conference of labour ministers of non-aligned and other developing countries in New Delhi endorsed the Uruguay round agreements for increasing economic opportunities for all countries. However, it not only denounced the "neo-projectionist" arguments, but virtually rejected outright the "social clause" sponsored by the West. The latter seeks to establish a linkage between international trade and enforcement of labour standards. The conference viewed the linkage as a "threat of emerging forms of protectionism which have the potential for neutralizing comparative advantages of developing countries and benefits resulting from the Uruguay round of trade liberalization".

The argument was that it was the industrialized West, which advocated free trade against socialist controls. But when the third world needed to minimize the social cost of structural adjustment by "adopting the appropriate social security measures" in the wake of economic reforms, the demand for labour and environment to influence terms of world trade could be seen as a dangerous move towards "extra-territorial laws". Social issues relating to employment, reforms in the quality of primary education, elimination of tribal child labour, investing more funds in primary education and upgrading of skills are linked to a society's prosperity. They cannot be made part of "extra-territorial" laws since these issues are linked to a country's overall economic and social development .However, last December India and 127 other nations accepted the World Trade Organisation declaration, linking trade with labour standards. True, the declaration issued a warning against the use of the clause for "projectionist purposes". But after the WTO pledges were endorsed, the third world needed to do something to show real progress in social reform. Governmental commitment in most third world countries to social and environmental standards is expedient (Nayeem,1997).

India is obviously keen to improve its image under international pressure as regards tribal child labour. The government asserts that tribal children are forced to work because their parents are poor. Here lies the problem. Tribal child labour keeps tribal children out of school and contributes to the growth of illiteracy. Industrial employers compete, with government support, with schools for tribal children. Middlemen from the same villages for a commission generally recruit those school age tribal children. Official policy in all developed and some developing countries dictates that no employer is permitted to employ child labourers and parents, no matter how poor, cannot keep tribal children out of school. So these countries have largely succeeded in stopping child labour and ensuring tribal children attend atlest primary level of school. True, Indian law prohibits the employment of tribal children in factories—but not in cottage industries, family households, restaurants or agriculture. The absence of strict, child labour laws, or the implementation of existing laws or provisions for compulsory primary school education, has meant that a little less than half of India's children between ages six and 14 are not in school (Lansky, 1997).

The tragedy is that government official, political and social activities and the Indian public say "we should not force poor parents to send their tribal children to school when society cannot provide employment for all educated adults". It seems to be a matter of social justice that tribal children of the poor be allowed to work. These phony arguments bolstered by a political consideration. Child labour legislation may jeopardise the interest of the employers enjoying political patronage. Both moral and practical rationales lie behind the state's non –action. The flip side to these arguments is that poor parents to believe their tribal children would benefit economical if they were in school. But in case of India, tribal children acquire skills thorough employment, not thorough formal education. Employers oppose enforcement of child labour legislation because tribal children are more pliable, work for lower wages are not unionized and have nimble fingers, which are useful in many crafts. Ironically, since independence every Governament appointed commission and all political particles and all political parties have talked of ending child labour and impairing composure education to all children up to 14 years of age. Yet activities and researchers in the Indies poverty explains this inactivity. Kerala is a case in point. It has a literacy rate of 85 prevent though it is percept income is not higher then the rest of the country. The real problem is that India speeds lower proportions of the gross nation product on education than most other developing countries. A larger proportion of the education budget is spent on higher education.

Policy failure in Ensuring Compulsory Education:

There is, formal, a widespread consensus about ending tribal child labour and establishing compulsory universal primary education for all tribal children up to the age of 14,a commitment that can be traced back to Gopal Krishna Gokhale's effort at the turn of the last century. So perhaps we can cite, India is a very first country, which thought towards a better plan to tackle tribal child labour problem effectively.

Spending some years during the early ages of the child hood in schools is highly essential for the effective socialization. Education is kind of immovable property of the society. Education plays a vital role in social cultural and economic progress of any society. Also cultural concept of education differs in different society. So there exists a high positive correlation between the level of educational attainment and the socio-economic standards of community life (Pati, 1992). Shandilya and Khan(2003) write "the social evil involved the employment of tribal children is also due to illiteracy and occasionally shifting towards lack of development of child's personality which continues beyond his / her child hood adult hood. There may also be yet another causes which may force tribal children to employment particularly when the society neglects the child and have indifferent attitude towards tribal children". In spite of enshrine free and compulsory education in the directive principle of state policies of our constitution, the educational backwardness of India even after 50 years of independence is quite glaring.

Compulsory primary education system is not yet fully implemented despite 93rd amendment to the constitution. Different Governments took more than 55 years to enact compulsory primary education in our country. Like western countries if, we could have brought compulsory primary education in the early periods of the independence, defiantly we would have minimize the rate of tribal child labour atlest by this time. Prof. Dak while writing the education to all say first "the existing disparities between and within sectors and among socio economic groups must be narrowed through the increased availability of educational facilities and service in relatively deprived sectors and the provision of incentives for increased access by deprived socio-economic groups"'. But in case of India the Governament is spending million dollars on higher education and few thousand rupees on primary education. The real economic cost of schooling to the poor must to the extent possible be reduced. While the manifold benefits of primary education cannot be denied, it must be qualified with the proposition that unless there are prospects of finding employment there is like to be an apathy on the part the poor parents to send their tribal children for education. (Datta,1991)

Perhaps one more reason that contemporary educationist is giving that inadequate motivation among poor parents is the major obstacles to universalisation of primary education. This lack of motivations probably the most continues and complexes as the issue involved range from the purely economic to border social and cultural consideration. Rather, it is the direct costs of schooling, which reduce the child's interest in education that primarily accounts for educational deprivation. In both the above phenomenon's reducing private costs of schooling and improving schooling quality and make learning is a joyful experience. The Government has to play a crucial role over here.

Vimal Rmachandra(1999) observes " It is widely acknowledged that a significant proportion of tribal children, especially those from underprivileged backgrounds and girls, either drop out of primary school or even if they attend school, learn very little Moreover, there is a wide gap between Governament and private school in different level of achievements. The active participation of tribal children in primary education hinges on a plethora of factors. Besides access a range of demand and supply issue influence why tribal children choose to attend school regularly. Thus the policy makers and education administrates should focus mainly on the formal school system and on improving access to education. The creation of backward and forward linkage is essential to creating an environment where every child not only goes to school but get some benefits from it." This is the aspect where, exactly Govt. policy makers and NGO's should focus on.

Experts have a opinion that until child get benefit from the school, Governament should seriously think about alternative income generation programme to those families or creative measures in order to lighten the burden on poor families. It is has been noted that there is no direct connection between rate if illiteracy and high incidence of tribal child labour. Some of the countries have largely succeeded in eradicating illiteracy but remain confronted by the tribal child labour, which some time very acute. This can be seen in some of the Middle Eastern countries.

Universalisation of Primary Education: Objections We Had

Till today three arguments widely raised in India against compulsory education the first is that since existing schools are unable to meet the needs of the poor, parents should not be forced to keep their tribal children in school. It is unfortunate that India has failed in successful address of problems in her primary education scenario. She is facing dedicates teachers and other resources. Paradoxically, state officials defend their reluctance to make education compulsory by pointing to their failure to improve the schools Till today the quality of the primary education in the state is disappointing.

The second objection was it may be difficult to enforce. Till today many laws have been enforced, why should be a compulsory education law be different?. Since, because state has to depend largely on its local officials who are working for lower wage like teachers, social workers,-etc and may be very difficult to divert them in a particular direction. But it should be noted that in countries that have made education compulsory, before India has soon become a norm in the local community. A norm more often enforced by community pressure than by authorities. This kind of scene can be seen in Kerala state. The third and perhaps the most persistent argument used in officials circles in India are tribal child labour cannot be tackled without first addressing the issue of poverty. As we have already noted, those who put forward this view argue that the nation must have wait until get increase her per captia income and poverty has been reduced. Only then families may think seriously to remove children from work. But however this argument has no place today as many Asian countries have eradicated child labour successfully by enforcing primary education (Weiner, 1996). Hence in case of India it may not be true to hold the view that households in economically advanced states spend more on education, though they have higher ability to spend. I, e the ability to spend and the actual level of spending do not go together.

How compulsory education should be?

The 1990 have seen the issue of universal of elementary education in India acquire urgency as never before. Before accepting the term universalisation of primary education we must take in to account why it is necessary. Probably we can say education is a basic human rights which positively impacts on overall development of the human being and thereby society. More then that literacy can empower the pole politically and economically. Also education will create an efficient work force in the country and thereby enabling many people to exploit economic opportunities (Reddy,1991). Finally it leads to increase in the per captia income of the people and hence three will be no necessary arises sending tribal children to work at any costs. Because of rapid increase in enrolment of tribal children to school there is a wide spread concern about the quality and design of the school system especially the performance of Govt. schools in India. Because studies have shown that an alarmingly large number of tribal children do not become literate even after four year of primary schooling hence it is argued that school effectiveness and actual learning have to be major rather then secondary concerns for universal of primary education. Also it is important to how effective schools are and success in learning depends not only on quality of the school inputs but on factors outside the school/s. There are wide variations in school quality in developing countries. Schools in developing countries some time can lack something as elementary and essential as a black board. Hence we can say that while research on school quality is necessary, it can become meaningful only if there is parallel research on the socio economic context. In a many developing countries and in India, the state sector still accounts for the much of educational delivery. In many countries, alternative NGOs schooling has often achieved better results. Here we are not discussing about quality of education among private schools, because all section of the society could not afford that costly education. Expert says since private schools would have enough resources to give high quality education to the rich state owned schools providing free education to the tribal children are suffering from the absence of essential resource to met cost of the education. While NGOs offer innovative alternative models, the coverage is as at small.

A small effort by sub-contracting related NGOs to carry out education programmes, the state sector is left to reproduce its higherarki and often-inadequate provision of education. Better State should learn some experiences from the NGOs. But the major hurdle is policy promotion by India's NGOs is still in a rudimentary form. India's NGO have, in the main, turned their attention to working with their clines rather than in organizing themselves as political lobbies to seek legislative a and programmatic changes. Few NGOs have decided what it is that they want Governament to do. NGOs should play a vital role within local communities in dealing with these issues especially by helping the Govt. in creating awareness about the value of education among socially excluded group. It will be only possible when both Govt. and NGOs from the prospective of community identities for advocating their secular interest in education and modern occupations. Hence this kind of mobilization of vulnerable sections of the society will better aware of the significance of the education for their tribal children and may send their tribal children to school (Weiner, 96). However this intervention should be implemented by the agencies working at grass root level. In some instance the success rate of some of anti tribal child labour programmes of both Governament and NGOs are very disappointing as per as Karnataka state is considered, because it seems to be framed by only officials with out any involvement of the poor. Thus, there was always a discrepancy between what is appropriate and useful, and what is actually given-leading to a relatively less than successful out come. Also many big NGOs are not trying to complement the Government effort's through new ideas, serving hard-to- reach area and constructive partnership with policy makers, but they are intended to substitute the Governament, which is highly impossible for ever. But revitalizing state provision by incorporating the lessons learns from the NGO experiences appeared to be promising way forward.

Here one question arises about the extent to which the schooling system itself reinforces pre-existing patterns of exclusion, was whether this reflects the particular logic of the model of universal education currently in force in the India. Hence there is a focus on one universal model, which, it is argued, would provide all tribal children with equal opportunities who belongs wide socio-economic background. It is thus premised on the existence of norms, standard, practice and procedures that are universally applicable. However the standardization of curriculum and teaching methods can also render abstract diversity in leering effects across castes and lass. It is argues that learning effects are also socially conditioned and standard applied need to be sensitive to the ways in which identities of exclusion and different life worlds can also effects on the learning process. Further standardization implies a static conception of tribal children's life world, and the imposition of unity concepts of *ideal child hood* is far from a reflection of the diverse realties that obtaining in India. Experts suggests that a strong case can be made for pluralist forms of educational provision within an overall frame work of comparability equivalence in educational standards rather than a single, homogenous model. Not only is this necessary in the context of diversity, but it would also enhance the speed of progress towards universal elementary education. Thus the emphasis of the education policy in these countries should be on national standards, and the state should ensure the regulation of non-state providers within this framework as the optimal route to overcoming inequalities in provision and distribution of resources.

Universalisation of primary education has a lot of drawbacks in case of long term vision of the government . This project has been sought to be achieved with in unrealistic time bounded frame that have led to very ambitious policy and many of them is really non-achievable targets in case of India, a country having wide diversities. This kind of policies gives downward confusions among grass root workers. More over achieving convergence's of policy and intervention between various departments especially department of labour and education at all levels, from national division, is still a concern in India.

One of the major problems in case of Indian education system that costs of educational provision is also a major concern. In India it has been increasingly dependent on western funding agencies. But no body is concerning primary education should be a cost effective. Reducing the unit costs of education is also necessary given that in India around 3/4th of total budget of education are spent on teacher salaries only. Hence state should include some of the NGOs approaches like (1) specially designed programmes to reach the unreached (2) set and proved model to provide quality education (3) basic criteria for efficient delivery. Also govt. should think about intimates that aim to provide formal education to marginalised comminutes addressing their specific social and cultural needs (Nambissan,1995). Non formal education schemes may be very useful to balance work and education thereby addressing reality of work in the lives of poor tribal children. This kind of schemes may useful urban working tribal children particularly girls, who have been bypassed by the formal system. All these programmes should be a model of decentralized community based school development, by ensuring a direct state –citizen engage ment over universal primary education. This kind of education can be viewed as supplementary to the schemes primary education for all (Kabeer and others, 2003).

From the above discussion we can draw two generalizations compulsory education should not be regarded merely as a duty, imposed by the state. When education is made a duty, parents, irrespective of their economic circumstances and beliefs, are required by law to send their tribal children to schools and it is the legal obligation of the very state to provide sufficient number of schools especially in rural areas with all essential facilities. More over as it is proved successfully by much Asian and western countries compulsory education is a necessary condition for the reduction and abolition of tribal child labour. As research found just not compulsory, a highly effective qualitative compulsory education is highly essential to minimize the child labour especially in case of India. We strongly propose that there should be lot of scope for vocational courses in the syllabus. In one country after another the phased extension of the age of compulsory education went hand-in-hand with a phased extension of restrictions on the employment of tribal children. If the school leaving age is lower than the age of admission to employment, children are likely illegal to seek employment, and the enforcement of tribal child labour law and acts rendered more difficult. Logically we can say it will be easier to administer the tribal children at school rather than to force the child labour laws and acts. It should be noted that no country has successfully ended child labour without address effective implementation of the compulsory education. Finally we can say compulsory primary education not only reduce inequality but also boosts growth in the long run (by creating human capital), directly reduce child labour immediately (through mass enrollment) and in the long run (through the decision on fertility and tribal children's education as educated adults). Further more study have reveled that negative relationship between adult literacy and child labour clearly demonstrates that schooling bears double dividends as it helps reduce tribal child labour both in short and long runs. Also it is found that educational polices which consciously target the enrollment of women will make a larger contribution to reducing tribal child labour as compared to promoting enrolment of both men and women in general (Ahmed,1999).

Hidden Face of Compulsory Education;

Besides all this, we can not categorically reject the limitations of the compulsory education programmes in a country like India. A big subcontinent having different culture and tradition the education polices and programmes can not be implemented uniformly through out the country. Most of the policies and programmes are culturally and geographically not specific. Although it has been long devoting a great chunk of its resources for promoting compulsory education and can boast of the lowest incidence of child labour in India, there will be still pockets of working tribal children which still thrive within its economy. It is also notable in this context that the tribal children who are said to have been brought into the fold of compulsory education often combine education with home based unpaid labour or seasonal work This kind of trend is more common among rural tribal children. Since normal; in India most of the schools are closed for more than around 170 days a year, education does not clash with the seasonality of the job (Datta, 2001).

Also the manifold benefits of primary education cannot be denied it must be qualified with the proposition that unless there are prospects of finding employment, there is like to be an apathy on the part of the poor parents to send their tribal children for education. Also it can be said that generation of a popular demand for primary education is contingent upon making education some thing people want and value, mere provision of schooling may with an allurement of mid day meals and fees concession may hardly keep the tribal children there unless parents are convinced that there are enough employment opportunities for their tribal children once they are out of schooling. More important is that on with primary education one can not get any attractive job in the future unless primary education is supplemented by the some higher studies. Family which is hit by poverty cannot wait for these extra unproductive and extra few years for their tribal children to become income earners. Hence it seems that a sustained desire on the part of these families to send their tribal children for primary education with the hope that they can continue for higher studies, is associated with an improvement in the economic condition of these families. Only a primary education and sustained move to make a tangible amelioration in the life style of the downtrodden section of our society; supported by the spread of a network of primary education can be expected to have a lasting impact on elimination of tribal child labour. Additionally, the socio-economic context, especially along the developmental dimension, is an integral part of school effectiveness .One the other hand, area type affects learning directly, by influencing poverty levels and also opportunities and motivation of learning. The impact of the area type on schools and learning is such that no description or analysis of schools can be meaningful without a parallel understanding of the area type. If initiatives to make elementary education universal are taken without the parallel measures as mentioned earlier, they may not fulfill the intended purpose. The absorption of educational inputs will be poor if a larger number of tribal children are simply not capable of deriving benefits from improved educational facilities. Plenty of resources could then be spent on elementary education without real results. At the same time, if some tribal children are, classified as poor achieves because of their socio-economic background, then their education may play a role that is the reverse of empowering. They may in fact be getting ready to become a problem educationally in the future. This is a danger, which is especially acute for tribal children belonging to backward class and tribes (Sharma, 1998).

Some Debatable Issue

Till now we have seen how compulsory education should be if we want to minimize the tribal child labour problem in case of India. But above discussion has raised lot debatable issues. Among them is that how the right to education could be effectively implemented in a context where tribal children's economic activity is believed many to be a response to basic family need. More then that the research should be focus on whether there was conflict between the ability of a poor family to meet its basic needs and to send its tribal children to school and if so, which should take priority.

Also there is a need to find out going beyond the household level, is the absence or inadequate provision of compulsory universal schooling simply a result of under-development and poverty or the direct reflection of misplaced national priorities and policies? And it is most necessary to get the clarification at what point with how rapid does growth have to be and what level of per capita income has to be reached, before anti-poverty objectives are seriously addressed and tribal child labour abolished in case of India. Then probably we will be In the position to answer whether is it possible to provide basic protection in the from of compulsory education and income security even at low levels of economic developments.

Concluding Remarks

What is the current state of education in India in comparison to other developing countries? India's state of education lacks effectiveness in yielding basic literacy in the population. It has been observed that "the overall condition of the education system can be a powerful influence on the supply of tribal child labour" (Grootaert and Kanbur 1995, 193). The 1991 Census of India shows that 64% of males and 39% of females are literate (The World Bank 1995, 113) — an increase of 17% and 14% respectively from the 1981 census (Census of India 1981 cited in Weiner 1991, 11). These increases seem significant, but India's overall literacy rate of 40.8% lags behind other developing countries such as China (72.6%), Sri Lanka (86.1%), and Indonesia (74.1%), all of which have Per Capita Incomes comparable to India's (Weiner 1991, 161). India's primary-school survival rate of 38.0% is also lower than China's rate of 70.0% and Sri Lanka's rate of 90.8% (United Nations Educational, Scientific, and Cultural Organization cited in Weiner 1991, 159). This indicates that few students are reaching fifth or sixth grade, and dropout rates support this conclusion. Dropouts rate measured by the Department of Education show that 35% of males and 39% of female's dropout (Government of India cited in The World Bank 1995, 113). What is the reason for these high dropouts rate and poor school survival rates? One possible argument given by Nangia (1987) is that "the pressing need for the child's earnings as well as low perceived advantages of school" cause parents to withdraw tribal children from school and deposit them in the labour force (p.182). In this case, poverty and the inadequacy of the school system play significant roles in causing tribal child labour, but also affect each other. Poverty forces high dropout rates, and thus no matter how good schools are, school survival rates and literacy rates will still remain low.

The concept of compulsory education, where all school aged tribal children are required to attend school, combats the force of poverty that pulls tribal children out of school. Policies relating to compulsory education not only force tribal children to attend school, but also contribute appropriate funds to the primary education system, instead of higher education. An example of a country where compulsory education has worked to reduce tribal child labour is Sri Lanka. The Sri Lankan government decided to enforce compulsory education in the 1920's and 1930's (Weiner 1991, 173). With this compulsory education policy, school participation rates rose from 58 percent in 1946 to 74 percent in 1963 (Weiner 1991, 173). The literacy rate also increased from 58 percent in 1946 to 86 percent in 1984 (Weiner 1991, 172). The corresponding result has been that the employment rate of tribal children in the ten to fourteen age group has shown a substantial decline from 13 percent in 1946 to 6.2 percent in 1963 (Weiner 1991, 174), and currently stands at 5.3% for males and 4.6% for females (International Labour Organization 1995, 113). These trends lead Weiner (1991) to the conclusion that "Sri Lanka has achieved a remarkably high enrollment rate, high retention rate, and a corresponding decline in child labour" (p.175).

The Indian State of Kerala distinguishes itself from the rest of India with its educational system. The government of Kerala allocates more funds to education than any other state, with a per capita expenditure of 11.5 rupees compared to the Indian average of 7.8 rupees (Weiner 1991, 175). It is not only the expenditure of more funds, but where the funds are used that make the difference. Kerala spends more money on "mass education than colleges and universities" (Weiner 1991, 176). No correlation exists between expenditure on education and literacy when comparing different countries because some countries, such as India, spend more funds on higher education than primary education (Weiner 1991, 160). Kerala's emphasis on primary education has lead to a dropout rate of close to 0%, a literacy rate of 94% for males and 86% for females (The World Bank 1995, 113), and a low child work participation rate of 1.9% (in 1971) compared to the Indian average of 7.1% in 1971 (Weiner 1991, 175). Weiner (1991) points out that "The Kerala government has made no special effort to end tribal child labour. It is the expansion of the school system rather than the enforcement of labour legislation that has reduced the amount of tribal child labour" .

Article 45 of the Constitution of India states that "The State shall endeavour to provide within a period of ten years from the commencement of this Constitution for free and compulsory education for all tribal children until they complete the age of fourteen years" (Jain 1985, 219). It is obvious that "the State" has not achieved this goal, shown by the literacy, dropout, and child work participation rates discussed previously. A National Policy on Education was adopted in 1986, and it addresses the need to "expand and improve basic education" (The World Bank 1995, 124). Recently, the central government implemented The District Primary Education Program (DPEP), in an attempt to act on the recommendations of the National Policy on Education. The program involves the subsidizing of approved investments, by the Government of India. The central government will provide a grant of 85% on expenditures by the states (The World Bank 1995, 123). Since these measures have been implemented very recently, results cannot be obtained and the effectiveness of the DPEP cannot be commented on at this time.

Continue of the debate around quantity verses quality of education still is on. Before this, policymakers should note that quality and quantity are intertwined and cannot be separated. It is real sense of urgency. Differences expressed pertained to the placement of priorities for the achievement of universal education, and is in turn related to the broader views held on the nature of the challenges. If state is really interested in the eradication of tribal child labour or atlest mind to minimize the problem it must and should seriously think about the quality of primary education at present. Probably a new population policy may help in this regard. Resources need to be targeted at expanding provision if Govt. think providing alternative income generation programmes to the poor parents who would like to send tribal children to work, then resource will have to diverted to making the curriculum relevant and of high quality. Given the manifest failure of the standard schooling system to include hard-to –reach tribal children, special efforts need to be made in this area and particular attention should be given to first generation learners. Some noted that high rates could put off many aspiring to secondary and higher levels of education, thus eroding the incentive to send tribal children regularly and consistently to school. Without providing of universal coverage and equivalent standards in terms of quality, it is not feasible or just to penalize parents who do not send tribal children to school. Clearly, meaningful and genuine universal elementary education is associated not only with universal access to well-functioning schools but also with certain out-of –school initiatives. Tribal children have varying capacities, apart from individual intelligence, depend on factors such as adequate nutrition good health and freedom to attend school regularly. It follows that thee prerequisite have to be ensured for effective and genuine universal education.

To conclude, how elementary education should be made universal is central to the concern for making it universal?. It is necessary to make sure that such education is effective. Apart from the need to scrutinize the education system, non-educational measures that prepare tribal children for education and facilities the process of learning are also needed. India is one of the countries having largest number of child labourers in the world, also country having highest percentage of dropouts at higher primary level. Poverty and overpopulation are intertwined with this problem (Sharma, 1998). At the same time, it has pioneered a number of different educational models for addressing the problems of hard to reach tribal children, models which reflect a shared value given to the welfare of tribal children and the need to ensure their right to education, but very different philosophies and modalities. If we seriously try with this model with some addition or subtraction suiting to our culture and traditions which are more effective and under what circumstances, we believe that the experiences, of India will have made a major contribution to a long standing problem beyond boundaries.

14

Educational Deprivation among Primitive Tribal Children of Karnataka: A Review

India is one of the major countries having larger concentration of tribal groups in the world. Among the tribals, primitive tribal groups are highly vulnerable. These groups are still isolated from the main stream of civilized society. They are small in number and still having pre-agricultural technology. The rate of literacy among them is extremely low. Different people are exploiting these primitive tribal groups in different ways. Both Govt. and NGOs have implemented several policies and programmes for the upliftment of these tribals. It was thoughtful of the Govt. of India to have constituted committees to suggest measures for the welfare and development of the Tribes implemented during different plan periods. But the result is not very significant and encouraging because of rigid traditional aspects of these tribals. Some time their dwelling places would be beyond reachable. Further the implementation machinery was faulty and development programmes could not be implemented properly. In this paper an attempt has been made to explore the present educational status and understand the vital for low rate of literacy in two identified primitive tribal groups of Karnataka State i,e *Jenu Kuraba* and *Koraga* Tribal development has been given one of the major attentions by all the Governments in India during all five years plans on account of the socioeconomic backwardness of the tribals. Also a lot of provisions have been brought into the Constitution to safeguard their basic interests. Planning Commission (1991) has remarked that 'tribal welfare should aim at the prospective within reasonable time and an advancement of the social and economic life of the tribes with a view to their gradual integration with the rest of country should be on a footing of equality'. It is noted that the total number of Scheduled Tribe (ST) population of India constitutes about 10.08 per cent of the total population as per the 2001 census. Out of this more than 63 per cent tribes are spread only in five States of the country. Recent study says the total number of such Scheduled Tribals is 643 in India (Singh, 1992). All Scheduled Tribe groups are entitled to have many benefits directly from the Governament, with reservations for them in many sectors of development. Moreover the Constitution enshrine a number of important provisions for the safeguard and promoting the interests of Scheduled Tribes in the country. Though number of efforts have been made for over all development of Scheduled Tribes it was noticed that some groups are still in the backward stage. Further the situation has deteriorated with administrative restrictions having been imposed on collection or utilization of forestland resources that the tribals traditionally depend upon. The major objective of this paper is to prepare a solid background for discussion for vanishing tribal education. Further this paper will look for such avenue where some of the suggested policy implications can play significant role in improving tribal education in general.

Who are the Primitive Tribal Groups (PTG)

The first attempt was made in 1931 to identify the PTG in the country. The group of tribals who have the following characteristic features have been classified into primitive tribal groups 1) still practicing pre-agricultural level of technology 2) extremely low level of literacy3) near stagnant or diminishing populations. Till today 75 groups have been identified in 16 states and Union Territories. The problems of Indian tribals can be classified into two types.1 problems of major tribes and 2 problems of primitive tribes. But in India both of them are mixed up together and that's why no significant achievement could be made in solving the problems of primitive tribes. In recent years they are facing some serious problems like lack of basic facilities including; poverty, illiteracy, lack of medical facilities, unreachable to NGOs, lack of essential agricultural technology etc. In the resent past Planning Commission had issued some guide lines to the States that tribal development plan should emphasize on the following aspects 1 elimination of expatiation of all form 2 rapid social and economic development 3 improving their organizational capabilities and narrowing down the gap between the levels of development of the tribals and others through by providing proper education. Also the Commission suggested that the Integrated Area Development Plan fousing on the specific problems of the tribal people must be implemented vigorously emphasizing on the cultural fabrics of the respective tribes. The major objective of this paper is to prepare a solid background for discussion for necessary action to be taken to improve the literacy rate of these two primitive tribals. Data collected through case studies, participant observation and focus group study among slected hamlets of these two tribals of Karnataka-India.Profiles of Primitive Tribals of Karnataka

Jenu kuruba and Koraga tribals have been identified as PTGs in the Karnataka State. Jenu kuruba tribe is concentrated around Mysore, Chmarajanagar and Kodagu districts of the state. Total population of this tribe is around 24654(2001Census). Literacy rate is extremely low. Usually they are living in hamlets made out of bamboo and huts with there own judicial system. They believe in magic, sorcery and witchcraft. Neither polygamy nor polyandry is practiced. Besides working with raton and bamboo, collection of minor forest products like herb, honey, roots and fruits are their major occupations. Poverty exists more in this group. Koraga is a very primitive tribal group in the Karnataka State. They are concentrated in Dakshina Kannada and some parts of the Udupi district of the state. They also live in some patches of Kerala and Karnataka border. The Koraga live mostly in rural areas. Experts has rightly said 'they were compelled to lead a segregated life from the immediate multi-ethnic, multi-religious neighborhood till few decades back owing to the sever untouchability prevailed in the region: To the great extent they very much believe in magic and witchcraft and local medicine men. Their total population is around 19784 (2001Census). Neither polygamy nor polyandry is observed. The Koragas remain extremely backward socially, economically and educationally. They have there own rich culture and traditional heritage. Their traditional occupation is basket making. Few percentage of the population lives in semi urban areas.

Education- A Tool for Development

Opening of the tribal areas in the wake of modern developmental process have brought in juxtaposition two distinct value systems – one based on inherent tradition and ignores and the other on technology and innovations. Harmonious synchronization of the two systems is highly essential for the rapid development of tribals (Jha, 1995). In this crucial moment education plays a vital role. Education is a backbone of every society. It is a tool for social change. In the past education was one of the main consideration for hierarchical classification in the Hindu society. Rapid population growth impedes educational developemnt in several ways. Most obviously it produces a rapid increase in the school age population. To spread the education among marginalised sections of society has been a formidable task in India. However, with the advent of modernization, the education of tribals has undergone a different phase. Under the influence of globalization, the tribal education and culture has been tremendously influenced .The uniqueness, of the tribal culture which enriches the country's culture mosaic, is fast disappearing and even getting distorted under powerful influences of the dominant urban culture. While dealing with the poor educational attainment of tribal children to formal schooling, researchers tend to emphasis the economic marginalization of these comminutes, their illiterate home environments, and inadequate facilities for education and culturally the alien nature of the school system. Lack of education is largely responsible for the exploitation and pitiable plight of the tribals. Due to this, the tribals have not been able to take advantage of new development. The above mentioned factors explain how level of education among the tribal children. Another important factor is the school process. This is most crucial because heavy drop outs and almost stagnation of tribal children within a year of admitting to primary school has been reported since last decade. A large proportion of the poorer tribal children, on account of the rising cost of the schooling and economic burden cannot afford to benefit from education. Most of the tribals tend to use their children for ancillary service that would bring in some added income for their starving families (Nagda, 1998).

According to the 2001 Census the average literacy rate of two PTGs is 28.6 per cent. It is very painful and to note that the literacy among these two tribals increased to only 7.45 per cent during the period 1961-1971. More unfortunate is that during the same period female literacy grew by less than three per cent. As per the table Jenu kuruba tribe has very low literacy rate when compare to the Koraga. Even though Jenu kuruba tribe is in a more advantage situation, its literacy rate is comparatively lower than Koragas. In both the cases female literacy rate is little bit higher than males.

Literacy Status of PTGs of Karnataka

PTG	*Total Population*	*Total Literates*	*Male Literates*	*Female Literates*	*Male*	*Female*	*Total*
Jenu kuruba	27597	4033	3172	2161	15.10	19.29	17.09
Koraga	11566	3543	1678	1865	27.82	29.38	28.06

(Source: Mohanty, 2002)

Enrollment of PTG students by sex in Primary Stage in Karanataka

Year	*Boys*	*Girls*	*Total Percentage*
2000-01	1876	1098	23%
2001-02	1798	1003	21%

2002-03	1894	987	17%
2003-04	2006	998	15%
2004-05	1983	1009	13%
2005-06	1872	991	11%
% growth rate			
Annual compound growth rate			

Reasons for low literacy rate

a) Disparity in the existence of the schools

Compared to the other major tribals of the state these primitive tribal groups are a more disadvantaged population. As for as non-existing facility within a habitation is concerned, one can find that other major tribes of the State are placed in a favorable situation relative to their total population. Looking at the disparity condition in terms of deprivation, more children of primitive tribal group school age children are deprived of a primary school within their habitations. Children belonging to the other major tribes like *Soligas, Betta kuruba* and *Malae kudiya* are in a better position than the PTGs thay have atlest one Ashram or Jeneral school within their habitations (Shukla, 1998). However so for as the number of habitations without a school is a concerned PTGs child are highly in a disadvantaged position. In general primitive tribal children should have to commute more than 3-Km distance to attend a school. In some case it is even more. Distance is also one of the major drawbacks in case of providing education to the people who are still away from modern world. Many of the parents don't like to send their children especially of their girl children to school, which is quite for away from their original habitation. Finally while a large population of the country school age children still face the disadvantage of distance between their own habitation and the location of a primary school, the more disturbing situation is this disadvantage is high in case of PTGs habitations in the tribe belt of Karnataka.

b) Language-A Medium of Instruction

The tribal situation in India presents a varied and complex picture and poses peculiar problems of social and economic development. Demographically speaking, there are more than 244 scheduled tribes with many sub-groups speaking some 100 languages /dialects. Most unfortunate thing is that major portion of government's resources is diverted to consensual provisions and little is left for the development of tribal education, language and culture of these two PTGs. The striking aspect that emerges from the scanty data on languages in primary education is the almost total absence of tribal language in schools. The attitude of our policies planners towards these tribal people appears to be one of assimilation. Little is being done to preserve their culture. Our policies scientists have almost all-major and minor tribes suffer with this kind of negligence. Not much work has been done to find out minimum and maximum resistance into their culture. Linguistic experts have made no attempt to standardize tribal languages by developing scripts, elaborating lexis and writing grammars and dictionaries in tribal languages. Till today there has not been any serious efforts to provide basic education in their respective mother tongues. No proper curriculums have also been framed based on tribal culture and tradition. Present education system does not orient the tribal children towards perusing their own mode of life. In phonology and syntax, the tribal languages are quite different from the medium of instruction like Kannada except in certain mutually borrowed lexical items due to their close contacts over a long period of time. This is one of the vital reason responsible for these PTGs poor literacy and dropout problem among tribal children (Pasayat, 1995).

c) Urban Bias

The success of one's education largely depends on the motivation. Basically tribals are living with low socio -economic status. Obviously the level of motivation and self-esteem will be comparatively low among tribal children. The main reason for this problem is current education system is more or less urban based non-tribal and absence of culture specific. Even though these tribals are emotionally attached to their local cultural norms Govt. has no interest in providing education which is more suited to the tribal children. Modern teaching methodologies, content of the text, appointment of non-tribal teachers and parameters for evaluations have become *Grains of Iron* to the low motivated tribal children. Implementation of uniform textbooks both for urban and tribal children are one more hit to them. The theory, concepts, values alien to tribal people is generally contained in the textbooks which generates negative attitude and a big blow to the learners' self-confidence. There is no attempt to take stock of the existing situation regarding instructional materials in tribal languages. Education policies documents also have not dwelt on the magnitude of tasks that are involved in the preparation of primers and textbooks for tribal children and have not outlined the concrete steps that have to taken in this direction. The increasing tendency for tribal people to retain the regional language as their mother tongue is only one indicator of their growing vulnerability in the face of these larger social processes (Verma, 1995).

The problem of dropout persists among all categories of children in both urban and rural India. However, in the context of children studying in Classes 1-10 the gap between the ST and total population of dropouts has widened from 1990-91 to 1998-99.The reduction in the dropout rates could b because of various incentive schemes run by the State Govt. for edition of ST children such as providing free textbooks, uniforms and scholarships in Govt. schools. But schemes such as those providing for hostels for ST boys and girls are not implemented fully by the State owing to lack of financial resources and therefor fewer ST children pursue high school education and very few up to the college level. The policies of reserving seats for ST students at higher education levels is not widely availed since a ledge number of ST students do not even reach those levels and dropout at lower levels of school education. Even the Ashram shools run by both Govt. and NGO are poory maintained and sometime lack even the basic facilities. Given the low level of literacy among the ST population, several children from these comminutes happen to be 'first generation learners' and in the absence of State support for heaping them to cope with studies, many children drop out of the schools. This disproportionately low representation of ST children at higher level of eduaion compounds the existing disparities among Indian society. Lack of proactive government in favor of the STs is not linked only to lack of resources. Govt. indifference and lack of political will are largely responsible for the state of affair (Mahendale,2001).

d) Inaction of teachers

Teachers are the real directors of every tribal school. There was a time in India where teachers were equal to the God. The major problem is that Govt. is recruiting teachers from the urban area to teach tribal children. A report say that only 0.56% of teachers is basically from either Anthropology or Sociology discipline. Majority of the teacher are from non-tribal community. Many of them have studied only in English medium schools and they even don't know the regional language properly. In this situation how one can expect to teach the relatively disadvantaged tribal children down to their level. More unfortunate thing is that many schools don't have teachers for all the subjects. Even though many NGOs are hiring teachers to teach at tribal schools many of them even don't have any basic degrees in education like BE.d/ TCH. Some of the teachers are prejudious about the performance of the tribal children. As they are the only literate persons having some political connections in the tribal areas, they neither fulfil their duties properly nor the concerned higher officers dare to take any action against them for dereliction of their duties.

e) What teacher says?

Many of the teachers are of the opinion that tribal children cannot understand the modern Kannada language. Content of the text is too standard to their level. Few of them will complain about the ignorance of the parents. More over teachers are facing many problems in the tribal areas. Proper residential and medicinal facilities are a nightmare. Higher education for their children some time will not be possible. Since many primitive tribal hamlets live deep in to the forest some time it will be humanely impossible to reach the school due to the lack of appropriate transport. More over feed back from the students is completely absent. No proper laboratory facilities to teach Science effectively. Teachers raised and brought up in a more sophisticated urbanized society would find it difficult to adjust themselves to the cultural shock that generates communication gap.

f) Parents' apathy

Tribal community feels childhood or adulthood largely depends not on the physical age but on the degree of responsibility that children could successfully fulfill. Apart from that children's responsibilities towards the family and the contributions they make are significant and much important while conceptualizing the above mentioned terms. In tribal society children from the early age will be engaged in cooking food, fetching water, siblings care, support in the field, collection minor forest food, grazing etc. Decision to give a chance to a child to spend happy childhood is not isolated from other aspects of household decision making nor are they purely household based. They reflect the norms and values of the wider community within which the tribal household is located and the social and economic possibilities which local contexts offer to different categorized of households. Hence, parents may think sending child to school means dislocation of traditional pattern of earning livelihood and of division of labour in their societies. Most vital problems of low literacy among tribal children is that children are considered by parents as economic assets to the family.

Education of tribal girl children is more neglected because of deep-rooted beliefs, traditions and mid-sets. Educationalist philosophers use the concept of false consciousness to refer to the existence of beliefs and values that individuals socialize into and operate upon. It can be argued from that the universalist perspective that the parents believe that girls need to be socialized into their adult roles as children nd the formal education has no meaning for them.

Universal Elementary Education for Tribal Children

The question of how elementary education can and be made universal has not received the attention it deserves. We think that issues should be highlighted. Recent study has shown that an alarmingly large number of children do not become literate even after four years of primary education especially in both rural and tribal areas (Sharma, 2002). Hence, total school effectiveness and actual learning have to be the central theme rather than secondary concern for universal education. Further, more important is that how effective schools are and successive learning basically depend not only on school level inputs but also on many vital factors outside the school. Basic infrastructures of Ashram Schools in tribal areas are worst than any thing in many southern districts of Karnataka. Many schools even don't have hard roofs. Hostels are ruining. Unavailability of play ground, lab and library and separate toilets are most common in many tribal schools where children of these two PTGs are learning. Absence of extra curricular activities makes children learning as a kind of unavoidable burden. Since tribal children are completely different from urban children or atleast from rural children learning should be a joyful experience for them other wise simply they may be dropouts. For genuine universal elementary education the impact of the wider context on schooling has to be understood in a better way.

Absence of Central Monitoring Unit

Absence of effective monitoring unit on the tribal schools is one of the major drawbacks in case of development of tribal education. Concerned inspecting staffs hardly visit to the tribal schools. Some time even only one time in a year. This makes teacher to lack commitment to their profession. Some people reported that teacher' visit one or two times in a weak to the schools only. This is also due to low level of motivation, inspiration and commitment among the inspecting staff, which are again matched, by the low level of motivation and interest among the teachers. This is the high time that Govt. should think to strengthen or establish Centralized Monitoring Unit especially for Tribal School and better unit chief from either Anthropology or Sociology background.

In the light of above discussion we may conclude that on one hand, economic backwardness is responsible for the low percentage of literacy in the younger generation and on the other social backwardness and lack of social consciousness are responsible for low percentage of children attending schools. When the school going children are few it can be well understood that higher education will be a rare phenomena in these PTGs. Hence, along with other development it is also necessary that we should create some awareness about significance of education among tribles the facilities available to them for education and the role of education in their upliftment of socially economically and politically condition of the tribal community.

Policies Implications

Some suggestions to handle the educational problems of Primitive Tribal groups are made based on the fieldwork and review of previous literature. These are brought out in this section.

1 There are many basic difference can be seen between major tribals and primitive tribals in case of India. Hence, the Govt. should bring a new educational policies especially for primitive tribals. It must be culturally and geographically specific. Moreover educational experts should be very sensitive while framing the policies which should not destroy the social solidarity of the tribes and kill their zest for life.

2 It is well revealed fact that modern education cannot cater to the basic needs of the tribes. Modern education system cannot deem to have held much relevance for

them since they are from the outer world. During our fieldwork it has been revealed that tribals consider 'culture as their first educator'. Hence there is a need to identify the areas of minimum and maximum resistance to innovations in their culture and vital linkage to their cultural fabric. Once we identify enough space we can imbibe education in to their culture.

3 It is the high time to have special education programme made for tribal children in consonance with the privileged cultural pattern and also in keeping with the needs and resources of the area concerned in order to secure the maximum amount of tribal children participation. Moreover new education programme should be in a the position to assert the existing perception, behaviour and action in education seeking process and culturally determined attitude towards use of different system of education.

4 The state Govt. should construct a Textbook Commission especially for tribal education developemnt. While framing the textbooks experts should focus on three-impordent prospectvies1 Linguistic 2 Instrumental 3 and the Culture. From the primary level itself all text materials should be in their respective mothertongue. There is need to evolve scripts, grammar, and as well as appropriate vocabulary to communicate 'school knowledge'. Proper training should be given in tribal language, culture and society to the non-tribal teachers working in the tribal areas.

5 Lack of good quality teachers in sufficient numbers resulting in high pupil teacher ratio may be an important factor in explaining the variations of educational status in these two PTGs in education. Given the inaccuracies in enrolments and the attendance/absence of teachers, probably pupil teacher ratio may not be efficient and meaningful variable representing the quality of tribal education.

6 Ashram Schools should have a multi-purpose complex. If possible there should be a provision for selling and buying of consumer goods and minor forest products. Further Ashram Schools initially must emphasis on the service rendered to the primitive tribals than on costly building. 'In the initial stage provision should be made for a Kacha thatched Ashram type building rather than a pucca building' (Monthy, 2003).

7 The socio economic context, along with the development dimension is an integral part of school effectiveness. On the other hand it is difficult to ensure good school quality in less developed tribal areas. On the other hand, it is found that area type affects learning directly by influencing poverty levels and also opportunities and motivation for learning. The impact of the area type on schools and learning is such that no description or analysis of schools can be meaningfull with out a parallel understanding of the area type (rural, hamlet of major tribals or primitive tribals).

The factors responsible for low educational status of tribal children in Karnataka are small and scattered habitations, geographical isolation, poor economic conditions, illiteracy of parents, lack of proper educational monitoring, education not related to needs of life, drab and uninteresting classroom experiences, engagement of children in collection of forest produce, unsuitable school hours, linguistic and cultural barriers, etc. The State strategies attempted at avoiding various managerial bottlenecks by creating adequate coordination between Tribal and School Education Departments, forming a Tribal Core Group at all level and by re-orienting the district officials about the tribal cultural specific problems, etc. Opening Alternative Schools, SSKs, NFE centres and Ashram schools giving priority to tribal habitations under DPEP would increase the accessibility of education to tribal children. Even though the State/district strategies claimed to have been assessing the learning needs of the tribal community, developing tribal sensitive pedagogic units by involving experts from TRI and SCERT and developing Bridge Language Inventory (BLI), subsequent discussion revealed that a little has been achieved in this regard and the pace of development is slow. In the first case the national component can contribute enormously by reviewing the existing State infrastructure to support these activities and providing the expertise wherever it is needed. Development of R.O.T.C as Resource Centre for Tribal Education for taking up local specific studies, research and evaluation work will in the long run support these diverse interventions in the area of tribal education. However the national component which supports there search work on tribal education can also share its information with R.O.T.C. Besides, with the help of information from R.O.T.C, researches supported by the national component can become need based. Assessments of training needs of teachers, VECs, MTAs empowering these bodies, mobilising community participation by using local tribal cultural strategies such as folk stories and dance were other attempts taken up by the State strategies. In other words, the State component for tribal education evolved separately and independently having it's own unique policies, structure and management system. A cell in SCERT on tribal education has been set up to look after training aspects and research. However, linking Tribal Welfare and Education Departments is and should be one of the major intervention strategies in Karnataka.

Conclusion

If we go through from the other angle, the problems of intensity of dropouts have been increasing day by day among tribal students. The next question is once they become dropouts what will be their next plan? What will be their day-to-day context? How do their parents react for this?. In our fieldwork it is revealed that many dropout children have become child workers. Many of them are working with their parents in the field and in some big estates. Of cource, there are many reasons for children dropouts even from the primary stage. Suppose if Govt. is ready to overcome all these problems modernize the tribal education system will parents send their children to school?. The Anthropological study on dynamic model of tribal child labour suggests that, their decision to send to work today depends not only on current consideration such as the marginal productivity of child'work but also on expected returns to work compared with alternatives such as school attendance. The finding that farm size increase dropout suggest that at given levels of household income, the return to work relative to the return to school is a significant determinant in sending their children to school. A naturally policy implication is therefore to invest in raising the return to education. In addition to general investment in improving school supply such measures may include reducing labour market discrimination against tribal women and raising awareness to reduce inhibiting social norms. Polices that improve the function of labour market in rural and tribal areas may reduce the dropouts, especially that of girls. Given the recent expansion of micro credit programmes, it is pertinent to note that developing tribal financial market many have positive spillover effects, encouraging development of land and labour market. The growths of tribal action market will not only counter the substation effect highlighted here, it may also generate overall income growth and reduce tribal inequalities. If so parents may not mind in sending their children to school.

While implementing the tribal development plans especially in case of education care should be taken to see that the cultural traits of primitive tribes are not disturbed with in the process of their interaction with the mainstream of nation life. More over a careful watch on the trends set in motion, which should not destroy the social solidarity of the tribes and kill their zest for life should be the part and parcel of every tribal developmental policies. Further there should be a lot of scope for prioritizing their needs, solving their own problems and raising their own resources to meet their urgent needs in all schemes by using their knowledge got from the schools. Finally it can be said that educational activities will have to be simultaneous with economic advancement in such areas as are in contact with urban and civilized, or partially civilized, centers. In such areas however, where the tirbals are not in such contact and are economically stable, education should have top priority. But in all such cases where economic disintegration has processed far and deep and the number of such cases is quite large economic rehabilitation must get very high priority.

15
Educating Tribal Children: Suggestive Lesson to the NGOs

The work of NGOs in the fields of health, micro-financing and alternative income generation programmes have also made important contribution in the effort to spreading education among tribal and rural India. However, unless NGOs make significant improvement in their performance in promoting sustainable livelihood for the poor their best efforts may not prove sufficient for empowerment through education.

Despite the formation of specific policies and projects for dealing with improvement of educational status of the tribals, and the implementation of a large number of programmes by the government and NGOs in pursuance of these policies, the impact on tribal education in the country is minimal. The basic reason for the failure of many programmes is that they are simply not designed to do so. All programmes, which will be implemented by the NGOs, should be geographically and culturally specific.

Experts are of the opinion that as long as prejudice continues to exist regarding value of education it would be difficult to reform them. Simple legislation is not enough. Since along with prejudice, acute economic crisis is the prime reason behind non-accepting of reforms through education the only method of convening parents is by compensating the family adequately for the loss of income. In this corner point, all NGOs must and should think rather than to provide some alternative income generation programme to assisting producers organizations. If NGOs seriously wants to be in this field and, if so, necessarily specialize and they should think much larger scale programmes and projects. Not only this, they should have high quality of human resource to mange themselves as organizations and their operations in a more

Since tribal education has some socio-economic touch NGOs should requires long term multi-pronged strategy to be carried out on a continuous basis. Although at policy level NGOs have been perceived as developmental agents, yet the scene at the grassroots level is not always in consonance with this subjectivity. It is so because base level Government functionaries some time see NGOs workers as outside encroaching/ occupying their space. (Baland and Robinson, 2001). And on other side few NGOs thinks different Government agencice are the main hurdles in their way. This may be the major weakness of many NGOs Their mutual interactions and even collaboration makes the effort more effective.

Here both Government and voluntary agencies should change their attitude and should be complimentary to each other and must take confidence in each other. The NGOs should make a lot of homework in making people's participation in educating and training to improve their of professional skills, overcoming behavior and cultural resistance of tribal communities may be preferably involved in tackling the problem of educational development and always they should try to became closer to the tribal people. Many NGOs believe economic compulsion is not only the reason why parents are not sending their children to school. The recent survey shows that more than 29.27% of tribal working children is the need to supplement the family income while only 7.56% of child worker were required to gain employment to earn a minimum living for their families. Only 1.56% are working part time, to finance their own education besides contributing to the inadequate family income. So all NGOs must think in the way of giving more and more low cost job oriented education and their by encouraging more women joining the work force besides empowerment of tribal women would go a long way in elimination prejudices about education.

Apart from parent's disinterest in education, the second main reason is the present pattern of education system in our country. Many tribal children are not attending schools because their parents want them to work for the reasons other than economic crises. For example child might lost his interest in the education, failed in the same class many times, corporal punishment by the teachers, parents might wanted to continue their family occupations in the early age, hanging with bad friends, threat of probable unemployment in the future, earn additional income to the family-etc. Hence NGOs should think about present education scenario and better concentrate on these topics.

Since many parents do not under stand the significance of the education, NGOs have to work to create awareness about the value of the education. As soon as possible NGOs should open *Home work centers* where any school going child can come and get help to complete his home work under the guidance of a trained teacher, and *Community play centers* where all children come and can play any games like carum, chess and volleyball-etc. if so few problems related to the educational aspects of can be solved. All children would have certain inherent skills. It is necessary to equip with certain skills suited their aptitude, NGOs should conduct most advanced type vocational training courses and must be more suitable to the dropout children because these dropout children are potential child laborers. These courses should be suited for child worker in general and in vocations for those working children who combine their work with studies. Also in order to provide opportunity to working girls for supplementing the family income NGOs should take some step to develop co-operative societies. Through this, young working girls having responsibility for organizing training, making raw materials, available and selling the products goods to the market.

Learning from others

Organizations like DEED, ROAD, CROSS and Cultural Survive are some of the important NGOs working on tribal education Issues and have valuable lesson from the field to others. Especially Rural Organization for Appropriate Development (ROAD) a Mysore- (Karnataka) based NGOs has successfully implemented all above mentioned programmes in its working area. But before learn any thing from others they have to concede that the work being done by agencies is addressing the same education related issues as the NGOs are trying to grapple with. But it is impordent to note that, each NGOs will have different ideas regarding poverty focus, community acceptance, beneficiary owner ship, funds, human resource, planing strategies-etc.

Resources from the Mainstream

1. Finances

Since almost all NGO's is totally depend on either foreign or Indian grants for their activities, it is necessary to rise capital from mainstream sources, such as the development financial institutions and the bank. If so it will have two benefits; first it will make NGO's more accountable in terms of effective use of money and also it opens much larger sources of funds that foreign and Indian grants. Almost all-financial institutions like SIDBI, ICICI, NABARD, IDIBI have by accumulated years of experience in funding NGOs through grants for experimental projects NGOs can approach these institutes to get fund as loans with longer than normal repayment and moratorium periods and lower interest rate or they can rise money from the corporal sectors.

2. Human resources

NGOs are known to have highly experienced and committed individuals. Many NGOs have good grassroots worker but not at middle levels. If so, the grassroots worker may not get any guidance and support. So NGOs should hire more experienced persons in education, Anthropologists and experts in other related field. If NGOs would like to move from direct implementing agencies to supporting producers organization, they need to have higher caliber of people at all levels is accentuate. Those in support roles have to be more versatile, having broad-based knowledge of various cultural factors which are hindering the tribal education programmes successfully (Basu, 1998).

3. Technology

As another step towards effectiveness in implementation educational related programmes NGOs need to have link with various technology generation institutions blessed with a very large scientific and technological research infrastructure in India. For example ICAR, IVTC (Institute of Vocational Training Center)-etc in addition to state level research and training institutes. Since education issue is related to more than one field NGOs should get a lot of technical support from these institutions. The presence of professionally trained staff in NGOs greatly facilitates this process of acquiring technology and adaptation to the local situation and to the poor tribal families.

Training should be relative to the ground situation and executed by the professionals only. Training techniques have to be related to the experience of the participants and must simultaneously appeal to their thinking and emotions. Behavioral games, stimulation's and case study basses discussions are some useful techniques and visit to other organizations will be also be useful.

4. Expertise

NGOs should have a vast pool of technical experts and professionals specialized in project finance, socio-economic analysis, training and capacity building, technical aspects, computing, tribal infrastructure, tribal financial institutions, planning, monitoring and evaluation-etc

5. Knowledge

As education is a complex phenomenon all NGOs should have certain useful concepts which have a bearing on successful educational related programmes like,

1. NGOs should understand social structure, caste and class problem, dynamic of social changes, political economy of resources and policies analysis of tribals (Verma,1996).
2. communication theory; diffusion of innovation; group dynamics and collective action; training and organization development; and any appropriate educational technology

6. Skills

Tribal education related specialist NGOs should have certain Following skills

- Wining, confidence of tribal people
- Building them to try out new ideas
- Conducting detailed feasibility studies
- Identifying and tying up with source of in puts
- Acquiring and adaptation of new educational technology
- Professional training to the staff and policies makers (Mahajan 1993).

Conclusion

In this paper a strong argument has been made that tribal education related NGOs should re-examine their approaches in this field due to it's inherent complexity and difference rather than relief and welfare programmes. They should exclusively focus on educated related issues only. If these kinds of NGOs could succeed in promoting sustainable livelihood for the poor, so that they can develop requisite level of expertise in tribal development related sub sectors. And NGOs must think of much larger scale projects and draw financial and human resource from the mainstream. Policies and projects should adopt a holistic approach, taking in to the consideration socio economic set-up of working area. They should also enter into collaborative relation ships with Governament agencies and other NGOs. NGOs try hard to solve grass-root level of problem and they should think in upgradtion of living standards and education status more particularly of the tribal women and children. More than this, NGOs should learn in employment generation in non-agricultural sectors will increase demand for quality education from the parents.

16
Servashikshan Abiyan (SSA) and Tribal Education: Issues and Prospects

The two main challenges in education of tribal children physical access to schooling at upper primary level and diverse socio-cultural context. In 2001, there were 14million tribal children enrolled in elementary schools as against 20.24 million in the 6-14 years age group. Thus 6.24 million children were still out of school in 2001. The cohort dropouts rate amongst tribal children was as high as 52.3% for primary and 69.5% for upper primary. For 20% of the habitations at the primary stage and 33% at the upper primary stage, access was still an issue in 2002.

Achievements of SSA I (2001 – 2006): SSA I addressed these issues with opening of1,33,000 primary schools and 1,06,000 upper primary schools from the date of reference of Seventh All India Survey (30 September 2002). Most of these schools have been provided to unserved habitations and tribal habitations are clearly benefited from it, thus, achieving almost universal access at primary level. Apart from this there are about 1,00,000 EGS centers that are providing education in unserved habitations. Moreover, based on the specific circumstances in which tribal's live, the norms for establishing primary schools have been relaxed to suit tribal areas in order to improve access to education. There has been an over all increase in the enrolment of children belonging to Scheduled Tribes. At the Primary Stage, against overall increase of 15% in enrollment, ST enrollment increased by25%, whereas that of ST girls increased by 36% against overall increases of 23% from 2000 to2004. At the Upper Primary Level against overall increase of 20%, ST enrolment increased by35%, whereas that of ST girls increased by 47% against girls overall increase of 30%. The dropouts at primary level declined by 10-percentage point.

Challenges for SSA II: About 1.66 million (2005) ST children are still out of school. Thus, the continued focus of SSA will be to bring in these remaining 1.66 million children in school and retain them at elementary stage. The decreasing trends in children being out of school, indicates that it will not be difficult to narrow these gaps. Though the reduction trends in dropouts have been at par with overall, the gap between the two (13 percent points) is a challenge. Reduction of this gap remains a key focus area in SSA. Physical access to schooling, especially at the upper primary stage, is still an issue in some parts of the country in remote tribal areas. Therefore, targeted coverage of all eligible habitations for the upper primary school facilities will be a priority. In some remote sparsely populated areas, it may be difficult to set up primary schools due to small number of children. This may necessitate residential schools/ hostels for which scope of SSA framework has been enlarged to include construction of residential schools in sparsely populated remote, hilly, desert and tribal blocks. Seasonal migration is common in several tribal areas. Facilities like seasonal hostels may need to be provided in all such blocks with high level of migration to help retain children in villages when parents migrate. Recognizing this the SSA framework has been amended to give focus to the issue of seasonal migration.

Strategies:1 Consultative Process of Planning:

SSA envisages a bottom-up approach of planning instead of a top-down approach, as it reflects the reality at the grassroots level. The planning process is participatory in nature and it also focuses on creating a sense of ownership among stakeholders, enhancing awareness and capacity building of programme personnel at various levels. The plans developed thus also, reflect local specificity. A Planning and Appraisal Manual sets out the processes for formulation of district (and state) plans, and for their appraisal by national teams. District plans are developed with incorporation of information from the habitation plans, on the basis of these findings as well as on secondary data. Every District Elementary Education Plan(DEEP) and Annual Work Plan is expected to articulate clearly the district's strategy and approach to tribal education and adopt specific programs and interventions to translate the strategy into action. It provides disaggregated data on tribal demography and education, spells out the educational problems of ST children, the interventions, quality improvement efforts, and convergence with programs of NGOs and other Government departments such as the Tribal Department etc. The assessment of problems related to the education of tribal children is made through household surveys and micro planning exercises.

Targeting: While the overall SSA strategy will continue to be in the same direction as in SSA I with regard to social equity, 74 districts with high tribal concentration have been identified for focused and targeted intervention and 52 districts identified by Ministry of Tribal Affairs are being targeted for focused attention on the tribal girl's education, infrastructure, and convergence with Ministry of Tribal Affairs. 13% of the total outlay provided under SSA is focused on 106tribal focus districts in the year 2007-08, 1.4.3 Monitoring and Evaluation: The Results Framework for SSAII provides for monitoring of Special Focus Groups, including tribal children. For each of the KPIs, the progress will be tracked on a disaggregated basis for each of the special focus groups. While in SSA I, the Results Framework focused on access and enrolment, in SSA II, this has broadened to include, transition, attendance and learning levels for each focus group. The Framework has also incorporated many process indicators, which contribute to quality.

The Programme: The Sarva Shiksha Abhiyan (SSA) is the flagship programme of Government of India (GoI), to achieve Universal Elementary Education (UEE) through a time bound integrated approach, in partnership with States. Launched in 2001, with a focus on decentralized planning and community ownership, SSA aims to provide useful and relevant education to all children in the 6-14 age groups by 2010. The over – arching goal of SSA is to bridge social and gender gaps in all education outcomes. The programme has completed five years of implementation, of which the last three years were in partnership with Development Agencies, namely, The World Bank, DFID and EC. The Development Partners are now in the process of preparing the second phase of their support to this programme, which they refer to as SSA II.: -Project Objectives and Components: The Development Objective (DO) of SSA II is to significantly increase the number of 6-14 year old children, especially from special focus groups, enrolled, regularly attending, retained at elementary stage and demonstrating basic learning levels. The progress on the DO will be monitored annually for the different social groups, i.e., Scheduled Castes (SC), Scheduled Tribes (ST), girls, minority community, Children With Special Needs, using the following key indicators:• Reduction in the number of out of school children from 9.6 million to 4.9 million;• Increase in enrolment of each social group with references to their respective shares in the population at national, state and district levels;• Improvement in attendance rates at primary and upper primary levels: There are two key thrusts of activities financed under SSA II – (i) Universalizing access and promoting equity; and (ii) Improving quality with equity. Both of these have significant importance for the education of the children from tribal communities, given their socioeconomic and cultural contexts.

III. Socio cultural and Political Context of Tribal Communities:

According to the 2001 census, the population of Scheduled Tribes in the country is 8.43crore, (84,326,240) constituting 8.2% of the total population of the country. Out of this, males are 4.26 crores and females 4.17 crores, accounting for 8.01% and 8.40% of the total population of respective groups. The ST population varies among the states. The main concentration of tribal population is in Central India and in the North-Eastern States. Nine1states together account for about four-fifths of the total tribal population of the country, but the tribal percentages of these states' population vary from about 5.5 to 31.8 per cent. On the other hand, several smaller states, notably in the northeast of the country, have much higher percentages (ranging from 64 to 95 per cent), but account for a small proportion of tribal people in the country as a whole. There are 698 tribes (with many overlapping communities in more than one State) as notified under Article 342 of the Constitution of India, spread over different States and Union Territories of the country. Each one of the tribes is associated with a specific geographic area, some more dispersed than other. Most have their own language, which is generally different from the 'mainstream' language of the state in which they live. While some tribal communities have adopted a mainstream way of life, at one end of the spectrum are 75 Primitive Tribal Groups (PTGs), who are characterised by:• A pre-agriculture level of technology; A stagnant or declining population;• Extremely low literacy; and• A subsistence level of economy. Tribal people tend to live in two main types of situations: (a) in 'mixed' (tribal and non-tribal) rural communities, within reach of educational and other opportunities and resources, and (b) inhabitations that are small in size and located in relatively inaccessible hilly or forested areas of the country. Majority of these habitations have less than 200 persons. The distribution of tribal people in these two types of settlement varies markedly by state, district and even block, calling for different strategies to be used in different areas to provide elementary education to tribal children. Demographically tribal habitations are small in size, scattered, and are sparsely populated. Because of this, most of these villages were bereft of basics infrastructural facilities like transport and communication. Formal education was also not available to these people and localities for a long time. The literacy rate for the ST communities was only 29.6 percent in 1991 as against the national average of 52.19 percent. In 2001 this has improved to 47.1 percent with female literacy improving from 18.2 to 34.8(Census 2001). According to Census 2001, there were 12.56 million ST children aged 6-10,and 7.68 million ST children aged 11-14 years in March 2001. 3.4Policy Framework: The 86thAmendment to the Constitution of India (2000) made educational fundamental right, calling for the State to provide free and compulsory education to all children between 6 and 14 years. At the same time Article 51 of the Constitution was amended to enjoin parents and guardians to provide education to their 6-14 year old children. Recognizing that the STs count among the most deprived and marginalized sections ofIndian society, a host of welfare and developmental measures have been initiated for their social and economic development. Tribal Sub-Plan approach came into existence as the main strategy for the welfare and development in the Five Year Plans. Along with core economic sectors, elementary education has been accorded priority in the tribal sub-Plan approach. Elementary education is considered important, not only because of constitutional obligation, but as a crucial input for total development of tribal communities, particularly to build confidence among the tribes to deal with outsiders on equal terms. A second important development in the policy towards education of tribals came with recommendations of the National Policy on Education (NPE) in 1986, which specified, among other things, the following:•Priority will be accorded to opening primary schools in tribal areas.•There is a need to develop curricular and devise instructional material in tribal language at the initial stages with arrangements for gradually adopting to regional languages.• Promising ST youths will be encouraged to take up teaching in tribal areas.•Ashram schools/residential schools will be established on a large scale in tribal areas. •Incentives schemes will be formulated for the STs, keeping in view their special needs and lifestyle. Educational Status: In 2001, there were 14 million tribal children enrolled in elementary schools as against 20.24million in the 6-14 years age group. The cohort drop out rates among tribal children was as high as 52.3% for primary and 69.5% for upper primary. The two main issues in education of tribal children that emerged were inadequate physical access and socio-cultural differences which came in the way of their participation in schooling. The Seventh All-India Educational Survey, 2002 shows that a total of 80 percent of tribal habitations have schools within / less than 1 km radius at primary level. Similarly, at upper primary level a total of 67 per cent habitations have been provided upper primary school within a radius of 3 Km. Thus for 20% of the habitations at the primary stage and 33% at the upper primary stage, access was still an issue.

Decentralized and Participatory Strategy

The SSA is a ten year long program for the GOI with specific goals as indicated earlier. The strategy and nature of interventions as described below will therefore largely continue to remain the same under SSAII, particularly since the emerging trends in educational out comes are positive. Based on lessons learned from SSA-I, there may be shifts in emphasis and scale, to be decided in a decentralized and participatory mode in consultation with the beneficiaries. Institutional arrangements and Capacity: The District and State Education Offices have officers specifically designated to ensure that the provisions for the special groups and for tribal areas and children are implemented. When necessary, the district units draw on the expertise of NGOs and other institutions, which have worked with tribal people in the field of education. Such expertise is available and is particularly useful in the community mobilization and pedagogical dimensions. Specialized institutions (such as the District Institutes of Education and Training) are also available to assist in the development implementation and management of activities as required. SSA staffs are trained to carry out the special activities in tribal areas with the necessary sensitivity and diligence. The districts with large tribal populations are specifically provided with Tribal District Coordinators. The educational system and several of the related institutions have outreach capacity, which will be utilized and developed as needed to serve tribal areas.

Specialists in tribal education are engaged, for example, in the planning and monitoring activities of SSA. Consultative Planning and Appraisal Process: The SSA planning process is completely decentralized and participatory, since it rests on habitation based planning. SSA emphasize area-specific, people specific and issue-specific planning and implementation of interventions to meet the learning needs of children. A Planning and Appraisal Manual sets out the processes for formulation of district (and state) plans, and for their appraisal by national teams. To quote from the Manual "SSA envisages the bottom-up approach of planning instead of the top-down approach in a decentralized manner, as it reflects the reality at the grassroots level. The planning process has to be participatory in nature as this type of planning not only creates a sense of ownership among the stakeholders, but also creates awareness and helps in the capacity building of personnel at various levels. The plans developed through consultative meetings and interaction with the community and target groups, at various levels, reflect local specificity. It is necessary that there be documentation of the process of the preparation of plan to evidence the fact that they have been prepared at the habitation level through participatory planning mode". This documentation is in the regional language since it emanates from and needs to accessible to the local communities. The main areas of emphasis in the planning section of the Manual are (a) Interaction with community and target groups (b) Consultative meetings(c) Micro planning exercises (d) Identification of Issues and Interventions and (e) target setting. In addition, this Manual has a separate section on Education of ST children, which includes a well-articulated Planners' Checklist and Appraisal checklist specifically for habitation based planning with tribal communities.Every District Elementary Education Plan (DEEP) and Annual Work Plan is expected to articulate clearly the district's strategy and approach to tribal education and adopt specific programs and interventions to translate the strategy into action. It provides disaggregated data on tribal demography and education, spells out the educational problems of ST children, the interventions, quality improvement efforts, and convergence between education activities and the programs of NGOs and of other departments such as the Tribal Department. The assessment of problems related to the education of tribal children is made through household surveys and micro planning exercises. District plans are developed with incorporation of information from the habitation plans, on the basis of these findings as well as on secondary data The consultative process at the grassroots level is thus an essential part of every habitation plan. It is the result of these consultative processes that provision of school facilities due to dispersed population, demands for teachers, additional classrooms, issues of migration, need for flexible timings, inability to meet the costs of schooling etc. are taken up. Some program initiatives taken in response to the expressed difficulties include setting up of short term residential programs for children of migrants, provision of more focused incentives like stationery, writing material, uniforms etc, setting up of residential schools or strengthening of existing Ashram Shala – residential schools, Tribal Welfare Department, provision of mobile teachers and seasonal camps for mobile communities etc. Review and appraisal of the DEEPs Annual Work Plans are technical, managerial and financial, and include a focus on issues relating to tribal education. The Appraisal teams include specialists in the education of the special focus groups, who sometimes carry outfield visits in addition to conducting 'desk appraisals'. The Project Approval Board, which approves the perspective, plans of the state and the annual plans of the districts critically examine the plans to ensure that the local issues – including tribal issues – are addressed through clear strategies and specific interventions. It may request the state/districts to reformulate the plan and/or to allocate more funds to the education of tribal children. Checklists focusing on ST children (as well as separate ones for other focus groups) have been formulated and have been included in the Manual. The key contents of these are as follows. The Planners' Checklist calls for special attention to: a special policy statement and strategy for education of ST children; provision of schools to "pockets of ST concentration"; inclusion and analysis of disaggregated data on ST children; special programs for urban ST children; community mobilization plans to ensure participation of ST children in education; in-service training of teachers to remove biases especially in classroom transactions; remedial measures to improve learning outcomes; innovations to improve learning levels; links with other schemes to address the problems of ST children. The Appraisal Checklist calls for special attention to the following during appraisal of the plans: presentation of disaggregated data on ST children; identification of un-served habitations and plans to provide them with school facilities; strategy to motivate the tribal community; availability of local and tribal teachers; capacity building of teachers to teach tribal children; the match between problems identified and interventions proposed; provisions for nomadic tribes; medium of instruction; attitudinal training of teachers; convergence with tribal department schemes; and the utilization of the allocation of Rs. 15 lakh per year for innovative strategies for ST children in the district. Planning teams at the State and district level have been sensitized to the approach and provisions in the SSA framework for the education of ST children. This is done through a multi – pronged strategy including direct training of Village Education Committee members and functionaries involved in planning at various levels by national, state and district level institutions including NGOs, community mobilization drives, Tribal coordinators are posted at the State Level and in tribal dominated districts to monitor SSA activities and to help incoordination with Ministry of Tribal Affairs. These coordinators also undergo training.

Plan of Interventions SSA:

Framework for implementation recognises the problems faced by children in the tribal areas are often different than that faced by children belonging to other areas. Hence, special interventions are needed in addition to the ones applicable for all children. Every activity approved under the SSA is based on the principle that it must identify the benefit that will accrue to children from these communities. The SSA, while providing a framework, provides flexibility to local units to develop context specific interventions based on local needs and contexts. Main categories of interventions include: Focus on Access to Elementary Education. Community Mobilisation and Participation • Awareness campaigns to increase enrolment.• Involving community leaders in school management committees to ensure a sense of ownership • Increasing the representation of ST members in Village Education Committees in tribal areas. •Engagement of community organizers from ST community to motivate and escort children from specific households, with a focus on schooling needs of children from specific households.• Training programmes for community leaders to develop capacities for school management and community mobilization and involving them in school management.• Deployment of tribal coordinators at the State level and tribal dominated districts to monitor SSA activities and interact extensively with the community and to help in coordination with Tribal Welfare Department. Special facilities and favorable norms for tribal areas• Setting up schools, Education Guarantee scheme centres (EGS) and alternative and Innovative education (AIE) centres within 1 km of all habitations for non enrolled children and dropouts, with relaxed norms (with 10-15 children)• Organizing special mainstreaming camps for out of school ST children under the AIE component.• Amending the school calendar in tribal areas to fit the availability patterns of local children. •Providing context specific interventions in the form of a hostel, incentives or a special facility as required •Attaching crèches and pre-school sections (anganwadis and balwadis) to schools in tribal areas to enable girls to participate in schooling by relieving them of sibling-care responsibilities.• . Special plan for nomadic and migrant population. • Employing community based teachers• Monitoring attendance and retention of children from weaker sections regularly • Provide flexibility in terms of timing, learning modalities, etc.• Provision of Rs. 15 lakhs to each district for special innovative activities to promote education for Scheduled Tribes.• Focus on ST girls through NPEGEL programme and KGBV scheme. 6.3 Focus on quality of education• Provision of free textbooks (up to Rs. 150 per child) to all ST children. • Textbooks in mother tongue for ST children in the beginning of primary education where they do not understand regional language.• Preparation of locally relevant materials for ST children.• Development of specific modules for training of teachers in tribal areas• Special coaching/remedial classes for improving learning outcome of ST children.• Deploying teachers from the local specific tribal communities, providing them special support according to their needs; and • Preparation of 'Bridge Language Inventory' for use of teachers.• Providing special training to non-tribal teachers to teach in tribal areas, including imparting knowledge of the tribal dialect.• In addition, provisions for all schools will also be available such as school and teacher grants, adequate Teaching Learning Equipment for primary and upper primary schools and20 days' in-service training each year for teachers.

Monitoring and Evaluation

The educational progress of ST children is monitored through the DISE based Education Management Information System (EMIS). EMIS data are analyzed at district and State levels and provide all relevant school strategies disaggregated by ST category. The EMIS relates school level data to community information gathered through surveys. Schools are encouraged to share all information with communities (including information on grants received). Notice boards are to be put up in schools for this purpose triggering both transparency and accountability to communities. In addition, the VECs or user groups, including tribal people, are responsible for continuous monitoring of activities in their areas, and provide feedback to local teachers and officials. The user groups also interact with local groups during their activities, such as village meetings, enrolment drives etc. Household surveys give disaggregated data for Scheduled Tribes by age, gender, drop out and neverenrolled. The Ministry has set up a Sub Mission for the Education of SC/ST children to monitor progress in terms of bridging social gaps in educational outcomes, identifying laggard districts, identifying good practices and promoting conceptualization and implementation of appropriate activities for SC/ST children. The SSA has established benchmarks for coverage and achievements during period of implementation, which would be used to monitor implementation progress. SSA has a detailed Monitoring and Evaluation Component in place in which research and academic institutions all over the country carry out continuous and comprehensive monitoring of SSA. The Quality monitoring tools cover school attendance and pedagogic aspects of tribal education. Autonomous Monitoring Institutes are involved in monitoring, the field aspects of SSA and their reporting format has special reference to Scheduled Tribes like:• Textbooks – Total number of children (district wise) to whom free textbooks are distributed in the State with a particular reference to STs. • Enrolment in Schools – Enrolment of children belongs to STs. • VEC - Representation of women and persons belonging to ST communities and the irregular participation in the VEC meetings. • KGBV and ST participation of girls etc. Evaluations are to be carried out by independent agencies to determine the impact of the SS Activities. Professional social scientists would be involved in the monitoring and evaluation activities. Evaluation reports are made public. The various research studies that are commissioned by GOI from time to time, seek disaggregated information about STs. The two independent studies whose report is finalized, i.e., Study on Out of School children and National Evaluation of KGBV, both have specific, mention about Scheduled Tribes. The following studies that are underway or are commissioned by GoI in 2007 also have specific reference to STs. • Study of Teachers' absence in Primary and Upper Primary Schools and provide information with regard to ST Teachers. • Study of Student's Attendance in Primary and Upper Primary School – provide information with regard to ST Students.• All India Sample Survey for estimation of Dropouts Rates - will provide information with regard to Drop out Rate of ST Students at elementary level.

During JRMs, the monitoring reports, studies and evaluations are reviewed. Particular attention would be paid to assessing progress on the following, through appropriate MIS and filed visits:• Opening and functioning of schools in tribal habitations in tribal and non-tribal are as;• Enrolment and retention of tribal children in schools in tribal and non-tribal areas;• Learning achievements of tribal children compared with other groups;• Availability of tribal teachers, teachers speaking the local tribal language, teachers training to deal with tribal children (attitudinal training), and administrators sensitized to tribal issues;• Availability of instruction and instructional materials in the local tribal languages;• Functioning of facilities such as CRCs and BRCs serving the needs of tribal children; and • Availability of other schemes and incentives to facilitate school attendance of tribal children. • Government of India has commissioned various independent studies to assess the functioning of different component under SSA. All these studies have special focus on scheduled tribe and shall provide disaggregated data on scheduled tribes.

Achievements of SSA to date:

SSA has opened 1,33,000 primary schools and 1,06,000 upper primary schools from the date of reference of Seventh All India Survey (30 September 2002). Most of these schools have been provided to unserved habitations and tribal habitations are clearly benefited from it, thus, achieving almost universal access at primary level. Apart from this there are about1,00,000 EGS centres that are providing education in unserved habitations. Moreover, based on the specific circumstances in which tribals live, the norms forest ablishing primary schools have been relaxed to suit tribal areas in order to improve access to education. For instance, Chhattisgarh has relaxed it's norms to the extent of establishing Gyan Jyoti Kendra in any unserved habitations where there are at least ten children of eligible age, Andhra Pradesh has started establishing schools in habitations where there are even twenty school-age children; Madhya Pradesh has steadily decreased population size norms to 25 children of eligible age, in order to open EGS centres, it is also upgraded more their 20,000

EGS centres that have operated successfully for more then two years. Under Innovation Head States like, Madhya Pradesh have strengthened Ashramshala (Residential schools opened by Tribal Welfare Departments in the States) schools with additional teachers and school / TLM grants. Also, residential schools have been opened for Girls in Tribal dominated districts. Similar residential schools have been opened in Arunachal Pradesh. This has resulted in improvement in the educational outcomes over the project period. Enrolment: There has been an over all increase in the enrolment of children belonging to Scheduled Tribes. At the Primary Stage, against overall increase of 15% in enrollment, ST enrollment increased by 25%, whereas that of ST girls increased by 36% against overall increases of 23%from 2000 to 2004. At the Upper Primary Level against overall increase of 20%, ST enrolment increased by35%, whereas that of ST girls increased by 47% against girls overall increase of 30%.

A national level study was launched in the year 2006-07 in 20 major States and the NCT of Delhi, to capture students' attendance. It provides disaggregated data by social category. The priority tables from 14 States with substantive tribal populations, given below shows that attendance among ST children is almost same as among students of other categories.

The DISE data shows an increasing trend in school completion rates among scheduled tribe students. At the Primary level, the dropout rates have reduced by 10 percent points both overall and for STs.. Remaining Challenges for SSA II. An independent study All India Survey of out of school children in the 6-13 years age group commissioned by GOI in 2005 estimated ST child population as 17.37 million, of this 1.66million were out of school, 9.54% of age cohort against national average of 6.94%. Thus, the continued focus of SSA will be to bring in these remaining 1.66 million children in school and ensure that they complete 8 years of education. The decreasing trends in children being out of school, indicates that it will not be difficult to narrow these gaps.9.2 The still persisting high drop out rates gap between overall and ST children (13 percent points) remain an issue of concern. Reduction of this gap remains a key focus area in SSA.

Physical access to schooling, especially at the upper primary stage, is still an issue in some parts of the country in remote tribal areas. But targeted coverage of all eligible habitations for the upper primary school facilities will be a priority. • In some remote sparsely populated areas, it may be difficult to set up primary schools due to small number of children. This may necessitate residential schools/ hostels.• Seasonal migration is common in several tribal areas. Facilities like seasonal hostels may need to be provided in all such blocks with high level of migration to help retain children in villages when parents migrate. Strategy: While the overall SSA strategy will continue to be in the same direction, 74 districts with high tribal concentration have been identified for focused and targeted intervention and 52 districts identified by Ministry of Tribal Affairs are being targeted for focused attention for girl's education, infrastructure, and convergence with Ministry of Tribal Affairs. The process of preparation of AWP&B each year includes consultations with various stakeholders, including NGOs working with dalits and tribal groups and social activists(Annex 3). The SSA programme will strengthen community ownership of educational activities through effective decentralization. This will involve Panchayati Raj Institutions, local tribal bodies, Village Education Committee (VECs), NGOs and women's groups. The programme will continue to involve tribal people in decision-making at several levels. At the district level, representatives of tribal people will continue to participate in the annual planning and local-level decision making, in oversight of the SSA activities, and providing feedback on the programme to field level staff. Both the SSA and local government systems call for and facilitate such involvement. At the block and village levels, locally elected ST representatives and teachers are members of VECs (which include the ST members of the local village panchayat) and other user groups such as School Management Committee, PTAs, etc. In predominantly tribal areas, ST men and women will continue to be involved in community mobilization efforts which include enrolment drives village meetings etc. Traditional tribal organization and local leaders are often involved in these activities. Local approaches to community mobilization will continue to be used, such as tribal fairs and festivals to promote education, and traditional media and art forms for communication. Finally, there will be an emphasis on recruiting tribal para-teachers as well as on selection of tribal candidates to fill vacant teacher posts in formal schools. Teachers will also be consulted in the preparation of district plans.

For girls, under the NPEGEL programme, special focus will continue to be given to education of girls from ST communities. The scheme is targeted to educationally backward blocks where the level of rural female literacy is less than the national average and the gender gap is above the national average, as also in blocks that have at least 5% ST population and where the ST female literacy rate is below 10%. Kasturba Gandhi Balika Vidyalaya (KGBV) schools will continue to be provided for girls in educationally backward blocks, where a minimum of 75% girls enrolled are to be from ST, SC, OBC Minority Communities. A total 2180 KGBVs (Residential Schools for older girls) have been sanctioned in the country out of which 457 KGBVs are located in Scheduled Tribe concentrated blocks. Total enrolment in all KGB is 80853, of which 23298 are Scheduled Tribe girls which is 29% of the total enrolment. Budgets: Favorable Norms for Tribal Areas. Focused attention is being given to those districts with concentration of tribal population(above 50%), with plans and budget allocations ensuring that these districts get proportionately higher share in allocations for primary and upper primary schools, additional classrooms, teachers, interventions for out of school children and overall allocations under SSA, NPEGEL and KGBV. In 2006-07 Rs. 1527 crores were allocated for these 74 districts, which amounted to 7.5% of the total outlay for the program. In 2007-08 special tribal focus districts have increased to 106 and funding to them to Rs. 2679 cr. (13% of total outlay). In addition, provision of Rs. 15 lakhs is made to each district for special innovative activities to promote education for Scheduled Tribes, The innovative programme can include on

Enrolment and retention drives. Special camps and bridge courses. Setting up special models of Alternative Schools, Monitoring attendance, Remedial / coaching classes. Providing a congenial learning environment inside and outside the school. The implementation schedule for activities in tribal areas would follow the general implementation schedule for the programme as a whole. Activities are planned and implemented in the districts on an annual basis.

Monitoring and Evaluation in SSAII: While the monitoring process and systems will continue to operate as previously, the Results Framework for SSA II provides for enhanced monitoring of Special Focus Groups, including the progress of children from tribal communities. For each of the KPIs, the progress will be tracked on a disaggregated basis for each of the special focus groups. While in SSA I, the Results Framework focused on access and enrolment, in SSA II, this has broadened to include retention and education efficiency indicators and learning levels for each focus group. The Framework has also incorporated many process indicators which contribute to quality. The Development Partners will be monitoring the programme through bi-annual Joint Review Missions on the basis of the enclosed Results Framework. The GOI in turn will be monitoring and reviewing the progress of the states on the basis of the same framework. Third party evaluations are also built into the design of the Results Framework. Disclosure: The Tribal Development Plan will be disclosed on the Ministry of Human Resource Development website by September 5, 2007. The Project Approval Board (PAB) minutes are already on the web site. These clearly indicate the commitments to tribals and the provisions made for the special focus districts as well as the state interventions for tribal children funded from the Innovations grant of Rs 15 lakhs. 13.2 The country's Right to Information Act allows for any citizen to seek information on any issue from the government by paying a very small fee and the government is obliged to provide the information. At all levels officers are designated for this purpose. Community mobilization activities also contribute to creating community awareness. Excerpts from SSA Manual for Planning and Appraisal Planning process.

At the outset, it is pertinent to mention that a solid database and clear visioning are essential for planning. SSA envisages the bottom-up approach of planning instead of the top-down approach in a decentralized manner, as it reflects the reality at the grassroots level. The planning process has to be participatory in nature as this type of planning not only creates a sense of ownership among the stakeholders, but also creates awareness and helps in the capacity building of personnel at various levels. The plans developed through consultative meetings and interaction with the community and target groups, at various levels, reflect local specificity. It is necessary that there be documentation of the process of the preparation of plan to evidence the fact that they have been prepared at the habitation level through participatory planning mode. The following steps are an integral part of participatory planning. Interaction with community and target groups The bottom-up approach will not only help the planning team to acquaint themselves with various problems, but may also provide an insight to the possible solutions. The commonality of problems across such meetings will help the planning teams to propose interventions accordingly. Interaction with community and target groups has to be ensured by involvement of target groups and community leaders in the constitution of habitation, block and the district level teams on one hand and by mobilisation activities and extensive visits of planning teams to every habitation – rural and urban (including slums) on the other. Such interactions not only provide an opportunity to be familiar with the problems of target groups and help in devising strategies to deal with these, but also mould the opinions of communities with the help of the good offices of community leaders. Consultative meetings: The consultative meetings with the officials at block and district levels would facilitate the core teams in formulating strategies to address the problems. These meetings would also facilitate convergence among various schemes being implemented or proposed by different departments. As the responsibility of implementing the programme rests with the educational administration of the district, it is essential to involve them from the planning stage itself. Documentation of consultative meetings and community interaction would enable the persons at the district and state levels as well as the appraisal teams to know about planning processes.

Micro planning Exercises: Once the planning teams are in place and their capacity building has been undertaken, the micro-planning exercise should be undertaken after the collection of data from various sources. This data would be an indicator of the existing situation and reflect the position vis-à-vis the goals and targets of the programme. It may be ensured that this data is invariably used for planning purpose. This data would form the basis to identify district specific issues. Identifications of issues and interventions.

Once the consulting process has taken place at various levels highlighting the problems and issues, the next step is to identify the problems and needs in the light of educational and general information and studies that have been conducted earlier. The assessment of the educational situation will lead to the identification of problems, needs and constraints of elementary education in the district. The problems related to access, enrolment, retention and quality of education need to be identified and reflected in the District Elementary Education Plan. Target setting. In order to meet the SSA goal of UEE, it is important to achieve the basic objectives of universal access, universal enrolment, universal retention and universal achievement within the stipulated time period. Various states are at various levels in the field of education. Thus, it may be possible for some states or districts to achieve the SSA goals before the target dates. It may, therefore, be essential for districts to set their own targets within the overall timeframe of the programme. The targets have to be set realistically in a phased manner. There is a need to set dis-aggregated targets (preferably block wise) for disadvantageous and other groups on the basis of gender. Targets can vary from district to district and within a district, from block to block.

Sub-Mission will review the performance of states on education of disadvantaged groups including Girls, SC/ST/ Minorities/Urban Deprived Children and Disabled Children as delineated under framework for implementation of Sarva Shiksha Abhiyan suggest and facilitate capacity building exercises that may be state-specific or in the nature of cross-state sharing workshops to promote best practices. • facilitate Government and NGO partnership in promoting elementary education for disadvantaged groups. • prepare a half yearly report that would be discussed in the Executive Committee of the National Mission for SSA.(ii)Tasks of the Sub-Mission (a) Inclusive Education• Suggest models of service delivery on inclusive education, which could be adopted by State SSA Mission Societies• Assist in providing a resource base on IE for states that require such assistance Provide inputs on material available on inclusive education, which could be utililzed by State SSA Mission Societies. • Facilitate development of barrier free access in the schools for all kinds of CWSN• Identify good practices for documentation and dissemination • Monitor implementation of IE in States, in quantitative, qualitative and financial terms.

Urban Deprived Children (b) • distinctive planning for urban areas in the form of urban/city specific plans/sub plans• identifying good practices for ensuring good quality education for deprived urban children• suggest organisation of workshops and meetings to share good strategies for enrolment, monitoring and quality education for deprived urban children• specifically review the work in States/UTs for the most vulnerable groups of deprived urban children including street children, children of construction workers, children working in shops, dhabas etc.• facilitate coordination between SSA State Mission with Municipal Corporations/other urban local bodies and NGOs.(c)Minority (Muslim) Education• strategies for promoting universal access enrolment and retention of Muslim children, especially girls. • tracking progress in access to schooling at primary and upper primary levels in Muslim dominated districts/blocks. • support to Madarasa/Makhtabs for teaching formal curriculum. • sharing good practices for promoting education of Muslim children. • facilitate data collection and research on education of children (6-14) from Muslim community. (d)Education of SC/ST Children• tracking progress towards bridging of social gaps in enrolment of primary and upper primary levels. • tracking progress in access to primary and upper primary schools in ST/SC dominated districts/blocks. • identifying districts where social gap is high or not reducing and facilitating of intensification of response strategies in those areas. • identifying good practices for enrolment and retention of SC/ST children in difficult circumstances. • promoting conceptualization and implementation of appropriate activities under the innovative fund for SC/ST children. (e) Education of Girls• tracking progress towards achievement of gender parity in enrolment at primary and upper primary stages. • facilitating a gender perspective in all planning and implementation aspects of SSA. • Identify and promote good practices in the area of girls' education. promoting good practices under the innovative funds for education of girls• promoting convergence of ICDS and other State programmes with SSA and NPEGEL for ECCE.

---

* Extracted from a website. Resources give greater acknowledged.

17

Educational Life Style of Tribal Children: A Case Study of Yarava's of Karnataka

Yarava's(tribe) are found in southern part of the Karnatka Literacy figure in the tribal settlement is very meager. Ot of 169 individuals only 81 children are studying. Lack of schools near their settlement and parent's desire to make use of their children to supplement family income in the form of labour are the main reasons for the high percentage of illiteracy lin this tribal settlement.

Compared to the tribal settlement, literacy is better in the two village. There is one government primary school (started in the year 1963). Total strength of this school is 36 of which 23 are boys and rest are girls. The school has one big hall with some wooden seats without back support or legs. Because of the scarcity of furniture some students sit on the floor. All the 1st, 2nd, 3rd and 4th standard classes are taught in the same large room by a single teacher. Details of each class strength is shown in the following. Among the 36 students, seventeen (47.22%) students are in the 1st standard; twelve (70.58%) students are attending classes regularly, and rest are irregular. Eight (47.58) are boys and rest are girls.

In the second standard the total strength is seven (19.44%) of which six (85.71%) are attending classes regularly and only one (14.29%) is irregular. All the students are boys.

---

* Study has done in few selected hamlets of the Yarava tribes in Kodogu district of Karnataka.

In the third standard, the total strength is five, of which four (80%) are boys and rest are girls (20%). In the 4th standard the total strength is seven (19.44%) of which six (85.71%) are regular to the classes and rest (14.29%) is irregular. All are boys. Study shows that in both first and second standard girls are greater in number than the boys, but in the third and fourth standard only boys are found. Older girls are apparently retained at home for households chores or to be engaged in lucrative labour.

Apart from the school information, the following table shows the literacy figure of the Yaravas in the this village in detail.

Among the 60 literates fourty-one (68.33%) are under primary school category. Twenty-seven (65.85%) are males, fourteen (34.15%) are females. Ten (16.67%) come under middle school category. All ten (16.67%) are males. Seven (11.67%) come under high school category. All the seven (11.67%) are males. Only one (1.67%) person is in the category of pre university courses. He is also a male. In the category of under graduate degree course only one (1.67%) person is a male. On the whole we can see more than 80%) are illiterates and rest are literates.

Compared to the tribal and the rural settlement, literacy figure is more than 50% in the urban centre i.e., Mysore city. Out of 612 persons in the 100 households 361 (59%) are literates and the remaining 521 (41%) are illiterates. Literates are categorized into primary, middle, higher schools, pre-university, under-graduates, post-graduates, diplomas, doctors, engineers, etc. The number of persons in each category is shown in the data and 4.

Among 92 (15%) under the primary education, twenty one (3.25%) come under first standard category, eight (1.13%) are males and thirteen (2.12%) are females. Thirteen (2.12%) come under second standard category. Five (0.13%) are males and ten (1.62%) are females. Thirty eight (6.20%) come in the category of fourth standard. Nineteen (3.10%) are males and another nineteen (3.10%) are females.

Out of ninety-five (15.4%) under the middle school level, thirty one (5.07%) are under the fifth standard category, twenty (3.27%) are males and eleven (1.80%) are females. Twenty-two (3.59%) are under the sixth standard category. Ten (1.63%) are males and twelve (1.96%) are females. Forty two (3.86%) come under the seventh standard category; twenty two (3.59%) are males and twenty (3.27%) are females.

Out of the one hundred and seven (17.5%) under the high school category, twenty (3.27%) come under eighth standard category; fourteen (2.29%) are males and six (0.98%) are females. Twenty-one (3.43%) come under ninth standard category; nine (1.47%) are males and twelve (1.96%) are females. Sixty-six (10.78%) come under tenth standard category. Forty-five (7.35%) are males and twenty-one (3.43%) are females.

Among twenty six (4.2%) under the category of pre-university course twelve (1.96%) are males and fourteen (2.29%) are females. Our of twenty eight (4.7%) under the under graduate course category, twenty one 3.43%) are males and seven (1.14%) are females. Out of six (1%) under the diploma course category, five (0.82%) are males and one (0.16%) is female. Among three (0.5%) under the doctors course category, two (0.5%) under the doctors course category, two (0.33%) are males and only one (0.16%) is female. No one has come under the engineering course.

A list of questions was distributed to the students studying S.S.L.C.* or above to get information regarding their choice of the course, kind of educational benefits they were getting, why they chose the particular subject for study and how much time they devoted to studies and household work. They were also questioned what they intended to do after their education, how their families thought with regard to religion, and the parents' treatment of their children. Their opinion towards their status was sought and they were asked whether it was the effect of discrimination by their classmates. They were asked this question since they belonged to the lower caste. Many of them were earning along with studies. So, questions were asked whether they liked that profession and how much they contributed for the house, as also how much time they were spending for sports and other games.

They were asked about playground facilities in their localities, kind of sports they were interested, their hobbies, kinds of papers and magazines they used to read, kinds of movies they liked.

Out of the 40 students who responded to the questionnaires, ten (25%) students are studying in S.S.L.C., sixteen (40%) students are in the pre-university course, another 10(25%) students are under the category of under-graduate courses, and the remaining four (10%) students are studying in post-graduate course.

Regarding the educational benefits like scholarships, free ship and merit scholarship it was found that 30 students were getting the benefits and the remaining 10 students who were getting educational benefits one (3.3%) was getting a merit scholarship and eight (26.3%) were getting scheduled tribes scholarship. One (3.3%) student was getting backward tribe scholarships. Nineteen (63.3%) were getting freeship facilities and the other (3.3%) student was getting a scholarship but she did not answer the questions or specify the scholarship.

The question "Why did you choose the particular course and what are you studying now?" was not applicable to 10 (25%) students because they are doing their S.S.L.C. course. Among the remaining, 4 (10%) students responded that the course is relatively easy, for another 12(30%) students the course consists of their favorite subjects, for another 12 (30%) the course is helpful in getting jobs, two (5%) have answered that, since they could not get admissions to any other course, they choose the present course.

To the question "How much time were you devoting to studies," eight (20%) students answered one hour a day, eighteen (45%) students answered two hours a day. Three (7.5%) students answered that they devoted three hours each day, six (15%) students stated that they spent four hours perday. Remaining five 912.5%) students answered that they spent more than four hours daily.

Again to the question., "How much time did you devote to domestic duties Eveready", ten (25%) students answered one hour, seven (17.5%) students said that it was two hours, eight (20%) students answered that they devoted three hours each day. More than four hours were claimed to being devoted to domestic duty by ten (25%) students and to the remaining two (5%) students, the above question was not applicable as they were staying in a hostel.

To the question "after your college/education what do you intend to do?", thirteen (32.5%) students answered that they would start earning their livelihood. Twelve (30%) students answered that they would continue their studies. Six (15%) students answered that they would like to get married after their studies. Three (7.5%) students answered that they were interested in taking up professional training after education. The remaining six (15%) students future plan was uncertain.

To the question on "The occupation which you would like to choose after completion of your students", twenty two (55%) have not responded. Two (5%) were interested in working as mechanics. One (2.5%) expressed his interest to do busyness after lhis studies. Four (10%) have indicated their desire to become teachers. One (2.5%) seemed interested to take up social work. Five (12.5%) were interested in going for employment in banks. Three (7.5%) were interested in becoming doctors, one (2.5%) was interested in becoming an engineer. The remaining one (2.5%) was interested in becoming police officer.

To the question "how religious is your family", fourteen (35%) students stated that their families were very religious. Twentyfive (62.5%) students wrote that their families were quite religious, remaining one (2.5%) said that his family was somewhat religious.

To the question on "how much did the parents love their sons or daughters", twenty five students answered that their parents love both their daughters and sons equally. Among them fourteen (35%) were boys and eleven (27.5%) were girls. Ten students answered that their parents loved their sons more.

Among them six were girls (15%) and four (10%) were boys. Another four (10%) boys answered that their parents loved their daughters more; only one (2.5%) girl answered that her parents loved their daughter more.

To the question on their opinion regarding who was being preferred to whom, twenty nine (72.5%) students answered that girls should be treated on equal terms always with the boys in the family as well as outside. Four (10%) students opined that more preference should be given to boys, while two (5%) students stated that more preference should be given to girls. Remaining five (12.5%) students were uncertain.

Responding to the question "in your view a woman should not take up a job," fourteen (35%) students opined "Yes", remaining twenty six (65%) students answered "No", Answering question "In your view, should a woman be treated as an equal in assigning jobs like men," thirty five (87.5%) students answered "Yes", and the remaining five (12.5%) students answered "No".

Replaying to the question "who financed your education", though eleven students stated to be getting scholarship, three (7.5%) students were not getting any finance from their parents apart from the scholarship. Six (15%) students said it was through their own earning. Eight (20%) students answered that part of their expenditure was from scholarship. Remaining 23 (57.5%) students stated that they fully depended on their parents for financial support.

Among the 40 students, four (10%) are full time employees and two were earning occasionally, eight students' earning was from scheduled tribe scholarship, one student's earning was through merit scholarship. Only one student's earning was from backward tribe scholarship. Another student also earned through scholarship (kind of scholarship she was getting was not stated in the questionnaire).

Among the pursuing their studies along with jobs, 4 were working in government officers, and one in a private firm. Four students were regularly giving money to their parents. One was giving money only occasionally to his parents. Another one inspite of his earning did not give money to his parents at all.

Regarding their financial contribution to their family it was found that two (5%) students were contributing ¾ of their earning. A quarter of his earning was contributed by another student. Two students contributed their whole earnings. The other boy was earning but not contributing anything to his family. Earning in the form of scholarship was not contributed by any student.

Answering the question "How would you describe your financial position", three students said it was "satisfactory" and two mentioned it to be difficult, land the remaining one answered it was comfortable. Students who earned money in the form of scholarship also felt it to be satisfactory.

Replaying to the question "whether they were engaged in any other occupation before the one in which they are engaged now," three boys answered "Yes" and the remaining boys who were earning answered "No". Those who answered "Yes" were salesmen early. Answering the question "did they like their job/ employment?" five students answered "Yes" only one answered "No". The above question was not applied to the remaining students. Further, three boys stated "it is interesting" and one boy stated that it was not interesting. The other one stated "it is repetitie". Remaining one answered "it is tiresome". The above question was not applied to the remaining students, since they were not working anywhere.

Recreation in every family has great significance. In fact recreation is necessary to release the extra energy and to gain grater strength. It makes the remained fresh and hence is essential.

Absence of regular recreation facilities, limited spatial mobility to get recreation from the outside and the economic condition of the tribal and rural Yaravas forced them to find their own recreation.

Both the tribal and rural Yaravas are busy from morning till evening. Since the tribal and rural Yarava settlements are nucleated in character, it is easy for them to organize indoor and outdoor games.

Gossip is an important activity to spend their leisure time. Boys find recreation in playing cards, and smoking beedies. Once in a way they take part in drams staged in their settlement, which gives a lot of recreation for the whole settlement.

During the time of harvesting almost all are busy in singing and teasing each other. This makes them to forget the tedium of work. In urban situation. Yaravas are not so busy form morning. Thus their leisure time is not seasonal. After their fixed duty hours, they are free. Students also become free in the evening.

To find out how students are spending their leisure time, questionnaires were distributed to get the details. Their answers helped the researcher to analyze that urban Yarava's are enjoying all sorts of recreational facilities like the radio, Cinema, magazines and sports like cricket, volley-ball, throw-ball, hockey, badminton, and kno-kno.

Apart from their earning, questions were asked about the interest they evinced in the field of sports. Responding to the question "How many hours have you allotted in your time table for games and sports"? twenty four (60%) students answered one hour each day. Twelve (30%) students stated two hours; two (5%) students claimed that they had earmarked three hours daily. Remaining two (5%) students spent more than three hours every day.

Replaying to the question "which of the following indoor games do you play?" Eight (20%) students answered "Yes" with reference to the fame "Sanake and Ladder" and the remaining thirty two students answered "No", as regards the same game. About chess, eight (20%) students replied in the affirmative and the remaining thirty two (80%) said "No". As to table tennis, twelve (20%) students answered "Yes" and the remaining twenty eight (70%) students answered "No". About carom board, thirty one (77.5%) students calimed that they played this game and the remaining nine (22.5%) students stated that they did not. The game of cards was played by twelve (30%) students.

Remaining twenty eight (70%) students did not play game of cards.

Responding to the question "which of the following outdoor game do you play", ten (25%) students answered "Yes" with reference to "Volley ball" and the remaining 30 (75%) students stated "No". Throw ball is played by twelve (30%) students and the other 28 (70%) students do not play this game at all. Hockey is played by three (7.5%) students do not play this game at all. The game Kho-Kho is played by eleven (27.5%) students. It is not played by the remaining twenty nine (72.5%) students. Only ten (25%) students play Badminton and the remaining thirty (75%) students do not play the above game. Cricket is played by thirteen (32.5%) (67.5%) students do not play the above game. Khabbadi is played by sixteen (40%) students and the remaining twenty four (60%) students do not play this fame.

Answering the question, "Do you have adequate playground for games and sports in your locality?" Twenty three (57.5%) students answered "Yes", the remaining seventeen (42.5%) students stated "No".

Answering the question "Did you participate in the following sports?" three (7.5%) students stated they participated in the district level sports. Five (12.5%) students stated that they had participated in the state level sports. Six (15%) students had participated in the "Dasara" sports. Eleven (27.5%) of the students had participated in the divisional level sports. The remaining fifteen (37.5%) students did not participate in any of the above sports.

Eleven (27.5%) students did not respond to the question on hobbies. One (2.5%) students answered that his hobby was to see imported cars and motor cycle magazines; another (2.5%) students stated that his hobby was painting. Fifteen (37.5%) students stated that they had "no hobbies", two (5%) students had the hobby of collecting cassette records, one (2.5%) students is philatelists and numatist. Reading is the hobby of two (5%) students. Another one (2.5%) student has the habit of drawing and reading fiction. Maintaining pen pals and collecting novels in the habit of another one (2.5%) student. Swimming is the hobby of another (2.5%) students. Painting and singing are the hobby of another (2.5%) student.

Responding to the question "Do you read newspapers daily?" Thirty six (90%) students answered "Yes", remaining four (10%ZZ) students have no habit of reading newspapers daily. Again to the question "Do you listen to radio regularly"? thirty nine (97.5%) students answered in the affirmative and the remaining one (2.5%) student does not listen to the radio daily.

Answering to the question "whether they participated in drama/debated/ music competition", eight (20%) students answer that they did participate in dramas. Two (5%) students participated in debates and four (10%) students participated in music. Only one (2.5%) students participated both in drama and debate. Four (10%) students participated both in drama and music. Twenty one (52.5%) students do not participate in any of the above competitions.

When asked about the kind of magazine they read, nineteen (47.5%) students stated that they read popular magazines like Sudha (kannada weekly), Prajamatha (Kannada weekly) and The Illustrated Weekly of India (English). Magazines that deal with religious issues are read by ten (25%) students. Thirty (75%) students do not read this kind of magazine. "Romantic" kind of magazine that deal with youthful love is read by nineteen (47.5%) students and the remaining twenty one (52.5%) students do not read such magazines historical magazines; for the remaining twenty two (55%) students it offers no attraction. Magazines with detective fiction is interesting to sixteen (40%) students but the thrillers offer no entertainment to the remaining twentyfour (60%) students. Film magazines are interesting to nineteen (47.5%) students and the remaining twenty one (52.5%) students do not read periodicals that deal with films and film personalities.

To the question, "do you write articles?" only three (7.5%) students answered "Yes" and the remaining thritys even (92.5%) students replied in the negative.

The last question was with regard to their attitude towards watching movies. Sixteen (40%) students stated that they loved movies with social themes and the remaining twenty four (60%) students were averse to seeing any kind of motion picture. Films with love themes are interesting to twenty (50%) students and the remaining are not interested in seeing above kind of films. Suspense films and thrillers are interesting to twenty there (57.5%) students and the remaining seventeen (42.5%) students are niot interested in this type of films. Films. Films with religious themes are interesting to twelve (30%) students and the other twenty two (70%) students are not interested in such films. Fifteen (37.5%) students are interested in watching historical films but twenty five (62.5%) students are not interested in seeing them. Films of lkpure humor and slap-stick are interesting to twenty one (52.5%) students, but such films of comic entertainment are not interesting to the remaining nineteen (47.5%) students.

The above data clearly shows about Educational life style of the Yarava children.

18

Tribal Education: A Frame work for Research, Monitor and Interventions

One of the weakest link in the chain is strong existence of caste system in the Indian society. Caste is a foundation stone of the Indian society. Without understanding the caste no one can properly understood the Hindu society and social institutions. Experts of the opinion that Varnas are the basic reasons for the existence of complex caste system in India. Brahmins have got first place in the social stratification of the Hindu law and Sudras have got a last place. These people have now recognized as SC under the Indian constitution. They represent 17.5 per cent of the total population of India

Education has limited connotation. It is largely concerned with the existing formal structure of education and the institutionalized methodology of imparting knowledge to individuals. Within this very system exist many sub-groups of individuals with specific needs and tribals are one of them. In fact tribals form a large group of individuals in the Indian society. For several historical, economic and social reasons the scheduled groups have remained economically backward and socially retarded even to this day. The ST population accounts for 8.6% of the total population of the country. There are many constitutional provisions and legislative support available for safeguarding the welfare and the interests of STs. In addition

* This paper based a National Workshop held in New Delhi on Tribal during 1995-96.

planned developmental efforts have also taken place through Five-Year plans. Despite the concern reflected in the Indian Constitution and the developmental efforts initiated for the welfare and the development of STs., their socio-economic and political development is still far below the others and therefore much more needs to be done in this direction, including their empowerment – educational, social, economic and political – with due regard to their special identity – culturally, habitation ally, traditionally – and in terms of the tribals' age-old rights and customs. The number of educational institutions in 1978, together with the number of pupils within the area covered by the plans for tribal development, is shown. The boarders accommodated in hostels were also given special coaching. The number of teachers in ashram schools were 1,171, and the number of teachers employed in primary, upper primary and high schools was 1,821. The number of students in receipt of post-matric scholarships was 1,950, 468 tribal students were admitted to reputable private schools and public schools, and 90 students were enrolled in the special residential school for tribals.

Suggested Action Plan under National Component

An action plan of national intervention for supporting the Statestrategies for tribal education in the gap areas identified in this seminaris suggested. The action plan can broadly be divided into:• Guidance in Policy Framing and Planning. •Capacity Building.• Pedagogic Intervention. •Monitoring and Evaluation. •Networking and Research.• Advisory and • Clearing-house role.

Guidance in Policy Framing and Planning

Since there is a need for flexible, desegregated area and group specific micro-level planning for tribal education an attempt imposing uniform pattern of planning by State strategies should not be discouraged by the national component. A gender component is missing from the State as well as national component for tribal education. Keeping in mind the wide gap between the literacy levels of tribal males and tribal females, the plan strategies for tribal education have to be further decentralized on the lines of gender both at State as well as district level. The national component along with evolving its own strategies should also guide the State strategies in this regard.

Capacity Building:

What the workshop made evident is that enormous help is needed to be extended to the State/district components of tribal education in capacity building. The national component should create orientation of capacity building at every level and impart training to the concerned persons to develop capacity at State / district / block level. The capacity building is the first step that should precede intervention programme so that the efforts are sustained and monitored in the right direction. The feasible approaches that could be part of national component for developing capacity at National/State/District/Block/Culture level are listed below. Identification and Training of Resource Group/ Persons Identification of resource group /persons and organising regular workshops with them at national and regional levels, in a constant effort to develop an understanding of the commonalities as well as the diversities of the problems of tribal education and chalking out more effective programmes to further the process would be the first activity that the national component should take up to build up capacity at State/district/block levels. The national component should have a national level core group exclusively for tribal education which will not only guide the State component in constituting the State core group for tribal education, but will also provide expert services to the State core group on different aspects of tribal education. Similar groups can be formed at district and block levels and the State component can provide training and guidance to district and block level core groups. The target group for training with central assistance is identified as consisting of:i)Members of State/District/Block/ Cluster level Core Group for Tribal Education. ii) State and district level administrators from Education as wellas Welfare Department.iii) Teacher Trainers i.e. persons from State and district level training and resource centres.iv) VEC/MTA/PTA members. The national component would assist the State in designing the training content (tribal culture specific information, items also on re-orientation), as well as developing modules for importing training to various target groups. The modules for teacher trainer, teacher and administrative officers should be different depending on the areas where these respective groups need to be trained or oriented.

Designing Teacher Training Modules

The national core group should assist the State core group in developing the training modules for teacher trainers as well as the teachers. The training modules should lay emphasis on the MLLs, activity based and child-centered teaching methods, and creation and use of tribal context specific teaching-learning materials. Besides, section of the training module for teacher trainers/teachers should also contain information on the following:i)Tribal specific culture.ii)Items on re-orienting the teachers towards tribals as a social group - placing emphasis on understanding tribal psychology .iii) Providing facts on grossly incorrect popularbeliefs about tribal children such as misconceptions about their low IQ.iv) Tribal ways of learning - i.e. use of more participatory and oral method in classroom teaching. Module on Multi-Grade Teaching Either a separate module can be developed with central assistance or a section on this can be included in the general module for training of teachers. However, it was realised that an overloaded training programme with an array of information might be detrimental to its objectives and thus there is a need to break the envisaged curriculum into parts and conduct separate training programmes over a year or two. However the training programme should begin with special orientation programmes in tribal areas. The details ofteacher training programme have already been chalked out from a National Sharing Workshop on "Teacher-Training" held in November, 1995 in New Delhi under the national strategies. The findings of this workshop can be re-designed taking into consideration the special needs of tribal children as well as tribal teachers.

Community Awareness Modules:

National component should help the State component in developing community participation modules for VEC/PT/MTA members. These modules should not only contain information on need and relevance of tribal and girl education but also on aspects like planning, administrative, and evaluation processes and the accountability of the school education even to bodies like VEC/PTAs. Once these bodies are empowered, they will be more demanding which will have an indirect supervisory control on the effective functioning of schools. As a result a real kind of participatory management process will emerge at the grass root level which will help in sustaining these educational efforts. Role of NGOs: The role of NGOs and allied groups such as traditional tribal systems like Guru-kulas in Karnataka, local tribal youth training groups, VECs etc. Can be multiple; they can help create a demand for education so that it becomes need based and is not thrust upon the tribals. These non-government and local bodies/groups can be used as an entry point to make inroads into the more difficult tribal groups so that their children come for education. They can assist in local based training, environment building, help in giving feedback about the teaching-learning material so that it becomes local knowledge based and local language based. Good projects sometimes fail because o lack of community acceptance. These groups can also help in identifying the actual issues with regards to reducibility of tribal children. In the area of retention, the NGO can help monitor attendance by putting one youth responsible for 10 children and checking drop-outs by checking quarterly and half-yearly charts. They can encourage the girl child by providing a room for younger siblings who are in their care and can help in developing quality performance infrastructure for teachers and students. Hence the national component can emphasize the role of NGOs and give the management of DPEP in cluster, to specific NGOs on an experimental basis - may be to one or two NGOs per State. The NGOs hould be asked to create alternatives. The national component can also have a national level NGO forum for preparing tribal areas specific training modules.

Pedagogic Intervention:

The tribal children were found to have difficulty in following the classroom teaching in the regional language in the initial school years. The problem was found to be more acute among the tribes who live in the geographically difficult areas and as a result have little or no exposure to regional language and the dominant culture outside their tribe Therefore, there is a need to prepare primers in tribal dialect on a priority basis to help such children at the initial stages of primary education. The national component was expected to help the States to develop mechanism to identify such tribal groups and to develop bilingual primers, supplementary reading material in tribal dialect, teacher's guide, etc. The national component should formulate a pedagogy unit specially for rendering expert service or training to the State / district level resource persons in developing these bi-lingual primers and supplementary reading material in tribal dialect. Besides, the non-contextually of the course curriculum has long been debated by educationist. The national component should provide the training to the district resource persons in identifying the course content which are incomprehensible and irrelevant for the tribal children and bring in changes by picking up examples from tribal cultures so that the desired concepts can be attained by the tribal children. The national component should also include training of teacher trainers and other resource persons in tribal dialect and languages. The national component can create an expert committee of linguists to help meet the specific needs of State / district strategies. Moreover, there is a need to evolve a clearer understanding of the specific needs of tribal children as well of concepts like activity-based child centered teaching-learning materials, textbooks having scope for local specificity, thereby promoting joyful learning among tribal children at all levels. The desirable approaches that could be part of the national strategy are listed below: (1) Identification and Training of Resource;

Persons, (2) Identification of resource persons which might include linguists, teachers, tribal experts, etc. as well as institutions such as TRIs, RIEs and SCERT for capacity building and organizing regular workshops with them at national and regional levels to identify the issues in developing textbooks for tribal children (such as inclusion of tribal specific content, making the textbooks child-centred and activity-based, promoting joyful learning, etc) and the need for adopting multiple methods in different combination (as per the requirements) for furthering the process. An assessment has to be made with regard to the training requirement of the resource persons or institutions at State levels who would be responsible for training and guiding the actual persons involved in developing the textbooks and supplementary teaching-learning material in tribal dialect. Broad basing Resource Network The national component can facilitate networking between DPEP efforts, and the efforts made by institutions (such as TRIs, RIEs, University Departments), NGOs and individuals to further the efforts made in development of relevant pedagogy for tribal children. National seminars can offer a platform to share and integrate thedisjointed efforts made by different resource groups/institutions and individuals on issues like:-•Development of bias-free local languages specific books.• Inclusion of tribal specific content. •Making these books competency-based. •Involving psycho-linguists, teachers, artists, NGOs, tribal experts etc. in textbook development.•Intensive orientation and sensitization of textbook writing teams, etc. and trailling and finalizing the textbooks. Technical Workshops and Regional Expositions The national resource group for tribal education would organize technical workshops on issues such as productions, specialists editing of textbooks, criterion for assessment of textbook contents, trailing of textbooks developed for tribal children, etc. Local fair can be organized to extract the tribal culture specific content that could be included in the textbooks.

Monitoring and Evaluation:

The national component on monitoring and supervision of the implementation of DPEP should treat tribal education as a special component. The experts associated with monitoring should be oriented to special aspects related to tribal education. Besides general monitoring, regular feedback from the State should be sought by the national component for monitoring the progress of special programmes of tribal education. The tools and strategies for evaluation of these special programmes would be developed taking into account the common and diverse education problems of tribal children.

The national component should seek periodical reports and review meetings from the State with regard to tribal education. Besides, the national component should train the concerned State/district/block level officials in monitoring and evaluating tribal education.

Networking and Research

It might be possible for the national component to facilitate networking through inventories of institutions, NGOs and individuals who can help. An effort to link DPEP efforts with universities and research institutions might also be undertaken. Networking national/state/district/block level efforts is necessary as tribal education needs different types of researches as a feed-back to plan programmes and policies to suit local needs and help in mid-term corrections of programmes. The research findings would be exchanged and shared among different States in order to gain from each other experiences. This requires coordination at the national level so that dissemination of information among the different States can take place; for example, different activities that are taking place in Assam can be disseminated to Kerala. There is a need to evolve a clearer understanding of the specific need so tribal children as well of concepts like activity-based child centered teaching-learning materials, textbooks having scope for local specificity, thereby promoting joy full earning among tribal children at all levels.

Advisor Role: Another supporting strategy under national component on tribal education would be advisory role of providing guidance and assistance for planning, implementation, monitoring and training related to tribal education programmes. The State can look up to national core group for advice on any aspect of tribal education either in planning and implementation or curriculum development or on any such related work.

Clearing House

The role of clearing house at national level will be documentation, collection and dissemination of research findings, innovations and information on other aspects of tribal education from different district/State, national and international agencies. The national component should provide a platform for cross-fertilization of ideas through organization of seminars and workshop. Workshops can be organized on themes which need to be immediately addressed by both national and state component in order to speed up the spread of UPE among tribals in DPEP States.

Conclusion

The National Strategies for tribal education under DPEP are an out come of various exercises. The workshop held on 19-20 March 1996 is one among them. The significance of the present exercise lies in the fact that the national strategy was evolved from the respective States expectations on the problems they faced in tribal education while implementing the programme. Besides, these kinds of exercises might help the national component to address more systematically the emerging needs of new DPEP districts/States. Moreover, this workshop has hopefully benefited the State/district strategies by making the national component more transparent and clearly spelled out.

In most of the Indian states there is no office or department is created exclusively to handle tribal education. The National authority should take notice of this and suggest a review of the State policy in the light of this. Providing expertise and developing capacity at State/ district levels to develop modules for training and orienting teachers in tribal culture and tribal dialect. National intervention is needed for development of Tribal learning material. The National component can provide expert help from NCERT or other language institutes for developing books and curriculum at State level within objective of providing "joyful learning" to the tribal children. Slow growth of education among tribals in many Indian states is due to small and scattered habitations over vast hilly terrain, inadequate cooperation among different departments like TWD, Forest Department, Panchayat, etc., involvement of tribal children in agriculture and household work, lack of parental motivation in enrolling children in schools, etc. The State/district strategies aimed at increasing intervention in the area of improving access, environment building, capacity building and empowering Vocation Learning Centers and Continuing Education Centers. etc. Alternative model of schooling should be adopted in all the tribal blocks under DPEP in order to improve access to schools. Motivating tribal parents through social awareness camping with the help of tribal NCC students of schools and colleges are also planned to reach out to the more difficult school age tribal children. Conducting a survey on migratory pattern of parents and starting of residential schools to retain the children whose parents seasonally migrate/or issuing certificates which are valid for continuing classes in new schools are suggested to help in bringing these other wise difficult to reach school age tribal children back in to the mainstream of education. It has increasingly been realised by the State/district strategies that empowering the teacher to buy teaching-learning materials worth Rs.500/-. orienting teachers to motivate tribal children towards formal education, monitoring effectively the existing welfare schemes and strengthening community participation will help in improving retention and learning achievements among tribal children. Intervention programmes have begun in this direction. With regard to the problem of medium of instruction in few states like Tamil Nadu have maintained that preparing tribal language linker is not necessary for the reason that almost all the tribals can speak and understand the regional language i.e. Tamil. However, the resource persons are not in agreement. Besides, the State was also silent about changes in the curriculum in the direction mentioned by other State teams however, added a few more points such as providing escort services with the help of MTCs as an innovation of DPEP, appointment and provision of special coaching for the tribal teachers recruited from the local areas, etc. Developing textbooks with crucial emphasis on socio-cultural milieu of the tribals and providing tribal culture specific in-service training to teachers and orientation programme to administrators etc. are the other interventions planned in the State

Further study has pointed out various lacunas in the education policy of most of the Indian states and expressed concern that the inter-tribal and intra-tribal disparities are not sufficiently reflected in the States component of tribal education. Hence National policies should assist the State component in re-orienting the community participation modules to make it more effective. •The Gender component of tribal education is not adequately addressed. National strategy should address this issue immediately. • States requires help from the national strategies for formulating training cells to motivate and improve the caliber of tribal teachers. National component also needs to provide expert services in developing training/ orientation module for the members of VLC/MTC and ECC. •The national component needs to remind the State component regarding the objective of utmost decentralizing of the planning processes and addressing the inter and intra-tribal and gender disparities at all stages of plan processes.

Tribal scenario in case of India seemed to have some unique features which need to be adequately addressed by the respective State as well as the national component of tribal education while planning for primary education. Negative parental attitude to education, lack of interest and motivation among teachers to problems of tribal children, lack of community participation, and language incomprehensibility are the major hurdles in spreading education among tribal children. The strategies for tribal education under DPEP include interventions in areas like increasing access to education, retaining tribal children in the school up to class V and in capacity building.

Conducting various camps to increase the awareness by using songs, skits, slogans, films and printed material developed mainly in local languages using existing structures like tribal bazaars and fairs for conducting intensive outreach campaigns to motivate tribals towards education, involving education in tribal pockets, adopting soft strategies to enter the tribal dominated tea estates and giving priorities to tribal areas must be undertaken for increasing accessibility of education to tribal children. The textbooks developed in little tribal language are in the final stages. The State strategy team should also plan to prepare teacher-training material in required language on priority basis. State strategy places equal emphasis on capacity building.

19

Trends in Voluntarism in Tribal Development in India

My emphasis is much more on voluntarism than on voluntary organizations as instruments of social change. I do not disregard the niches that market forces and state and public agencies leave unfilled, but I argue that these niches can be filled not only by their third sector or voluntary organizations but by the "developmental deviants" or "entrepreneurs" or "volunteers." These volunteers, while remaining in the mainstream public or market organizations, can create new alignments between social needs and institutional support. The excessive attention on voluntary organizations by aid agencies seems misplaced insofar as these agencies almost completely neglect the DVs.

By supporting only NGOs, agencies reduce pressure on public and market agencies for reform and self-renewal. NGOs led by managers or leaders who are often from an urban context, by their own creativity, suppress or fail to nurture the creativity of the local disadvantaged. Social change thus becomes more and more dependent on external leaders.

Tribal development as part of social change is defined here as a process of expanding the decision-making horizon and extending the time frame for appraising investment and consumption choices by tribal disadvantaged people collectively, and not necessarily at the village level but at even higher levels of aggregation.

Sustainable processes will require correspondence between people's *access* to resources, *ability* to convert access into investments (that is, skills for using resources), and *assurance* of future returns from present investment (vertical assurance) and about others' behaviour vis-à-vis one's own (horizontal assurance or collective rationality). The changes in the network of access, ability, and assurance for DVs and the people have to be achieved simultaneously.

Voluntarism may affect any one or more subsets of the developmental triangle of access, assurance, and ability of the people and thus may remain restricted in its impact. The propositions that follow deal with the way that voluntarism has been related to the process of social change in India. Given the range of experiences, it is indeed a synoptic account.

Process of Voluntarism

1. Voluntarism triggered by a natural crisis such as flood, drought, or cyclone may legitimize the entry of outsiders in a given region, but depending upon the mobilization process, NGOs that emerge in response to such crises often diversify into other areas of social development and remain community oriented rather than class oriented.

Several church-based NGOs came into existence when international aid agencies offered relief at the time of the Bihar famine in the 1960s. Most of the relief was in the form of consumables such as foodstuffs, clothes, and medicine. The organizational structure for the distribution of this aid was different from the structure for managing durable assets such as rigs for drilling wells, transportation, and buildings. The move from relief to reconstruction attracted many young people. Instead of going back to pursue their professional careers, they remained behind to organize people, manage food for work programs, drill wells, or provide health and education facilities.

Many aid agencies sought legitimacy through relief but subsequently indulged in other interventions. The reaction of state agencies was to incorporate such volunteers or voluntary organizations as appendages of public relief and development programs. Such incorporation also took place in many NGOs, which came into the picture much later. An interesting feature of these organizations was that having begun with a community approach (relief was needed by all), they continued to use an eclectic approach to development.

Social conflicts were merely noted by some and participated in by others. The institutionalization of voluntarism in intermediary support or funding organizations or grass-roots organizations gave a techno-managerial start to the intervention strategies. A negative feature of such aid was that in regions prone to frequent natural calamities, people started losing their self-help initiative. State relief in the form of employment or food was not linked with a mobilization of voluntarism among the people. Dependency so created made the task of many radical NGOs even more difficult. People could not understand why mobilization around a radical ideology should be a reason for forging immediate material benefits.

2. *Voluntarism triggered by man-made disasters such as the Bhopal tragedy* can *get caught in the dilemma of legitimizing the state's indifference by becoming part of urgent relief and rehabilitation vis-à-vis questioning the basis of the tragedy and the complicity of the state in its consequences.*

(Gupta,2005)

Ravi Rajan (1988) while analyzing rehabilitation and voluntarism, observed four distinct styles: (1) intervening organization took on the provision of relief and rehabilitation as its primary task, became dependent on the government, and with the diminution in the governments' own commitment to the cause, soon collapsed; (2) volunteers served as "conscience keepers," pursuing change through systematic research reports; (3) trade union activists demanded charge of the industrial plant to provide employment through alternative use of plant and machinery; and (4) perhaps the most significant strategy by volunteers was to reject the idea of voluntarism as propounded by the state. Rather, voluntarism was redefined to include sustained mobilization the struggle for better relief, access to medical data, questioning the scretiveness of the part of the government, legal activism and questioning the right of the government to give such a low priority to the life of the poor. Voluntarism of this nature is difficult to mobilize in backward tribal areas given the dispersed nature of settlements and weak social articulation, low media attention, and poor networking among interventionists.

> 3. *Voluntarism as manifested in the 1960s by a protest against agrarian disparities (in the form of a violent leftist movement, known as the naxalite movement) and by social reconstruction (initiatives by students, professionals in the mainstream organizations, and voluntary organizations) has undergone a sea of change in the wake of recent economic liberalization.*
> (Ranjan, 2001)

Radical groups using violent means of social change have sought support essentially from Maoist philosophy. After the Chinese aggression in 1962, covert support to these groups increased, and income disparities intensified after the first phase of the green revolution. Technological change had provided the spur for a large number of young people, particularly from West Bengal and Andhra Pradesh, to plunge into the field of violent social change. The attempt was to annihilate rich farmers and other symbols of perceived oppressive classes or those considered class enemies.

Another stream of volunteers who entered the field of tribal development came with innovative ideas for providing relief during the 1964-1966 drought in different parts of the country. These volunteers became crucial instruments of social dynamics. The war in 1965 with a neighboring country led to a slowing down of U.S. aid to India. The search for indigenous alternatives became intense, and the legitimacy of voluntarism increased.

The period between 1966 and 1972 was full of economic crises. The economic environment in the preceding decade had been aimed at the closure of the Indian economy through import substitution. Droughts, wars (1965, 1971) devaluation of currency, and inflationary pressure created an environment of social unrest in the organized and unorganized sectors. Death from starvation was supposed to have been eliminated (almost) after the drought of 1965-1967. Maharashtra state started an employment guarantee scheme during the drought of 1972. In the wake of large-scale violence in 1966 and 1967 by left-wing radical groups, the report of a confidential inquiry committee by a committed civil servant (Appu) set up by the Home Ministry argued for an immediate thrust toward target group oriented programs of tribal development suited to location or ecology and class-specific need.

The Small and Marginal Farmer and Agricultural Labourer Development agencies, the Drought-Prone Area Programme, and the Tribal Development and Hill Area Development plans followed. Decentralized development in the policy was accompanied by greater political centralization from 1970 to 1977. A movement based on Gandhian values that called for total social revolution was spearheaded by Jaya Prakash Narayan in 1973 and 1974. It attracted a large number of young people, particularly in Gujarat, Bihar, and Maharashtra, and many of these young people continued with voluntary work.

The government declared a state of emergency from 1975 until 1977, after a prolonged railway strike, and even urban people realized for the first time the implications of a non-democratic coercive state. Voluntarism was also sought out as a sign of despicable deviance. People has the option of being incorporated into the repressive state structure or being jailed or victimized. The post-1977 phase of change in political continuity through the single-party rule brought many Gandhians committed to decentralized development into the mainstream. Tax concessions for voluntary initiatives by commercial companies were introduced for the first time by the Janata government in 1978, and many innovative organizations came into being. A number of developmental volunteers who worked in commercial organizations found this an opportunity for exploring new organizational space. Some misused this option but many did not.

For the first time, professionals and young activists were offered competitive salaries in addition to autonomy for work unheard of in mainstream organization by and large. These events were also accompanied by a change in the policy of international aid agencies, which started shifting from funding better implementation of government programs bureaucratically to better implementation by NGOs. It was unfortunate that creative avenues in the NGOs. It was unfortunate that creative avenues in the NGOs got generally fossilized because of their proximity to the state and their participation in implementing standardized programs.

A change of government in 1980 and the restoration of rule by the Congress party led to the expected withdrawal of tax concessions; the centralization of voluntarism (companies could contribute to the Prime Minister's fund for tribal development and seek fresh grants from it for action programmes); the halting of the direct transfer of funds from a commecial balancel sheet to the social (less easy to account) balance sheet; the standardization of developmental programs such as the Integrated Tribal Development Programme (IRDP); the withdrawal of higher allocations to the IRDP for backward areas and putting them on par with other areas; and the merger of earlier adaptive or responsive programs into a standardized IRDP, with credit-linked subsidy as the dominant mode of relationship.

Another interesting development was the return of naxalite (radical Maoist leftists) underground workers to the mainstream was non-violent but articulate strategists of social change. For the first time, several ex-naxalites sought election in 1977 and some were elected.

The social space for alternative development was filled by volunteers with varying backgrounds, ex-radicals, liberal or social democrats who were dissatisfied with the workings of the state and wanted to influence the distribution of resources. Enthusiastic urban activists who after looking for a career, failed to get one and returned to a mainstream profession rather quickly; young professionals with technical or other disciplinary backgrounds who launched action-research projects or supported other professional groups, retired civil servants, ex-Gandhians, lawyers, and so on, who formed independently or with the support of aid agencies large NGOs; and quasi-state organizations promoted to provide technical, financial, marketing, or other support to NGOs, artisans, and other beneficiaries of state-sponsored developmental programs.

At the time when social space for volunteers was widening, opportunities for career growth in mainstream organizations also begin to increase. The first phase involved the growth of the banking sector after nationalization in 1969. A large number of bright young men and women with backgrounds in science, the humanities, or engineering joined banks, insurance corporations, and other such systems. "Brain drift" as opposed to "brain drain" took a heavy toll by depriving academic disciplines of bright students and luring some professionals on the margin away from other direct social development systems. (Raiha, 2006)

The post-1980 boom in the consumer goods industry and the continued growth of banking and other public and private ventures further increased the flow of young people toward such careers. The opportunity cost of those who chose to work in NGOs did indeed increase.

The question we want to address next is "What are the processes by which voluntarism in mainstream organizations can complement the efforts of NGOs not merely in bringing about social change on the micro-level but also in influencing public policy in favor of the disadvantaged?"

Implications for Action and Research

Generating extra-organizational space for developmental volunteers within mainstream organizations is a necessary condition for sustainable social development. One study on bank and NGO cooperation for poverty alleviation in backward regions noted that there was no NGO working in the fifty most backward sub-regions of Gujarat. State organizations like the National Bank could not gain credibility in supporting NGOs if they did not provide the opportunity for exploration and experimentation to volunteers within their system. NGOs often did not recover even the operating costs of many services from people. In the process, such NGOs remained perpetually dependent upon aid agencies. Moreover, accountability of the NGOs in regard to the poor was so low that most NGOs did not aim at inducting poor people into their own management structures.

One nationalized bank invited its clerks to volunteer for two years in a village development program in an area of their choice without any loss of seniority upon their return. This triggered numerous innovative experiments by DVs.

The hands of DVs in technology generation, adaptation and diffusion system working on unpopular problems of larger social concern needed just as much attention. How can professionals who disregard professional rewards and devote attention to such problems but cannot put pressure for reform on their own organizations be sustained? Empowering them will require recognition of their voluntarism by a body of concerned scholars and activists. No national award has been given to date to any bank officer for initiating innovative schemes. So much so that about ten million rupees for new innovative schemes for tribal development provided at the national level remained unspent because no system existed for identifying and recognizing DVs within the mainstream system.

Can the capacity of urban people to manage their own affairs be provided by urban volunteers who come from very different cultures? The poor do not cooperate with developmental organizations because they are not recognized as possessing any *richness* in terms of their cultural and moral fiber. The findings of our research are seldom shared with those from whom we collect data (Gupta, 1987a, 1987b). Involving the tribal poor as co-researchers of social phenomena, building upon cultural roots of voluntarism, and showing respect for common property institutions can change this situation. Acknowledging local initiatives can spur their transformation into innovations. Documenting people's knowledge and identifying the scientific merit of some sustainable resource management alternatives can rekindle people's experimental ethic.

Institution building requires the dispensability of external leadership, the recognition of an inverse relationship between status and skills and the discrediting of values that generate helplessness. "Lateral learning" among developmental volunteers and NGOs can be triggered to provide empirical basis for building a "theory in and of" action.

Concepts of voluntarism such as zakat among Muslims, gupt dan (anonymous charity) among Hindus, Kar Seva (voluntary labour for the common good) among Sikhs, and so on, are examples of the positive bases on which different religions build organic institutions. Different languages have words like *andi* (Haryanavi) and *dhuni* (Hindi), implying a person obsessed with ideas generally for the social good. Why has appreciation for this trait vanished? Anonymous voluntarism, a unique and long-standing tradition of the east, has been absorbed by voluntary organizations that believe that voluntarism can only exist in their types of organizations. This vision is limited, because it denies the possibility of institutionalizing culture throughout a full range of institutions, not just voluntary organizations.

Finally, neither NGOs nor the developmental volunteers can succeed unless those long-ingrained values that inhibit change among tribal poor people are brought into question.

Voluntarism in tribal development in India has not been accompanied by pressure for policy change except in regard to environmental issues. Often action at the local level has not been linked with lobbying at the macro level. Recognizing that the state and markets perform better if kept under constant check, developmental volunteers within the organizations will have to serve a sort of "insurgent" function so as to align, anonymously, with grass-root activists, NGOs and professionals. International agencies can strengthen local social change by broadening local ideas and innovations into global thinking and by providing global space for developmental volunteers to validate their hypotheses. Right Livelihood awards constitute one such source of international recognition. If the tribal poor of India could communicate with the homeless in America, surely the cultures of deprivation would provide the basis for collection action. Social innovators and DVs around the world are struggling for similar space in a society where one does not have to go through a phase of unbridled accumulation followed by guilt, charity, and benevolence for the have-nots.

Sustainability in nature and society requires players, whistle blowers, spectator rules and creative chaos. DVs are arguing that the losers in a game should not lose the right to play on the same field again. Asking them to play only on separate fields (in the form of volags) will eventually rob the game of the chaotic waves of sorrow and joy. Should we let it convert the spectators into warriors?

Source: Taken from "The Nonprofit Sector In the Global Community: Voices from Many Nations", A Publication of Independent Sector, Washington, pp. 422-437.

Bibliography

Ambasht, 1970 'A Critical Study of Tribal Education', New Delhi: Chand & Co.

Anjali Kurane 2005 Socio-economic development among the Warlis of Maharashtra in Dimensions of research in Anthropology Vol.2 Serial Publication Delhi.

Basu, Ashok Ranjan and Nijhawan Satish. (1995) *Tribal Development Administration in India.* New Delhi: Mittal Publications.

Chatterjee, 2000 Educational Development of Scheduled Castes: Looking Ahead, Gyan Publishing House, New Delhi.

Chacko, M. Pariyaram (2005) *Tribal Communities and Social Change.* New Delhi. Saga Publications.

Chaudhri, D.P. (1997), 'Female Tribals and Gender Bias in Tribal Education in Indian States: 1961-1991.' The Indian Journal of Labour Economics, Volume 40, no.3, pp. 493-505

Dash, K. N. (2004) *Invitation to social and cultural Anthropology*: New Delhi, Atlantic Publisher and Distributors.

Dash, K. N. (2004) Invitation to social and cultural Anthropology: New Delhi, Atlantic Publisher and Distributors.

Deshmukh, B. A. (2004) *Tribal Education. New Delhi*: Sonali Publications.

Deshmukh (2004) Tribal Education, Sonali Publication, New Delhi.

Gupta, Danda, 1984, *Tribal Education in India*, Anthropological Survey of India, Calcutta

Kailash, G (1993) 'Tribal Education and Occupation: Dynamics of Impact and Change', New Delhi: Nank Publication

Kumar A. (2002) Tribal Development in India, Sarup and Sons, New Delhi.

Kamlesh Mann. (1996) *Tribal women: on the Threshold of twenty-first century.* New Delhi, M.D. Publication PVT. LTd.

Kothari, B, Vijaya, P G, Chand S & Sharma, R (2000): *A Review of Primary Education Packages in Madhya Pradesh,* Indian Institute of Management, Ahmedabad.

Kumar, K, Priyam, M & Saxena, S (2001): *Looking Beyond the Smokescreen: DPEP and Primary Education in India,* Economic and Political Weekly, Vol. 36 No. 7

Kailash, G 1993 'Tribal Education and Occupation: Dynamics of Impact and Change', New Delhi: Nank Publication

Lieten, G.K., A.K. Karan & A.K. Satpathy (2005), Children, School and Work: Glimpses from India. New Delhi

Leclercq, F (2003): *Education Guarantee Scheme and Primary Schooling in Madhya Pradesh,* Economic and Political Weekly, Vol. 38 N0. 19

Mathur, H.M., (1996) 'Anthropology and Development in Traditional Societies', New Delhi: Vikas Publishing.

Malhotra, O.P. (1998) *Tribal Education: Impact of Education on Tribal Life and Adjustment,* New Delhi. Cosmo Publications.

Mishra, S 1998 'Education of Tribal Children in Inida' (Internet)

Mathur, H.M., (1996) 'Anthropology and Development in Traditional Societies', New Delhi: Vikas Publishing.

Mohanty, P.K (2002). "*Development of Primitive Tribal Groups in India,*" Kalpaz Publication: New Delhi

Manmatha (1994) Tribal Education: New Perspectives, Gyan Publishing Kundu House, New Delhi

Malhotra, O.P. (1998) *Tribal Education: Impact of Education on Tribal Life and Adjustment,* New Delhi. Cosmo Publications.

Meenakshi (2004) Policies and Strategies for Tribal development. Rawat Publications, Jaipur and New Delhi.

Makhan jha, 1995, "*An Introduction to Indian Anthropology,*" Vikas Publishng House, New Delhi

Prakash 2006 Development of Indian Tribes. Discovery Publishing House. New Delhi.

Patel, Tara. (1984) *Development of education Among Tribal Women.* Delhi: Mittal Publications.

Patel, M. L. (1994). "*Development and Dualism of Primitive Tribes",* M.D Publications: New Delhi

Rao and Vaidehi Status of tribal education in TN, *Kurukshetra* 2004

Rajarshi Roy (2007) Ethno – Pedagogy, Education of tribes, teacher's training, and juxtaposition of status, Shipra Publications, Delhi.

Rajarshi Roy (2007) Ethno – Pedagogy, Education of tribes, teacher's training, and juxtaposition of status, Shipra Publications, Delhi.

Rao and Vaidehi Status of tribal education in TN, *Kurukshetra* 2004

Raina, V (2002): *Point by point response by Vinod Raina to the Note circulated by R.Gopalakrishnan, Secretary to the Chief Minister, Government of Madhya Pradesh, detailing the Government's case for closing down HSTP,* at url http://www.cisl.columbia.edu/grads/presi/EKLAVYA/HSTPreportResp.html posted in 2002, accessed on 2nd February 2006.

Raina, B (2006): *Anti-Reservation Protest: Shoring up Privilege,* Economic and Political Weekly, Vol. 41 No. 20

Rammurthy, A (1990): *Shiksha, Sanskriti Aur Samaj (Education, Culture and Society),* (in Hindi) Shrambharati, Munger.

Sen, K M (2000): *Bharater Shanshkriti (The Culture of India),* in Bengali, Viswabharati Publications, Santiniketan.

————————— (2000): *In the Wonderland of Primary Education* in *From Your School to Our School,* Rajiv Gandhi Shiksha Mission, Government of Madhya Pradesh.

Sujatha, (1994) 'Quality education Educational Development among Tribes,' New Delhi: South Asian Publishers.

Sujatha, (1994) 'Quality education Educational Development among Tribes,' New Delhi: South Asian Publishers.

Sharma, S. (2002). "Tribal Welfare and Development" Sarup and New Delhi: Sons Publications.

Singh, B. (1977). "Tribal Development at Cross Road" *Man In India.* 57(3): 229-247.

Shama, S. Ram. (1996) *Women's Education: A Conceptual Framework.* New Delhi: Discovery Publishing House.

Shah, P. Vimal and Patel Tara (1985). *Social Contexts of Tribal education.* New Delhi: Concept Publishing Company.

Sharma S. Ram. (1996) *Education of Women of Scheduled Castes and Scheduled Tribes.* New Delhi: Discovery Publishing House,.

Singh Bhupinder and Mahanti Neeti. (1995) *Tribal Education in India.* New Delhi: Inter- India Publications.

Sah 2004 Tribal Issues in India, Rawat Publication, Jaipur and Yatindra Singh Sisodia New Delhi.

Singh 1982 Economics of the tribes and their transformation, Concept publication.

Shah, P. Vimal and Patel Tara (1985). *Social Contexts of Tribal education.* New Delhi: Concept Publishing Company.

Sharma S. Ram. (1996) *Education of Women of Scheduled Castes and Scheduled Tribes.* New Delhi: Discovery Publishing House,.

Singh Bhupinder and Mahanti Neeti. (1995) *Tribal Education in India.* New Delhi: Inter- India Publications

Shukala, (1998.) 'Education of Indigenous People', www.google search.

Shama, S. Ram. (1996) *Women's Education: A Conceptual Framework.* New Delhi: Discovery Publishing House.

Saxena, *Draft National Policy on Tribals: Suggestions for Improvement*

Sharma, S. (2002). Tribal Welfare and Development. New Delhi: Sarup and Sons Publications.

Singh, B. (1995). "Tribal Development and Education: Are they at Cross Road" *Man In India.* 77(3): 229-247.

Von Fürer-Haimendorf, Christoph. *Tribes of India: The Struggle for Survival.* Berkeley: University of California Press

Verma, R.1995. "*Indian Tribes Through the Ages*," Publication Division, Ministry of I and B, Governament of India.

Vidut Joshi 1998 Tribal situation in India: Issues in Development, Rawat Publication, New Delhi.

Vinoba Gautam, 2003, Education of tribal children in India and the issue of Medium of Instruction: A Janshala experience

Vargheses, 1993 'Quality in Primary Education' New Delhi: BR Publishing House

Wazir, Rekha (ed.) (2000), The Gender Gap in Basic Education. NGOs as Change Agents. New Delhi: Sage Publications

Weiner, Myron (1991), The Child and the State in India. New Delhi: Oxford University Press

Vargheses(1993) Quality in Primary Education. New Delhi: BR Publishing House.

Index

D

Y